# The Rodale Cookbook

# The Rodale Cookbook

by Nancy Albright
Chef-Manager of Fitness House,
the Rodale Press Dining Room

jacket and interior design
by John K. Landis

photography by
T. L. Gettings and Robert Griffith

Rodale Press Book Division
Emmaus, Pennsylvania 18049

International Standard Book Number 0-87857-071-3

Library of Congress Card Number 73-5161

Manufactured in the United States of America

Book Designer: John Landis
PB-402
First Printing—October, 1973
Second Printing—January, 1974
Third Printing—October, 1974
Fourth Printing—October, 1974
Printed on recycled paper

**Acknowledgements:**

Special thanks to editor, Joan Bingham, for pulling all the ends together.

Our appreciation to the following business establishments who provided materials for photographs used in this book.

The Mill Shop
Emmaus, Pennsylvania

Merritt Lumber Company
Emmaus, Pennsylvania

The China Barrel
Wescosville, Pennsylvania

# Table of Contents

The Rodale Cookbook

# FITNESS HOUSE

## The Fitness House Rodale Cookbook

fitness house

The Rodale Cookbook

Rodale Cookbook

fitness house

Rodale Cookbook

Rodale Cookbook

fitness house

FITNESS HOUSE

# Introduction

In many ways this cookbook is the story of Fitness House Kitchen and our Fitness House staff. As I leaf through the recipes, they bring various people to mind. Some started on our staff three years ago and are no longer with us, but they have made essential contributions. Carol Van Horn developed our Almond Crunch (the best granola I've ever eaten), our Carob Almond Cake, Brazil Nut Torte and so many more; Betty Royer who, without batting an eyelash at the prospect of making rye bread using no wheat flour, came up with a beautiful crusty round loaf, the original of our present Fitness House rye; Daisy Fatzinger, who especially loves making soups—her old-fashioned chicken rice soup and her potato soup make frequent appearances on our menu due to popular request.

The story began in February, 1970 when Rodale Press purchased a large, charming, old house in Emmaus. It was to become the home of the magazine *Fitness for Living* and thus was named "Fitness House." For years, Bob Rodale had been thinking about starting a dining facility that would offer, not only the tastiest, but the most nutritious meals possible. Since the main floor of the house was largely kitchen and dining rooms, it offered a good opportunity to put his idea into practice on a sizable scale. So Fitness House Dining Room was opened to Rodale Press Employees and their guests, and I was asked by Bob Rodale if I would manage it. My answer was an unhesitating yes.

I have had a special interest in food all of my life. As a child, I never lacked a healthy appetite. Over the last 25 years, my profession as a cook has brought me fascinating experiences in England, Switzerland, and all over America.

Cooking is a creative art and one I find satisfying and fulfilling. It is also a tangible, important way to care for people. I believe that a good cook can make the difference between a happy and unhappy marriage or home.

Since I have come to Fitness House, an extra dimension—an organic awareness—has been added to my convictions as a cook. Having had only a nodding acquaintance with the organic food movement, I had everything to learn. Operating an organic kitchen represented a challenge, but an intriguing one, which appealed to my pioneering spirit. I learned that we would use (as much as possible) only food which had been grown without chemical fertilizers, pesticides, herbicides or insecticides—food which had been grown in soil fed naturally—that we were to start with basic ingredients and do our own cooking, avoiding most processed foods and thus avoiding the wide assortment of preservatives and additives. This is, of course, the way our grandmothers cooked.

I found that honey is a quite satisfactory substitute for sugar. I was encouraged to experiment with grains and flours, other than wheat, and to use unsaturated oils for cooking and salads, instead of animal or hydrogenated fats. I was introduced to brown, unpolished rice and peanut flour. I learned the value of wheat germ, sunflower seeds, dried peas, beans of all kinds, and that amazing little legume, the soybean. Nuts, I discovered, were important sources of protein, vitamins and minerals—instead of just nibblefood.

I knew that chocolate was not a particularly healthful food but I love it, so I was delighted to find out that there is a delicious substitute that comes satisfyingly close to chocolate—carob, or as it is sometimes called, "St. John's Bread."

Some of the grains we use at Fitness House are: millet, corn, barley, oat, rice, buckwheat and rye. We use potato starch and potato flour, as well as arrowroot and cornstarch for thickening agents and sometimes in baking. J. I. Rodale's theories about milk and wheat gluten are the reason for our limited use of them. He was convinced that we Americans put too much emphasis on these two foods, and that many common physical disorders— allergies, in particular—can be traced back to our heavy consumption of them. We do use powdered skim milk occasionally, the non-instant kind, which is high in protein, low in fat, and an excellent source of calcium.

We have found several sources of organically grown meat and I'm sure it can be found almost anywhere, with a little searching. I particularly enjoy the trips out into our beautiful Pennsylvania countryside to visit the farms and pick up the meat firsthand. We have found it exceptional—lean, tender and delicious. More and more farmers across the country are going organic and more of this good meat will be available as time goes on.

We are fortunate to get our eggs, potatoes, turkeys and fresh vegetables in season from the Rodale Experimental Farm. Also our next door neighbors at Fitness House have made a good-sized naturally-fertilized, no-spray vegetables patch available to us. We never peel these organic vegetables. When the recipes in this book use vegetables or fruits and specifically state "unpeeled," we expect that you will use your own judgment and peel the vegetables or fruit if it is not organically grown, rather than consume the poisonous spray residues on the skins. Some recipes call for lemon or orange rind; this should simply be omitted unless the fruit is free of spray.

It is such a joy to cut a firm, crisp cucumber into a salad, skin and all, with no worry about the greasy, waxy coating you generally find on the supermarket variety. And now such organically grown produce is becoming more readily available. There is a large wholesale organic distributor near us who gathers in fruits and vegetables from all over the country and supplies the Philadelphia, New York and Washington areas. In Washington, D.C. almost every store in a large chain of supermarkets is supplied with organic produce from this source.

When you cook vegetables, use as little water as possible. Cook them just until tender, and drain them immediately, saving the water for soup. Or sauté the vegetables in a bit of oil, covering them briefly at the end, to steam until tender. This preserves the vitamins and minerals *and* the flavor and texture.

Confusion abounds when it comes to the subject of oils and the methods by which they are processed. Since we exclusively use oil for cooking, rather than hydrogenated (solid at room temperature) fats, we have learned through experience which oils are best for cooking and which make the best salad dressings and desserts. We recommend unrefined oils because they are most apt to retain their nutrients and to be free of chemicals.

The term "cold-pressed" can only apply to olive or sesame oil, since these are the only two materials which yield enough oil without first being heated. Other unrefined oils have been pressed after being heated to a temperature of 200°-250°F.

Safflower oil is the mildest flavored, and the best one to use for desserts and salad dressings such as mayonnaise. It is also rich in linoleic acid, considered the most important of the unsaturated fatty acids. Olive and sesame oils are fine for oil and vinegar dressings, although olive oil is highly-saturated and should be used sparingly. We sometimes use a combination of safflower and olive oils in our salad dressings.

Corn, soybean and peanut oils are good for sautéing. They will add distinctive flavor to the dish being prepared and should be selected accordingly. Cottonseed oil should be avoided because of the large amount of pesticide customarily used on the plant.

At Fitness House we make our own mayonnaise, catsup, yogurt and cottage cheese, so we can be sure they contain no chemical preservatives, colorings or flavorings. Recipes for each of these are included in this book.

Brewer's yeast, sometimes called Nutritional yeast, is a non-leavening yeast grown especially for human consumption. It is an excellent source of vitamin B, and we add it to some of our breads, meat loaves, beverages, and cookies for extra nourishment.

Salt, whether labeled "Sea Salt" or not, should be used in moderation. We use as little salt as possible in our recipes, because of its unhealthy effect on the circulatory system.

We use Tamari soy sauce because it is made without monosodium glutamate (MSG), sugar or carmel flavoring.

The honey we use in making our recipes is raw and unstrained, in order to preserve its natural nutrients. The wheat germ is also raw, since toasting destroys some vitamins.

Whenever dried apricots, prunes, peaches or raisins are called for in recipes, they should be unsulphured, naturally dried. If they look dark and shriveled to you and seem tough to chew—that's because you are used to the ones which have had their color and texture preserved artificially. When you use unprocessed dried fruits at home, soak them briefly in water to tenderize them. You will soon discover what a delicious flavor they have.

Peanut butter can be made easily with a blender. This gives assurance that it has not been hydrogenated and the valuable unsaturated fats are still intact.

When sherry is called for in a recipe, it should be the very dry kind, unless you have made your own wine, using a minimum of sugar.

When vanilla is called for, use either a vanilla bean (incomparable in flavor!), or pure vanilla extract, not the imitations.

I have touched only briefly on the various foods we use at Fitness House. At the beginning of each of the following recipe sections, we will go into more detail concerning the specific recipe ingredients.

Mine was the envied experience of a cook starting out in a newly-equipped kitchen. I had been cautioned from the beginning to buy stainless steel pots and pans, rather than aluminum, because J. I. Rodale often wrote that the aluminum tends to migrate into foods cooked in it. We do have some cast iron skillets and pyrex pie plates, but most of our equipment is stainless steel. It meant spending more money in the beginning, but stainless steel is less likely to become contaminated or wear out. Washing stainless steel pots and pans is also a lot less painful than washing aluminum ones.

The electric blender is an absolute must for the organic kitchen. We make mayonnaise almost daily, purée our soups, mix our salad dressings, coarse-grind nuts and put the blender to endless other uses.

We have two electric mixing machines—one large, with a grinder, a slicer and purée attachments, and a smaller one. We have a juicer and a small nut grinder.

Before I leave the subject of equipment, I would like to caution anyone who is thinking of buying a microwave oven not to do so. The U.S. Bureau of Radiological Health has set official government safety standards for these ovens. But the danger is that they very often leak radiation above the level considered safe. A government pamphlet, "Facts About Microwave Radiation" carries the disconcerting recommendation that the cook stay at least a full arm's length away from any of these ovens in operation!

People seem to enjoy working in Fitness House Kitchen. Maybe it is the friendly, informal atmosphere, which exists throughout Rodale Press. I think it is also because we are all caught up in the challenge and importance of the task we have taken on.

Our present staff consists of:

*Peter Noga*, a young man from Brooklyn with innate good-cooking sense and a creative flair;

*Yvonne Malloy*, who spent 16 years in Ireland where her 6 children were born, now bakes breads for us, using some of the wonderful recipes she learned over there;

*Kathy Kelly,* whose specialty is baking carob Brownies and who is also very good at remembering where I put something—like an odd screw for example—when we really need it;

*Linda Koch,* a high school student who works with us part time and has developed into an efficient and artistic salad maker;

*Rose Stutzman,* who came to Fitness House from a college course in home economics because she wanted experience in cooking with organically-grown foods.

Kathy was in on the beginning of the Fitness House Kitchen in spring, 1970. She and I were the entire staff then. We were expecting to feed 15 people a day, at the most. But very soon after opening, the numbers grew to 25, then 30, and now we feed up to 40 daily. At Fitness House there are two dining rooms seating 16 and 22 respectively, plus a patio which seats about 24 at redwood tables and benches—a favorite spot on nice spring and summer days. People serve themselves, buffet style.

Very early in our work it became obvious that there simply weren't enough recipes that fit the kind of cooking we planned to do. We realized the need for creating our own recipes and testing them before putting them on the menu. As a result, we now have quite a collection of original recipes, each one carefully tested in our kitchen. People were constantly asking how we made this or that dish, so it was natural that this cookbook would follow.

Two people who deserve a lot of thanks for the work are Carol Van Horn, whom I mentioned earlier and who tested and developed many of these recipes, and Faye Martin. Faye, a talented cook and gourmet cateress, has worked tirelessly to standardize all of the recipes in this book—originating and testing many of her own in the process.

We are in the forefront of a cultural food revolution. Our traditional American eating habits are being looked at with new eyes. I believe the direction this revolution takes in the future largely depends on each one of us.

What do we want from the food industries—artificial, instant, convenience foods and quick snacks? Do we want Bacos instead of bacon—Tang instead of orange juice? I don't! Something inside of me is repulsed by the idea of food made out of chemicals.

There is an innate rightness about nature's way and something basically sane and rewarding about our working with it. I know you will agree when you've had the opportunity to try a few of the recipes from the pages that follow.

Fitness House, the Rodale Press Dining Room

conversation over lunch at Fitness House

dining on the Fitness House patio

← Bob Rodale, president of Rodale Press, at the buffet

from left to right,
Nancy Albright,
Linda Koch,
Peter Noga,
Yvonne Malloy

# Cooking Hints

This is a quick check list excerpted from the chapter introductions that follow. It offers some simple pointers on how to get the most flavor and nutrition out of the foods you serve. For more specific detail, turn to the appropriate section of the book.

## APPETIZERS, SNACKS, NUTS & SEEDS

1. Shelled nuts and seeds should be stored in a refrigerator or freezer. Because of their high fat content they tend to become rancid if kept too long at room temperature.

2. Brazil nuts and cashews are best eaten raw. Peanuts—any nut or seed, for that matter—can be roasted easily at home. Peanuts require approximately 30 minutes in a 300°F. oven and sesame seeds will toast in 15 minutes in a 350°F. oven.

3. Nuts and sunflower or sesame seeds make a good garnish for salads and vegetable dishes.

4. Caraway, dill, celery and mustard seeds (whole or ground) are valuable seasoning. substitutes for salt.

5. Make your own peanut butter by putting 2 cups peanuts in a blender container and blending for one minute. Gradually add 1/4 cup oil, a tablespoon at a time, watching carefully and scraping down the sides of the container with a rubber spatula frequently.

cooking hints

6. Cashew or sesame "milks" are good mixers in beverages or desserts. To make the milks, just add 1 cup of cashew nuts or ¾ cup sesame seeds to 4 cups water, in a blender container, with honey to taste and blend at high speed for 2 minutes. Sesame milk should be strained.

**SOUPS** 1. Vinegar added to simmering soup stock (2 tablespoonfuls per quart of water) will help dissolve the calcium in the bones, allowing it to pass more readily into the liquid.

2. Soup stock should be made at least a day in advance and refrigerated overnight, so that the fat particles which rise to the surface can be skimmed off.

3. Chicken fat, skimmed from chilled chicken stock, can be refrigerated for future use in sautéing vegetables or making sauces.

4. Extra soup stock can be frozen in bread pans. The frozen block is then removed from the pan, and wrapped and stored in the freezer for future use.

5. Before adding vegetables to soup, sauté them in oil or chicken fat. This seals in their flavor and keeps them firm.

6. Left-over rice, bulgur or buckwheat groats add flavor and body to a soup.

7. When making cream soups with skim-milk powder, be sure to use a wire whisk, rather than a blender, to mix the powder with water. This prevents curdling when the milk is added to the hot liquid.

cooking hints

**SALADS AND SALAD DRESSINGS**

1. Leafy vegetables, exposed to the light at room temperature, can lose half of their vitamins B$_2$ and C in a day, so refrigerate them at the first opportunity.

2. While fresh, organically-grown vegetables are not always available, fresh sprouts from beans or seeds can be grown easily in three days and they make a nutritious addition to a salad.

3. You can make basic oil and vinegar dressing in 6 minutes. It will cost ⅔ of the price of a commercial dressing and it will be fresh and free of chemical additives.

4. Mayonnaise and yogurt, combined, make a good base for delicious salad dressings. Using yogurt instead of sour cream provides a creamy consistency without the high fat content. This dressing has the extra protein of the yogurt and egg, plus the nutrients in the oil.

**MEATS, POULTRY AND FISH**

1. Meats are their tenderest and juiciest when cooked slowly using low to moderate heat. This is true of roasts, steaks, poultry and fish, whether they are baked, roasted or broiled. The reason is simple: protein toughens at a high temperature.

2. Never boil meat. When making soup from meat, keep the heat low so the soup is "simmering." Boiling toughens meat.

3. Organ meats are nutritionally superior to other meats but they are especially perishable and should be used at once or frozen.

cooking hints

4. Fish needs less cooking than meat—as little as 10 minutes for broiling a fillet and no more than 30 minutes for baking a whole fish.

**SOYBEANS, EGGS, CHEESE**

1. Soybeans require at least 8 hours of soaking and 2-3 hours of cooking—longer than any other legumes.
2. Freezing soybeans after soaking lessens the amount of time needed to cook them.

**VEGETABLES**

1. Cook vegetables for as short a time as possible, using a minimum of water, in a tightly-covered saucepan over a medium-high heat. Many of the vitamins are water-soluble, so never soak vegetables in water. Wash them quickly and peel, chop or slice them just before cooking. If you know the vegetables have not been sprayed with insecticides, do not peel them.
2. Save the nutrition-rich water in which vegetables have been cooked. Use it in soups or gravies.
3. Vegetables should be salted after, not during cooking. Salt tends to draw the natural juices, containing flavor and nutrients, out of the vegetables into the water.
4. An excellent way to cook vegetables is to sauté them in oil so that they retain their natural color and firmness.
5. A vegetable should be served immediately after it is cooked to avoid any unnecessary loss of nutrients. Instead of reheating left-over vegetables, serve them cold as part of a salad.

cooking hints

**GRAINS**
1. Serve bulgur (cracked wheat) pilaf, millet souffle, cornmeal polenta, or buckwheat kasha with meat, as an interesting alternative to potatoes.
2. In flavor and food value, brown rice is superior to white rice. It should be cooked so that all of the nutritionally valuable water is absorbed, leaving a fluffy, somewhat dry, rice.
3. A blend of oat and soy flours makes a good coating for oven-baked chicken.
4. A blend of rice and soy flours is a good thickening agent for gravy, sauces or soups.
5. Cornstarch, potato starch and potato flour are fine substitutes for wheat flour as thickening agents and for use in some cakes and cookies.
6. The combination of oat and barley flours makes delicious pie crust.
7. Though it contains less gluten than wheat, rye flour can be substituted for wheat in breads and as a thickening agent in meat gravies. It is excellent for dredging liver or kidneys before sautéing them.
8. Raw wheat germ, rich in protein and vitamin E, can be used instead of breadcrumbs in savory dishes and added to toppings for desserts.

**BREADS**
1. To make your own "enriched" bread at home, substitute 2 tablespoons of soy flour and 2 tablespoons of raw wheat germ for 4 tablespoons (¼ cup) of white flour.
2. When using soy flour for baking, turn the oven temperature 25 degrees lower than usual, since

soy flour browns at a lower temperature than other flours.

3. Store whole grain flours in a cool, dry place, or in a refrigerator or freezer.

4. It is important that the ingredients for making bread be at room temperature before mixing them. If the flour has been refrigerated, it can be heated in the oven at 250°F. for 20 minutes; stir it after 10 minutes.

5. Yeast is a living organism. It stops growing if it is chilled and overheating kills it. The liquid in which the yeast is dissolved must be lukewarm.

6. Adding 1 teaspoon of honey to the dissolving yeast will hasten the action because yeast feeds on sugars.

7. For the rising process, dough must be in a draft-free, warm, humid room. If such a place is not available, warm your oven briefly. Turn it off, and put the dough, covered with a damp cloth, into the oven. Place a pan of water on a lower oven shelf for humidity.

8. If bread comes out with a "yeasty" or "sour" taste, either the dough was allowed to rise too much before being stirred down, or it was not kept warm enough while rising. It is not the result of using too much yeast.

9. Whole grain breads are more apt to stick to the bread pan than ordinary bread, so oil your pan generously.

10. If you plan to store homemade bread longer

cooking hints

than a few days, it should be frozen. It tends to dry out in the refrigerator.

**DESSERTS**   1. Raw, unstrained honey may be substituted for sugar in almost any recipe. Use half as much honey as the amount of sugar required in the recipe. From our experience, clover honey is the mildest flavored and thus the best to use as a general sweetener.

2. Honey will keep indefinitely. If it is too thick or becomes grainy, set the jar in a bowl of hot water and stir the honey from time to time, until it has thinned and the crystals have dissolved. Do not heat honey as that will destroy some of the nutrients.

3. If honey is substituted in a recipe, remember that it is a liquid, so more flour or dry ingredients may have to be added to produce the right consistency.

4. Safflower oil, the mildest-flavored of the unrefined oils, is substituted for hydrogenated shortening in our desserts. Because oil is a liquid, the ratio of wet ingredients to dry in the recipe must be adjusted accordingly.

5. Carob tastes very much like chocolate, has a little more than half the calories, one-hundredth the amount of fat and two and one-half times the amount of calcium.

6. Carob has a somewhat raw taste which disappears if it is mixed with hot water, or heated

cooking hints

briefly in a double-boiler. Carob dissolves better in oil than in water.

7. Date "sugar" (ground, dried dates), makes an excellent natural sweetener which can be used in fruit crisp toppings, cookies and date desserts.

8. Assorted dried fruits (unsulphured) and mixed nuts and seeds make an attractive, nourishing dessert.

9. Delicious and unusual cakes can be made using ground Brazil nuts, almonds, sunflower seeds and soy grits instead of flour.

**OILS**

1. Safflower is the mildest-flavored of the unrefined oils, so it is the best one to use in desserts or salad dressings, such as mayonnaise.

2. Corn, soybean and peanut oils can be used for sautéing. Their distinctive flavor will add to the dish being prepared and the oil to be used should be selected with this in mind.

**MISCELLANEOUS**

1. Brewer's yeast, sometimes called Nutritional yeast, is a non-leavening yeast grown especially for human consumption. It is an excellent source of vitamin B and can be added to meat loaves, stews, soups, breads, and cookies as a natural way of enriching them.

2. Tamari soy sauce is made without monosodium glutamate (MSG), sugar or caramel flavoring.

# Supplements to enrich your foods

Looking for new ways to add nutrition to your family's favorites without springing an unfamiliar recipe on them? Check this chart for nutritional additions you can use in your favorite recipes. It's an ideal way to make the most of poor appetites.

| Supplement | Rich Source of | Can Be Added To |
|---|---|---|
| Wheat Germ | Vitamin E | Cereals<br>Casseroles<br>Cakes<br>Toppings for desserts<br>Breads<br>Salads |
| Sprouts | Vitamins A and C | Salads<br>Soups<br>Omelettes |
| Nuts and Seeds (Ground and Whole) | Potassium, Protein, Phosphorus | Snack Dishes<br>Cereals<br>Salads<br>Desserts |
| Soy powder; soy grits | Protein | Stews<br>Meat Loaves<br>Breads<br>Beverages |
| Brewer's yeast (sometimes called Nutritional yeast) | Vitamin B-complex | Beverages<br>Soups<br>Casseroles<br>Breads |
| Kelp, dulse, other powdered seaweed | Iodine | Soups<br>Salads<br>Casseroles<br>Meat dishes |

## Natural Foods vs. Processed Foods

What does it cost you (in time and money) to serve natural foods rather than processed foods? What do you gain (in food value) and avoid (in chemical additives)? The following chart shows enlightening comparisons that will help you in deciding on the kind of food you want to serve your family.

| OD | Tang | Orange Juice (Frozen) | Orange Juice (Fresh) | Cheerios | Almond Crunch Cereal (Homemade) |
|---|---|---|---|---|---|
| ST | 1 cup 5¾ ¢ | 1 cup — 10¢ | 1 cup — 18¢ | 10 oz. — 49¢ | 10 oz. — 45¢ |
| GREDIENTS | Sugar | Water | Orange Juice | Oat Flour | Oatmeal |
| | Citric Acid (for tartness) | Orange Juice (Concentrated) | | Wheat Starch | Coconut |
| | Calcium Phosphate (Regulates tartness and prevents caking) | | | Sugar | Almonds |
| | | | | Salt | Sunflower seeds |
| | Gum Arabic (Vegetable gum provides body) | | | Calcium Carbonate | Raisins |
| | | | | Sodium Phosphate | Wheat Germ |
| | Natural Flavor | | | Sodium Ascorbate | Honey |
| | Potassium Citrate (Regulates tartness) | | | Artificial Color | Water |
| | Vitamin C | | | Niacin | Oil |
| | Cellulose Gum (Vegetable gum) | | | Iron | Sesame seeds |
| | Hydrogenated Coconut Oil | | | Gum Acacia | |
| | Artificial Flavor | | | Vitamin A Palmitate | |
| | Artificial Color | | | Vitamin $B_6$ | |
| | Vitamin A | | | Riboflavin | |
| | BHA (A preservative) | | | Thiamin | |
| | | | | Vitamin D | |
| | | | | Vitamin $B_{12}$ | |
| | | | | BHT (To preserve freshness) | |
| EPARATION ME | 30 SECONDS | 1½ MINUTES | 2 MINUTES | NONE | 2 HOURS* |
| | | | | | *Preparation-Time needed refers to batch-size recipe. Approx. 3 lbs. or 15 ½ cup servings. |

continued on next page

| FOOD | Sunbeam Stone-Ground Whole Wheat Bread | No-Knead Bread Whole Wheat (Homemade) | Mayonnaise (Hellman's) | Mayonnaise (Homemade) | Salad Dressing (Oil & Vinegar) Kraft |
|---|---|---|---|---|---|
| **COST** | 1 lb. — 41¢ | 2 lb. loaf—47¢ | 1 quart — 89¢ | 1 quart — $1.20 | 8 oz. — 43¢ |
| **INGREDIENTS** | Flour<br><br>Stone-ground whole wheat flour<br><br>Water<br><br>Wheat Gluten<br><br>Sugar<br><br>Vegetable Shortening<br><br>Yeast<br><br>Non-fat dry milk<br><br>Salt<br><br>Honey<br><br>Yeast nutrients<br><br>Mono & Diglycerides<br><br>Ethoxylated Monoglycerides<br><br>Hydroxylated Lecithin<br><br>Sodium Stearoxyl-z Lactylate<br><br>Artificial Color<br><br>Calcium Propionate (A preservative) | Whole Wheat Flour<br><br>Water<br><br>Wheat Germ<br><br>Molasses<br><br>Honey<br><br>Yeast<br><br>Salt<br><br>5-lb. bag whole wheat flour and 8 oz. yeast bought at health food store | Vegetable Salad Oil<br><br>Fresh whole eggs<br><br>Vinegar<br><br>Water<br><br>Fresh-frozen-egg-yolks<br><br>Salt<br><br>Sugar<br><br>Lemon juice<br><br>Spices | Oil<br><br>Egg<br><br>Vinegar<br><br>Dry mustard<br><br>Salt | Soybean oil<br><br>Vinegar<br><br>Onion juice<br><br>Lemon juice<br><br>Salt<br><br>Flavor<br><br>Propylene Glycol Alginate<br><br>Calcium Disodium<br><br>Edta to protect flavor |
| **PREPARATION TIME** | **NONE** | **20 MINUTES TO PREPARE 2 HOURS TO RISE** | **NONE** | **6 MINUTES** | **NONE** |

| Salad Dressing (Homemade) | Carnation Instant Breakfast | High-Protein Milk Drink (Homemade) | Beechnut Baby Food (Carrots in Butter Sauce) | Baby Food (Puréed Carrots) | Orange-Pineapple Jello |
|---|---|---|---|---|---|
| 8 oz. — 26¢ | 6 cups — 77¢ | 6 cups — 82¢ | 4½ oz. — 8¢ | 4½ oz. — 6¢ | 2 cups — 14¢ |
| Oil | Non-fat dry milk | Eggs | Carrots | Carrots | Sugar |
| Vinegar | Sucrose | *Skim milk powder | Water | Water | Gelatin |
| Lemon juice | Corn syrup solids | Water | Light brown sugar | | Adipic Acid (for tartness) |
| Salt | Lactose | Yogurt, plain | Sugar | | Sodium citrate (controls acidity) |
| Onion juice | Vanilla extract | Honey | Butter | | Fumaric Acid (for tartness) |
| | Magnesium hydroxide | Pure vanilla extract | Salt | | Artificial and natural flavors |
| | Sodium Ascorbate | | | | BHA (A preservative) |
| | Ammonium Carrageenan | *Non-instant skim milk powder bought at health food store | | | U.S. Certified color |
| | Artificial flavors | | | | |
| | Ferric Ortho Phosphate | | | | |
| | Vitamin E Acetate | | | | |
| | Vitamin A | | | | |
| | Niacinamide | | | | |
| | Calcium Pantothenate | | | | |
| | Manganese Sulfate | | | | |
| | Basic copper carbonate | | | | |
| | Pyridoxine hydrochloride | | | | |
| | Thiamine Mononitrate | | | | |
| | Riboflavin | | | | |
| | Folic Acid | | | | |
| | Potassium Iodide | | | | |
| | Vanillin | | | | |
| | Ethyl Vanillin | | | | |
| 6 MINUTES | 30 SECONDS | 12 MINUTES | NONE | 10 MINUTES | 5 MINUTES |

continued on next page

| FOOD | Orange-Pineapple Gelatin (Homemade) | Betty Crocker Hamburger Helper (Potato Stroganoff) 5 servings — | Beef-Potato Stroganoff (Homemade) | Yogurt, Plain (Dannon) | Yogurt (Homemade) |
|---|---|---|---|---|---|
| **COST** | 2 cups — 21¢ | $1.38 | 5 serv. — $1.36 | ½ pint — 29¢ | ½ pint — 9¢ |
| **INGREDIENTS** | Pineapple Juice (unsweetened)<br><br>Water<br><br>Frozen Orange Juice<br><br>Honey<br><br>Gelatin | Dehydrated vegetables (potatoes, onion, garlic)<br><br>Sour Cream solids<br><br>Salt<br><br>Vegetable shortening<br><br>Enriched flour (bleached)<br><br>Bouillon<br><br>Hydrolyzed vegetable protein<br><br>Sugar<br><br>Natural & artificial flavorings<br><br>Lactose<br><br>Dextrins<br><br>Beef extract solids<br><br>Sodium caseinate<br><br>Beef fat<br><br>Caramel color<br><br>Monosodium glutamate<br><br>Potassium and Sodium phosphates<br><br>Citric acids<br><br>Mono and Diglycerides<br><br>Disodium inosinate<br><br>Guanylate<br><br>Freshness preserved with Sodium sulfite<br><br>BHA and Propyl Gallate in Propylene Glycol | Hamburger<br><br>Potatoes<br><br>Beef Bouillon<br><br>Onion<br><br>Yogurt<br><br>Oil | Fresh, partially skimmed, homogenized, pasteurized milk<br><br>4 percent non-fat Dry milk<br><br>Yogurt culture | Water<br><br>Skim milk powder<br><br>Yogurt culture |
| **PREPARATION TIME** | 6 MINUTES | 30 MINUTES | 20 MINUTES | NONE | 4 MINUTES TO PREPARE 8 HOURS TO PROCESS |

| Green Beans (Canned) | Green Beans (Fresh) | Fruit Cocktail (Canned) | Fruit Cup (Fresh) | Campbells Chicken Rice Soup (Condensed) | Chicken Rice Soup (Condensed) (Homemade) |
|---|---|---|---|---|---|
| 8 oz. — 26¢ | 8 oz. — 25¢ | 16 oz. — 35¢ | 16 oz. — 26¢ | 10½ oz. — 18¢ | 10½ oz. — 50¢ |
| Green beans | Green Beans | Peaches | Orange | Chicken stock | Chicken |
| Water | | Pears | Banana | Rice | Water |
| Salt | | Seedless Grapes | Canned Pineapple (unsweetened) | Cooked Chicken meat | Carrot |
| | | Pineapple Tidbits | | Carrots | Celery |
| | | Halved Cherries, artificially colored red | | Salt | Onion |
| | | Heavy syrup | | Chicken Fat | Brown rice |
| | | | | Celery | Parsley |
| | | | | Monosodium Glutamate | Bay leaf |
| | | | | Potato starch | Salt |
| | | | | Sugar | Peppercorn |
| | | | | Dehydrated onions | |
| | | | | Flavoring | |
| NONE | TO PREPARE FOR COOKING 10 MINUTES | NONE | 5 MINUTES | 5 MINUTES | 12 MINUTES TO PREPARE 2½ HOURS TO COOK |

# Food Substitutions

**Minor substitutions among cooking ingredients can make major changes in flavor and nutritional value. Many cooks are unaware that they have a choice of flours, sweeteners, milks and oils. Look over the list of possibilities and try something new!**

| Foods | Fitness Kitchen Substitutes |
|---|---|
| Sugar | 1. Honey<br>2. Date sugar (ground dates) |
| Chocolate | Carob |
| Animal (Hydrogenated) Fats (Lard, shortening, etc.) | Unsaturated oils including:<br>1. Olive oil<br>2. Corn oil<br>3. Soybean Oil<br>4. Peanut Oil<br>5. Sunflower Seed Oil<br>6. Safflower Oil |

**White Flour**

Flours made from vegetables, nuts, seeds and whole grains including:

1. Soy flour
2. Rye flour
3. Potato flour
4. Corn flour
5. Millet flour
6. Barley flour
7. Buckwheat flour
8. Peanut flour
9. Sunflower Seed Meal
10. Brown Rice flour
11. Oat flour
12. Whole Wheat flour

**Whole Milk**

1. Soy milk from soybean
2. Soy milk from soyflour reconstituted with water
3. Powdered skim milk (non-instant)
4. Nut milks

**Thickening Agents (Flour)**

1. Brown Rice flour
2. Soy flour
3. Potato Starch
4. Potato flour
5. Arrowroot
6. Cornstarch
7. Rye flour

**Leavening Agents Baking Powder and. Baking Soda**

1. Yeast
2. Eggs
3. Sour dough starter

# What you get in what you eat

Do you want to emphasize a specific nutrient in the meals you prepare — more dishes rich in B vitamins, protein or iron? Do you want to know which foods to avoid if you're cutting down on calories? Consult the chart below for a valuable picture of the nutritional makeup of most familiar foods.

Consumption based on 100 grams edible portion (about 3½ oz. serving)
Source: Composition of Foods, Agricultural Handbook #8, U.S.D.A.

| Food | Calories | Protein grams | Carbohydrate grams | Calcium mgs | Phosphorus mgs | Iron mgs | Vitamin A I.U. | Vitamin B₁ thiamine mgs | Vitamin B₂ riboflavin mgs | Vitamin B₃ niacin mgs | Vitamin C ascorbic acid-mgs |
|---|---|---|---|---|---|---|---|---|---|---|---|
| Asparagus | 26 | 2.5 | 5.0 | 22 | 62 | 1.0 | 900 | .18 | .20 | 1.5 | 33 |
| Beans Lima | 345 | 20.4 | 64.0 | 72 | 385 | 7.8 | trace | .48 | .17 | 1.9 | — |
| Snap | 32 | 1.9 | 7.1 | 56 | 44 | .8 | 600 | .08 | .11 | .5 | 19 |
| Broccoli | 32 | 3.6 | 5.9 | 103 | 78 | 1.1 | 2,500 | .10 | .23 | .9 | 113 |
| Cabbage | 24 | 1.3 | 5.4 | 49 | 29 | .4 | 130 | .05 | .05 | .3 | 47 |
| Carrots | 42 | 1.1 | 9.7 | 37 | 36 | .7 | 11,000 | .06 | .05 | .6 | 8 |
| Cauliflower | 27 | 2.7 | 5.2 | 25 | 56 | 1.1 | 60 | .11 | .10 | .7 | 78 |
| Celery | 17 | .9 | 3.9 | 39 | 28 | .3 | 240 | .03 | .03 | .3 | 9 |
| Corn, sweet | 96 | 3.5 | 22.1 | 3 | 111 | .7 | 400 | .15 | .12 | 1.7 | 12 |

| | | | | | | | | | | | |
|---|---|---|---|---|---|---|---|---|---|---|---|
| **Cucumber** | 15 | .9 | 3.4 | 25 | 27 | 1.1 | 250 | .03 | .04 | .2 | 11 |
| **Eggplant** | 25 | 1.2 | 5.6 | 12 | 26 | .7 | 10 | .05 | .05 | .6 | 5 |
| **Garlic** | 137 | 6.2 | 30.8 | 29 | 202 | 1.5 | trace | .25 | .08 | .5 | 15 |
| **Kale** | 53 | 6.0 | 9.0 | 249 | 93 | 2.7 | 10,000 | .16 | .26 | 2.1 | 186 |
| **Lettuce** | 13 | .9 | 2.9 | 20 | 22 | .5 | 330 | .06 | .06 | .3 | 6 |
| **Onions** | 38 | 1.5 | 8.7 | 27 | 36 | .5 | 40 | .03 | .04 | .2 | 10 |
| **Peas** | 340 | 24.1 | 60.3 | 64 | 340 | 5.1 | 120 | .74 | .29 | 3.0 | — |
| **Peppers, sweet** | 22 | 1.2 | 4.8 | 9 | 22 | .7 | 420 | .08 | .08 | .5 | 128 |
| **Potatoes** | 76 | 2.1 | 17.1 | 7 | 53 | .6 | trace | .10 | .04 | 1.5 | 20 |
| **Pumpkin** | 26 | 1.0 | 6.5 | 21 | 44 | .8 | 1,600 | .05 | .11 | .6 | 9 |
| **Radishes** | 17 | 1.0 | 3.6 | 30 | 31 | 1.0 | 10 | .03 | .03 | .3 | 26 |
| **Soybeans** | | | | | | | | | | | |
| raw, dry | 403 | 34.1 | 33.5 | 226 | 554 | 8.4 | 80 | 1.10 | .31 | 2.2 | — |
| cooked | 130 | 11.0 | 10.8 | 73 | 179 | 2.7 | 30 | .21 | .09 | .6 | — |
| **Sweet Potatoes** | 114 | 1.7 | 26.3 | 32 | 47 | .7 | 8,800 | .10 | .06 | .6 | 21 |
| **Tomatoes** | 22 | 1.1 | 4.7 | 13 | 27 | .5 | 900 | .06 | .04 | .7 | 28 |
| **Turnips** | 30 | 1.0 | 6.6 | 39 | 30 | .5 | trace | .04 | .07 | .6 | 36 |
| **Grains** | | | | | | | | | | | |
| **Barley** | 349 | 8.2 | 78.8 | 16 | 189 | 2.0 | — | .12 | .05 | 3.1 | — |
| **Buckwheat** | 335 | 11.7 | 72.9 | 114 | 282 | 3.1 | — | .60 | — | 4.4 | — |
| **Bulgur** | 359 | 8.7 | 79.5 | 30 | 319 | 4.7 | — | .30 | .10 | 4.2 | — |
| **Corn** | 348 | 8.9 | 72.2 | 22 | 268 | 2.1 | 490 | .37 | .12 | 2.2 | — |
| **Millet** | 327 | 9.9 | 72.9 | 20 | 311 | 6.8 | — | .73 | .38 | 2.3 | — |
| **Oats** | 390 | 14.2 | 68.2 | 53 | 405 | 4.5 | — | .60 | .14 | 1.0 | — |
| **Rice** | 360 | 7.5 | 77.4 | 32 | 221 | 1.6 | — | .34 | .05 | 4.7 | — |
| **Rye** | 334 | 12.1 | 73.4 | 38 | 376 | 3.7 | — | .43 | .22 | 1.6 | — |
| **Wheat** | 330 | 14.0 | 69.1 | 36 | 383 | 3.1 | — | .57 | .12 | 4.3 | — |
| **Wheat Germ** | 363 | 26.6 | 46.7 | 72 | 1,118 | 9.4 | — | 2.01 | .68 | 4.2 | — |

continued on next page

32

| Food | Calories | Protein grams | Carbohydrate grams | Calcium mgs | Phosphorus mgs | Iron mgs | Vitamin A I.U. | Vitamin B₁ thiamine mgs | Vitamin B₂ riboflavin mgs | Vitamin B₃ niacin mgs | Vitamin C ascorbic acid-mgs |
|---|---|---|---|---|---|---|---|---|---|---|---|
| **Nuts** | | | | | | | | | | | |
| Almonds | 598 | 18.6 | 19.5 | 234 | 504 | 4.7 | — | .24 | .92 | 3.5 | trace |
| Brazil Nuts | 654 | 14.3 | 10.9 | 186 | 693 | 3.4 | trace | .96 | .12 | 1.6 | — |
| Cashews | 561 | 17.6 | 29.3 | — | — | .4 | — | .43 | .25 | 1.8 | — |
| Peanuts | 564 | 26.0 | 18.6 | 69 | 401 | 2.1 | — | 1.14 | .13 | 17.2 | — |
| Pecans | 687 | 9.2 | 14.6 | 73 | 289 | 2.4 | 130 | .86 | .13 | .9 | 2 |
| Walnuts (English) | 651 | 14.8 | 15.8 | 99 | 380 | 3.1 | 30 | .33 | .13 | .9 | 2 |
| **Seeds** | | | | | | | | | | | |
| Pumpkin | 553 | 29.0 | 15.0 | 51 | 1,144 | 11.2 | 70 | .24 | .19 | 2.4 | — |
| Sesame | 563 | 18.6 | 21.6 | 1,160 | 616 | 10.5 | 35 | .98 | .24 | 5.4 | — |
| Sunflower | 560 | 24.0 | 19.9 | 120 | 837 | 7.1 | 50 | 1.96 | .23 | 5.4 | — |
| **Fruits** | | | | | | | | | | | |
| Apples | 58 | .2 | 14.5 | 7 | 10 | .3 | 90 | .03 | .02 | .1 | 4 |
| Apricots | 51 | 1.0 | 12.8 | 17 | 23 | .5 | 2,700 | .03 | .04 | .6 | 10 |
| Bananas | 85 | 1.1 | 22.2 | 8 | 26 | .7 | 190 | .05 | .06 | .7 | 10 |
| Cantaloupe | 30 | .7 | 7.5 | 14 | 16 | .4 | 3,400 | .04 | .03 | .6 | 33 |
| Cherries | 70 | 1.3 | 17.4 | 22 | 19 | .4 | 110 | .05 | .06 | .4 | 10 |
| Dates | 274 | 2.2 | 72.9 | 59 | 63 | 3.0 | 50 | .09 | .10 | 2.2 | — |
| Grapes | 69 | 1.3 | 15.7 | 16 | 12 | .4 | 100 | .05 | .03 | .3 | 4 |
| Oranges | 49 | 1.0 | 12.2 | 41 | 20 | .4 | 200 | .10 | .04 | .4 | 50 |
| Peaches | 38 | .6 | 9.7 | 9 | 19 | .5 | 1,330 | .02 | .05 | 1.0 | 7 |
| Pears | 61 | .7 | 15.3 | 8 | 11 | .3 | 20 | .02 | .04 | .1 | 4 |
| Pineapple | 52 | .4 | 13.7 | 17 | 8 | .5 | 70 | .09 | .03 | .2 | 17 |
| Plums | 66 | .5 | 17.8 | 18 | 17 | .5 | 300 | .08 | .03 | .5 | — |
| Strawberries | 37 | .7 | 8.4 | 21 | 21 | 1.0 | 30 | .03 | .07 | | |

| Food | | | | | | | | | | | |
|---|---|---|---|---|---|---|---|---|---|---|---|
| **Muscle Meats** | | | | | | | | | | | |
| Beef (choice) | 301 | 17.4 | 0 | 10 | 161 | 2.6 | 50 | .07 | .15 | 4.2 | — |
| Veal (medium fat) | 190 | 19.1 | 0 | 11 | 193 | 2.9 | — | .14 | .25 | 6.4 | — |
| Lamb (choice) | 263 | 16.5 | 0 | 10 | 147 | 1.2 | — | .15 | .20 | 4.8 | — |
| Chicken (roast) | 239 | 18.2 | 0 | 10 | 176 | 1.6 | 920 | .08 | .19 | 6.7 | — |
| Turkey | 218 | 20.1 | 0 | — | — | — | — | .07 | .16 | 8.1 | — |
| **Organ Meats** | | | | | | | | | | | |
| Liver | | | | | | | | | | | |
| beef | 140 | 19.9 | 5.3 | 8 | 352 | 6.5 | 43,900 | .25 | 3.26 | 13.6 | 31 |
| calf | 140 | 4.7 | 4.1 | 8 | 333 | 8.8 | 22,500 | .20 | 2.72 | 11.4 | 36 |
| chicken | 129 | 19.7 | 2.9 | 12 | 236 | 7.9 | 12,100 | .19 | 2.49 | 10.8 | 17 |
| Heart (beef) | 108 | 17.1 | .7 | 5 | 195 | 4.0 | 20 | .53 | .88 | 7.5 | 2 |
| Kidneys (beef) | 130 | 15.4 | .9 | 11 | 219 | 7.4 | 690 | .36 | 2.55 | 6.4 | 15 |
| Sweetbreads (beef) | 207 | 14.6 | 0 | — | 393 | — | — | — | — | — | — |
| Brain | 125 | 10.4 | .8 | 10 | 312 | 2.4 | 0 | .23 | .26 | 4.4 | 18 |
| **Salt-Water Fish** | | | | | | | | | | | |
| Bluefish | 117 | 20.5 | 0 | 23 | 243 | .6 | — | .12 | .09 | 1.9 | — |
| Cod | 78 | 17.6 | 0 | 10 | 194 | .4 | 382 | .06 | .07 | 2.2 | 2 |
| Flounder | 202 | 30.0 | 0 | 23 | 344 | 1.4 | 587 | .07 | .08 | 2.5 | 2 |
| Haddock | 79 | 18.3 | 0 | 23 | 197 | .7 | 304 | .04 | .07 | 3.0 | — |
| Halibut | 100 | 20.9 | 0 | 13 | 211 | 1.1 | 587 | .07 | .07 | 8.3 | — |
| Herring | 176 | 17.3 | 0 | — | 256 | 1.0 | 449 | .02 | .15 | 3.6 | — |
| Mackerel | 191 | 19.0 | 0 | 5 | 239 | — | — | .15 | .33 | 8.2 | — |
| Perch | 118 | 19.3 | 0 | — | 192 | .9 | — | — | — | — | — |
| Salmon | 217 | 22.5 | 0 | 79 | 136 | 1.8 | — | — | .08 | 7.2 | 9 |
| Sardines | 160 | 19.2 | 0 | 33 | 215 | .8 | — | — | — | — | — |
| Snapper | 93 | 19.8 | 0 | 16 | 214 | .7 | 323 | .17 | .02 | — | — |

# A Lesson in Nutrition

One February day, a Home Economics teacher at a local high school brought 17 of her students to lunch at Fitness House and they learned about the differences between quick-lunch hamburgers and organic foods. Daisy Fatzinger went out and bought a typical McDonald's meal. She weighed each item, and determined the nutritional values from a U.S. Department of Agriculture chart. The same was done with the meal served at Fitness House that day. The comparison speaks for itself.

| | Calories | Protein | Fat | Carbohydrates | Calcium | Iron | Vitamin A | Vitamin B₁ | Vitamin B₂ | Niacin | Vitamin C |
|---|---|---|---|---|---|---|---|---|---|---|---|
| **Two Rolls** | 290.52 | 9.39 gm | 3.45 gm | 54.43 gm | 75.60 mg | 2.59 mg | — | .27 mg | .18 mg | 2.48 mg | — |
| **Two Hamburgers** | 171.60 | 14.53 | 12.18 | — | 6.60 | 1.82 | 24 I.U. | .02 | .10 | 2.04 | — |
| **French Fries** | 180.84 | 2.83 | 8.71 | 23.76 | 9.90 | .85 | — | .08 | .05 | 2.04 | 13.86 m |
| **Shake** | 389.12 | 12.28 | 11.05 | 57.34 | 379.36 | .25 | 537.60 | .12 | .56 | .25 | 2.56 |
| **Totals** | 1,032.08 | 39.02 gm | 35.39 gm | 135.53 gm | 471.36 mg | 5.51 mg | 561.60 I.U. | .49 mg | .89 mg | 6.81 mg | 16.42 m |
| **Soybean Soup** | 124.14 | 10.52 | 5.70 | 10.39 | 86.38 | 2.39 | 283.6 | .29 | .11 | 1.10 | 14.51 |
| **Brown Rice** | 123.12 | 2.56 | .65 | 26.47 | 10.94 | .54 | — | .11 | .01 | 1.60 | — |
| **Meat Loaf** | 265 | 41.20 | 9.45 | 10.6 | 30.8 | 4.78 | 1,405.8 | .32 | .69 | 3 | 20.5 |
| **Salad** | 30.65 | 1.90 | 5.80 | 6.24 | 47.43 | 1.52 | 2,956 | 2.26 | .11 | .78 | 33.48 |
| **Onion Dressing** | 69.65 | .30 | 7.54 | 1.97 | 4.88 | .04 | 52.46 | .002 | .01 | — | .88 |
| **Brownie, Carob** | 154 | 3.68 | 10.56 | 15 | 27 | .87 | 85.18 | .94 | .04 | 1.75 | .18 |
| **Brownie, Butterscotch** | 148.6 | 5.45 | 7.25 | 15.78 | 75.65 | 1.65 | 227.76 | .07 | .12 | 1.43 | .55 |
| **Totals** | 915.16 | 65.61 gm | 46.95 gm | 86.45 gm | 283.08 mg | 11.79 mg | 5,010.80 I.U. | 3.99 mg | 1.09 mg | 9.56 mg | 70.10 m |

**Where you can buy Natural Food Staples**

If you are not accustomed to buying foods, such as soy flour, Nutritional yeast, sunflower seeds and wheat germ, you will find this availability chart helpful. You may be surprised that many of the staples can be purchased in supermarkets, most others are stocked in any of the Natural Foods Stores that have sprung up in just about every town. Those items not available locally can be ordered by mail. A list of Sources for Natural and Organic Foods begins on page 448. Choose the one closest to you for fastest service.

| Item | Supermarket | Natural Foods Store | Mail Order |
|---|---|---|---|
| Almonds | ☑ | ☑ | ☑ |
| Apricots (dried, unsulphured) | | ☑ | ☑ |
| Arrowroot | | ☑ | ☑ |
| Barley Flour | | ☑ | ☑ |
| Brazil Nuts (raw) | ☑ | ☑ | ☑ |
| Brewer's (nutritional) yeast | | ☑ | ☑ |
| Brown Rice | ☑ | ☑ | ☑ |
| Buckwheat Flour | | ☑ | ☑ |
| Bulgur | | ☑ | ☑ |
| Caraway Seeds | ☑ | ☑ | ☑ |
| Carob | | ☑ | ☑ |
| Cashews (raw) | | ☑ | ☑ |
| Coconut (unsweetened) | | ☑ | ☑ |
| Corn Meal | ☑ | ☑ | ☑ |
| Corn Oil (unrefined) | | ☑ | ☑ |
| Cornstarch | ☑ | | |
| Date Sugar | | ☑ | ☑ |
| Dates | ☑ | ☑ | ☑ |
| Dry Milk | ☑ | ☑ | ☑ |
| Eggs | ☑ | ☑ | |
| Figs | ☑ | ☑ | ☑ |
| Garbanzo Beans | | ☑ | ☑ |
| Gelatin, unflavored | ☑ | ☑ | |
| Groats | | ☑ | ☑ |
| Herb Teas | | ☑ | |
| Herbs | ☑ | ☑ | |
| Honey | ☑ | ☑ | ☑ |
| Kidney Beans | ☑ | ☑ | ☑ |
| Lentils | ☑ | ☑ | ☑ |
| Millet | | ☑ | ☑ |
| Molasses | ☑ | ☑ | ☑ |
| Mung Beans | | ☑ | ☑ |
| Oat Flour | | ☑ | ☑ |
| Oatmeal | ☑ | ☑ | ☑ |
| Olive Oil | ☑ | ☑ | ☑ |
| Peaches (dried) | | ☑ | ☑ |
| Peanut Butter | ☑ | ☑ | ☑ |
| Peanut Flour | | ☑ | ☑ |
| Peanut Oil (unrefined) | | ☑ | ☑ |
| Peanuts | ☑ | ☑ | ☑ |
| Pinto Beans | | ☑ | ☑ |
| Potato Flour | | ☑ | ☑ |
| Potato Starch | | ☑ | ☑ |
| Prunes (unsulphured) | | ☑ | ☑ |
| Pumpkin Seeds | ☑ | ☑ | ☑ |
| Raisins (unsulphured) | | ☑ | ☑ |
| Rice Flour | | ☑ | ☑ |
| Rice Polish | | ☑ | ☑ |
| Rye Flour | | ☑ | ☑ |
| Safflower Oil (unrefined) | | ☑ | ☑ |
| Sesame Oil | | ☑ | ☑ |
| Sesame Seeds | ☑ | ☑ | ☑ |
| Soy Flour | | ☑ | ☑ |
| Soy Grits | | ☑ | ☑ |
| Soy Powder | | ☑ | ☑ |
| Soybeans | | ☑ | ☑ |
| Split Peas | ☑ | ☑ | ☑ |
| Sunflower Seeds | | ☑ | ☑ |
| Tamari Soy Sauce | | ☑ | ☑ |
| Vanilla Beans | | ☑ | ☑ |
| Vinegar | ☑ | ☑ | ☑ |
| Walnuts | ☑ | ☑ | ☑ |
| Wheat Germ | ☑ | ☑ | ☑ |
| Whole Wheat Flour | | ☑ | ☑ |
| Yeast, Dry, Baker's | ☑ | ☑ | ☑ |
| Yogurt | ☑ | ☑ | ☑ |
| Yogurt Culture | | ☑ | ☑ |

ALMONDS

peanut butter

JULEP APPLE

cranberry JUICE

PINEAPPLE JUICE

seeds

Melon Cooler

Sunflower Seeds

Cheese Balls

CASHEW

cranberry relish

Seeds

peanut butter

Snacks

1.

## Appetizers, Snacks, Nuts, Seeds, Relishes & Beverages

Appetizers have an established place in the American diet, whether as finger food at the cocktail hour, or as a first course at dinner. At Fitness House we think of them as important food, not just a trifle to please the eye or tickle the palate.

Our recipes for Chicken Sesame Balls, Mexican Bean Dip and Eggplant Spread, made with all-natural ingredients, offer a refreshing change from the highly-processed, commercial hors d'oeuvres. We serve them with crisp cucumber, green pepper, carrot, celery sticks, cauliflowerets and radish roses. Young zucchini and summer squash can be cut into sticks for a colorful and unusual addition. Tasty crackers are surprisingly simple and quick to make. You mix, roll, cut and bake and that is all there is to it. We make them in various shapes and top them with different herbs or seeds.

Crackers are cut and placed on cookie sheet for baking.

The combination of homemade peanut butter and whole-grain bread can't be beat for a snack that is really a nourishing meal in itself. *Homemade* is the key word that will save you money and assure you of a product free of stabilizers, emulsifyers and preservatives. You can roast the peanuts quickly in your oven, and once they are cool, simply blend them in your blender. A bit of oil added at the beginning may be necessary to facilitate the blending. At Fitness House, we make many nut and seed butters in this same way.

We have developed a granola type cereal which we call Almond Crunch. It is equally delicious eaten with milk or fruit and fruit juice or simply as a snack just as it is. It's so simple to make, even children can do it. Some like to munch it while watching television.

A dish of raw cashew nuts (cheaper and better for you than roasted), or sunflower seeds and fruit frequently adorn the table at Fitness House to satisfy our snackers.

For the inveterate "sweet-tooth," our recipes include a number of delicious confections (found in the dessert section) which combine seeds, nuts and soy flour with a bit of honey, dried fruits or carob. These, though not low in calories, are high in protein.

Nuts and seeds are without doubt the most convenient high-energy snacks. Ounce for ounce, they supply almost twice the amount of nutrients of any other food. Most common nuts contain about 10 to 25 percent protein. Peanuts are highest in protein closely followed by cashews and walnuts.

Nuts, of course, are actually hard-shelled seeds and all seeds are a rich source of the B vitamins, vitamin E and the minerals—phosphorus and iron. With the exception of almonds and sesame seeds, however, most nuts and seeds are lacking in calcium. For this reason we serve nuts and seeds with vegetables and fruits that are rich in calcium. A frequent dessert at Fitness House is a platter of dried fruits served with a bowl of mixed nuts and seeds.

We use a lot of sunflower and sesame seeds in cereals, snacks, vegetables, salads, breads and desserts. Several of our tortes contain ground nuts or seeds instead of flour. Homemade nut butters make delicious spreads, dips or fillings for celery sticks. Peanut flour adds protein as well as a unique flavor to cookies, pie crust, and bread.

Nut milk is perhaps a surprising idea, but it can be made from any nut or seed. All you need is a blender, water and a strainer—plus, of course, the nuts. Cashew milk or sesame milk are examples of the unusual items you can make. Nut milk can be used to contribute important nutrients as well as the exotic flavor to many beverages and desserts. Try our recipes for Cashew-Carob Pudding and Sesame-Orange Mandalay.

We have worked hard to develop a snack for our Rodale executives to take along on their business trips. It is based on our Almond Crunch Cereal recipe, but in order to avoid sending them off with a bag of cereal under one arm, we had to make a "bar" version of it.

Because of their high potassium and low sodium content, we find that dill, caraway, celery and mustard seeds are valuable as seasoning substitutes for salt. Pumpkin seeds, also high in potassium, have a higher content of iron than any other seed and are rich in vitamin B. Pumpkin seeds are often added to Fitness House salads, to give a special crispy crunch. We also use them as a garnish for many dishes.

We are very enthusiastic about sunflower seeds at Fitness House. Some nutritionists call them the miracle food, and with good reason: they contain more protein than any other seed; they are rich in the unsaturated fatty acids, they have an especially high vitamin E content. Seasoned sunflower seeds, raw or toasted, are particularly delicious. You can nibble them happily, knowing you are storing up precious nourishment.

Because of their high fat content, nuts and seeds can become rancid if kept in a warm or damp place. They should be stored in the refrigerator or freezer where they will keep indefinitely.

In warm weather a cold beverage is the perfect appetizer. At Fitness House we sometimes serve Melon Coolers (delicious made with either cantaloupe or watermelon), or fresh carrot or tomato juice, as a starter before the meal. Our Watercress-Pineapple Cocktail is popular because of its refreshing, tangy taste and beautiful color. What a pleasant way to consume all those precious "dark green leafy" nutrients!

One beverage which is an ideal snack is the High Protein Milk Shake—vanilla, carob, orange or banana flavored. You might want to experiment with other fruits or flavors. Made with skim milk powder and soy flour, it is a low fat, high protein food. If you add Nutritional yeast or seeds and nuts, it is an excellent way to get your B vitamins in their natural proportions.

Mulled hot drinks, such as apple or pineapple juice flavored with spices, are always welcome on a cold evening when friends drop in for a visit. Equally satisfying and popular are the herb teas, particularly peppermint, chamomile and rose hips.

Those who have been making-do with coffee-tea-or-milk (or soda) will make some exciting discoveries among our beverage recipes.

see color photograph

## Almond Crunch Cereal

Preheat oven to 225° F.
3 cups uncooked, old-fashioned, rolled oats
1½ cups dry coconut shreds, unsweetened
½ cup wheat germ or soy grits, if preferred
1 cup sunflower seeds
¼ cup sesame seeds
½ cup raw honey
¼ cup oil
½ cup cold water
1 cup slivered, blanched almonds
½ cup raisins (optional)

In a large mixing bowl, combine rolled oats, coconut, raw wheat germ or soy grits, sunflower seeds, and sesame seeds. Toss ingredients together thoroughly.

**2**

Combine honey and oil. Add to dry ingredients, stirring until well-mixed. Add the cold water, a little at a time, mixing until crumbly.

**3**

Pour mixture into a large, heavy, shallow baking pan which has been lightly-brushed with oil. Spread mixture evenly to edges of pan.

**4**

Place pan on middle rack of a preheated oven and bake for 1½ hours, stirring every 15 minutes. Add one cup slivered almonds and continue to bake for one-half hour longer, or until mixture is thoroughly dry and light brown in color. Cereal should feel crisp to the touch.

**5**

Turn oven off and allow cereal to cool in oven. If raisins are to be added to cereal, do so at this point.

**6**

Remove cereal from oven—cool and put in a tightly-covered container. Store in a cool, dry place.

**7**

Serve plain or with fresh fruit.

Yield:  8 cups.

## Banana-Peanut Butter Appetizers

3 ripe bananas
1/2-3/4 cup peanut butter
1/4 cup orange juice
1 cup finely-chopped peanuts, peanut flour or
　　　unsweetened, shredded coconut

Peel bananas and slice in two, lengthwise.
Spread each half with peanut butter and put
back together. Brush with orange juice.

Roll bananas in finely-chopped peanuts,
flour or coconut. Cut into one-inch pieces.
Spear with toothpick if desired.
Use as an appetizer or to garnish a fresh fruit
salad.

Yield: 14 to 16 pieces.

## Cheese Ball

1 lb. cheddar cheese, grated
1 small can (8¾ oz.) crushed pineapple,
　　　drained (save juice)
1 tablespoon mayonnaise
1/2 teaspoon mustard
1/2 cup finely-chopped walnuts

Combine all ingredients and mix thoroughly
with a fork. Add some pineapple juice, if
necessary, to make mixture soft and moist
enough to handle.

Form into a large ball and roll in walnuts
until completely coated.

Serve with whole grain crackers.

Yield: one 6-inch ball.

# Caraway-Corn Crackers

Preheat oven to 325°F.
2 cups white corn meal
$\frac{1}{2}$ cup whole wheat flour
$\frac{1}{2}$ cup raw peanut flour
$\frac{1}{2}$ cup wheat germ
1 teaspoon salt
2 tablespoons caraway seeds
1 tablespoon sesame seeds
$\frac{1}{3}$ cup oil
$\frac{2}{3}$ cup boiling water, or enough to bind batter

Combine dry ingredients.

Stir in oil gradually.

Add boiling water slowly and mix batter thoroughly.

Place batter by teaspoonfuls on unoiled baking sheet. With spatula or fingers, shape into flat circles about $1\frac{1}{2}$ inches in diameter.

Bake in preheated oven about 20 minutes.

Remove from sheet and cool on wire rack.

Yield: About 5 dozen.

## Cheese Petit Choux

Preheat oven to 400°F.
½ cup cold water
¼ cup oil
¼ teaspoon salt
½ cup sifted potato flour
½ cup shredded cheddar or Swiss cheese
3 eggs

Combine cold water, oil, and salt in a medium saucepan. Place over medium heat and bring to a boil. Remove from heat. Using a wooden spoon, quickly stir in the potato flour, all at once.

**2**

Return saucepan to low heat and stir vigorously until mixture forms a ball and leaves the sides of the pan (about one minute). Remove from heat and add shredded cheddar or Swiss cheese and blend until cheese melts.

Put mixture into a mixing bowl.

**4!**

Add eggs, one at a time, beating well with an electric beater after each addition. Beat until batter is smooth.

**5**

Drop batter by scant teaspoonfuls, two inches apart, onto ungreased cookie sheets.

**6**

Place in a preheated oven and bake for 20 to 25 minutes or until puffs are nicely-browned. Remove from oven and transfer puffs onto a wire rack, away from drafts, to cool.

**7**

To serve: Using a sharp knife, cut off top of puff. Spoon Chicken—Sesame Ball filling into puffs and replace tops. (See recipe in this section.)

Note: Puffs may be prepared in advance and stored in freezer until ready to use. (Store in an air-tight container.) Remove from freezer several hours before filling. Place puffs on a cookie sheet in a preheated 250°F. oven for 15 to 20 minutes to crisp. Remove from oven; cool. Fill puffs as directed in Step #7.

Yield: About 40 tiny puffs.

# Herb Crackers

Preheat oven to 400°F.
1/2 cup rye flour
1/2 cup corn flour
3/4 teaspoon salt
1/2 tablespoon nutritional yeast
1/4 teaspoon dill weed
1/4 teaspoon tarragon
1/4 cup oil
5 tablespoons cold water
1 tablespoon caraway seeds

Mix dry ingredients and herbs.

Mix water and oil. Add to dry ingredients, stir with fork until ball is formed.

Roll out on floured board and cut into squares or diamond-shaped pieces. Top with caraway seeds.

Bake on lightly-oiled cookie sheet at 400°F. for about 8 minutes.
Yield: Approximately 2 dozen.

*Appetizers,*
*Snacks,*
*Nuts*
*and Seeds*

## Chicken-Sesame Balls

1 cup finely-chopped, cooked chicken*
    (see recipe in poultry section)
1 tablespoon finely-minced onion
1 tablespoon minced parsley
½ teaspoon curry powder
½ teaspoon prepared mustard (optional)
¼ teaspoon paprika
3 tablespoons mayonnaise
⅓ cup toasted sesame seeds

Fresh parsley sprigs

In a small bowl, combine chicken, minced onion, minced parsley, curry powder, prepared mustard and paprika. Mix ingredients together. Add mayonnaise, one tablespoon at a time, mixing until thoroughly blended. Taste and correct seasoning.

Form into balls, using one teaspoon of mixture for each. Cover and refrigerate until thoroughly chilled.

Meanwhile, toast sesame seeds in a 325°F. oven until lightly-browned.

**4!**

Remove chicken balls from refrigerator, roll them in toasted sesame seeds and place on a serving dish. Cover and refrigerate until ready to serve. Garnish with fresh parsley sprigs.

*Note: Cooked turkey breast may be used in place of chicken, if desired.

Yield: Approximately 24 balls.

# Corn Pone or Corn Crackers

Preheat oven to 325°F.
3 cups cornmeal
¼ cup peanut flour (ground raw peanuts)
1 teaspoon salt
¼ cup peanut oil
1 cup boiling water—plus 2 tablespoons or
          more until batter holds together
Parmesan cheese (optional)

Combine dry ingredients.

Stir in oil gradually.

Add boiling water slowly, mixing with spoon and finally kneading dough. Keep adding water until dough holds together.

With your fingers, flatten rounded teaspoonfuls of batter on an oiled cookie sheet. If a cracker is desired, flatten it as thin as possible. If a thicker, larger corn pone is desired, use more dough and don't press it quite as thin.

**5**

Bake in 325°F. oven for 40 minutes, or until it is slightly golden around the edges.

**6**

Remove from pan while still warm. Cool on a rack and store in an airtight container. Note: Parmesan cheese can be sprinkled on top of crackers before baking them, if desired.

Yield: Approximately 5½ dozen crackers or 3 dozen corn pones.

# Christmas Confetti Dip

⅔ cup yogurt (see recipe in salad section)
½ cup mayonnaise (see recipe in salad
     section)
2 tablespoons chopped chives
2 tablespoons finely-minced onion
2 tablespoons chopped green pepper
2 tablespoons freshly-snipped parsley
2 tablespoons chopped pimiento
½ teaspoon powdered kelp
⅛ teaspoon paprika
dash of cayenne

Mix yogurt and mayonnaise in a small bowl.

Add chives, onion, green pepper, parsley, pimiento, kelp, paprika and cayenne. Blend together thoroughly. Taste and adjust seasoning.

Cover and place in refrigerator to blend flavors.

Pour dip into small serving bowl and place in center of large serving dish surrounded with rye-sesame crackers and fresh pieces of celery, carrot sticks, cauliflower flowerets, cherry tomatoes and green pepper sticks.

Yield: About 1⅓ cups dip.

# Eggplant Spread

1 eggplant, about 1½ pounds
2 tablespoons olive oil
1 clove garlic, minced
1 medium onion, thinly-sliced
1 cup sliced green pepper (¼-inch by 2-inch
      length)
1 teaspoon salt
½ teaspoon freshly-ground pepper
¼ teaspoon paprika
½ teaspoon kelp powder
1 cup yogurt
Thin slices of dark rye bread cut into small
      wedges

Wash and peel the eggplant. Dice and set aside.

Heat two tablespoons olive oil in a heavy, ten-inch skillet over medium heat. Sauté minced garlic and thinly-sliced onion for about one minute. Add diced eggplant and green pepper slices and sauté until vegetables are tender, but not brown—stirring occasionally. (To tenderize vegetables more quickly, cover skillet tightly and cook for 5 to 10 minutes, remove cover.) Season vegetables with salt, ground pepper, paprika and powdered kelp.

**3**

Remove from heat and pour mixture into a medium-size bowl to cool. Stir in the yogurt; adjust seasoning. Cover and refrigerate to allow flavors to blend.

**4!**

Serve cold as an appetizer. Sprinkle paprika over top. Arrange wedges of rye bread around spread.

Yield: Approximately 2 cups.

*Appetizers,*
*Snacks,*
*Nuts*
*and Seeds*

## Dry-Roasted Soybeans

Preheat oven to 350°F.
1 cup dried soybeans
3 cups water
1 teaspoon salt

Wash soybeans and remove any foreign
particles. Add three cups of water to soybeans
and soak overnight in refrigerator.

**2**

Pour soybeans and liquid used for soaking
in a large, heavy saucepan. Add more water
to cover. Place over medium heat and
bring to a boil; lower heat and add salt, cover,
and simmer one hour. (If desired, one-half
teaspoon oil may be added to soybeans
to keep mixture from boiling over.)

**3**

Remove saucepan from heat and drain
soybeans thoroughly; (reserve liquid for
soup). Pour into a shallow pan and bake in
a preheated 350°F. oven for 45 minutes
to one hour or until soybeans are brown.
Remove from oven and sprinkle with salt
while warm.
Yield: 3 cups.

## Hi-Energy Bar

Preheat oven to 300°F.
2 cups almond crunch cereal (see recipe in
        grain section)
2 eggs, well-beaten

In medium-size mixing bowl, combine cereal
and eggs. Mix thoroughly.

**2**

Spread carefully on lightly-oiled cookie
sheet, pressing into oblong shape about 6
inches by 8 inches and $\frac{1}{4}$ inch thick. Press
firmly to be sure bars will hold together.
With sharp knife, cut into bars $1\frac{1}{2}$ inches
wide and 2 inches long.

**3**

Bake for 20 minutes in preheated oven.
Remove from oven and allow to cool for 5
minutes, then break apart (or re-cut). Cool
completely, wrap individually and store
in covered container.

Yield: 15 bars.

# Guacamole

2 ripe avocados, peeled and seed removed
1 small onion, grated
3 tablespoons lemon juice
½ teaspoon kelp powder
½ teaspoon chili powder
2 tablespoons catsup (optional)
¼ cup mayonnaise

Mash the peeled avocados in a bowl, with a fork, until smooth; or cut the avocados into small pieces and place them with all ingredients except mayonnaise, in a blender. Blend until almost creamy—do not blend too long as the mixture will not keep its shape.

**2**

If guacamole is prepared using a fork, season with grated onion, lemon juice, kelp powder, chili powder and catsup; mix well. Adjust seasoning.

Form mixture into a mound and cover with a thin layer of mayonnaise to keep from becoming dark; refrigerate, covered, until ready to serve.

**4!**

Just before serving, stir the mayonnaise (which covered the guacamole) into the mixture until no trace of mayonnaise remains.

**5**

Serve on crisp lettuce leaves as an appetizer; garnished with fresh cherry tomatoes or tomato quarters, celery sticks, cauliflower pieces and rye crackers.

Yield: Approximately 2 cups.

## Mexican Bean Dip

1 cup dried, red kidney beans
water to cover
½ teaspoon salt
¼ cup oil
1 cup shredded cheddar cheese
½ teaspoon kelp powder
1 teaspoon chili powder

Wash kidney beans, remove any foreign particles. Place them in a medium-size bowl and cover with water. Allow to stand at room temperature about one hour. Add more water, cover and place in refrigerator overnight.

**2**

The following day, transfer kidney beans with liquid to medium-size saucepan. Add more water to cover kidney beans. Place over medium heat and bring to boil; reduce heat, add one-half teaspoon salt, cover, and simmer over low heat until tender.

Remove from heat and drain kidney beans, reserve liquid.

**4!**

In medium-size skillet, heat ¼ cup oil. Add drained kidney beans and mash with potato masher until smooth. Add ⅓ cup of reserved bean liquid to help make a smoother mixture, adding more liquid if beans appear to be too dry. Stir constantly.

**5**

Add shredded cheddar cheese, kelp, and chili powder, stirring constantly until cheese melts. Taste and adjust seasoning.

**6**

Pour mixture into a chafing dish or heated casserole and serve hot with corn pone or corn crackers. (See recipe in this section.) If mixture gets too stiff for dipping, thin with a little more of the bean liquid.

Yield: Approximately 3 cups.

# Nuts and Seeds

1 cup unblanched almonds
1 cup raw cashew nuts
1 cup walnuts
1 cup Brazil nuts
1 cup sunflower seeds
1 cup pumpkin seeds
$\frac{1}{2}$ cup sesame seeds
2 cups raisins (optional)

All nuts should be raw and unsalted. Toss together and serve.

Yield: 4-6 cups.

# Sesame Crisp Crackers

Preheat oven to 350°F.
1 cup oat flour
$\frac{3}{4}$ cup soy flour
$\frac{1}{4}$ cup sesame seeds
$\frac{3}{4}$ teaspoon salt
$\frac{1}{4}$ cup oil
$\frac{1}{2}$ cup water

Stir together flours, seeds and salt. Add oil and blend well. Add water and mix to pie dough consistency.

Roll dough on floured surface, to $\frac{1}{8}$ inch thickness. Cut into squares or triangles and place on an unoiled baking sheet.

Bake at 350°F. until the crackers are crisp and golden brown (about 15 minutes).

Yield: 3-4 dozen crackers.

*Appetizers,*
*Snacks,*
*Nuts*
  *and Seeds*

## Peanut Butter

Preheat oven to 300°F.
2 cups raw peanuts, shelled
¼ cup oil
¼ teaspoon salt

Spread shelled raw peanuts in a shallow pan.
Place in a preheated oven, on middle rack,
and roast for 30 to 35 minutes. Stir
occasionally during baking. Check brownness
by removing skins from a few nuts. If you
have purchased peanuts without skins, you
will not have to roast them so long.

Remove from oven and cool.

Transfer roasted peanuts to an electric
blender and blend about one minute.
Gradually add the oil, one tablespoon at a
time, blending thoroughly. Stop blender from
time to time and push large pieces of peanuts
away from sides of blender with a rubber
spatula. Add salt.

**4!**

Spoon peanut butter into jar with tight-fitting
cover and store in refrigerator for several
hours before using. Peanut butter becomes
firm upon standing for several hours.

NOTE: The above recipe may be prepared
with a meat grinder, using the finest blade.
Stir oil into peanut butter to thin.

Yield: one and one-half cups.

# Sunburgers

Preheat oven to 350°F.
½ cup grated raw carrots
½ cup celery, chopped fine
2 tablespoons chopped onion
1 tablespoon chopped parsley
1 tablespoon chopped green pepper
1 egg, beaten
1 tablespoon oil
¼ cup tomato juice
1 cup ground sunflower seeds
2 tablespoons wheat germ
½ teaspoon salt
⅛ teaspoon basil

Combine ingredients and shape into patties.

Arrange in an oiled, shallow baking dish.
Bake in a moderate oven until brown on top;
turn patties and bake until brown. (Allow
about 15 minutes of baking for each side.)

Yield: About 4 servings.

# Sunflower-Seed Snack

Preheat oven to 350°F.
1 lb. sunflower seeds
3 tablespoons oil
¼ teaspoon cayenne
3 tablespoons tamari soy sauce
½ teaspoon celery seed, ground
¼ teaspoon paprika

In shallow pan, combine sunflower seeds with
other ingredients. Mix together and bake
in a moderate oven for 20 minutes, stirring
after 10 minutes.

Remove pan from oven and drain sunflower
seeds on paper towels to remove excess oil.

Cool and store in tightly covered container.

Note: If recipe is doubled, be sure to bake
a little longer (30 to 35 minutes).

Yield: Approximately 2 cups.

# Appetizers, Snacks, Nuts and Seeds

## Sesame-Rice Cereal

¾ cup raw brown rice
1 cup skim milk powder
3½ cups water
1 teaspoon salt
2 tablespoons sesame seed meal, (whole
      sesame seeds briefly ground in
      blender)
1 tablespoon nutritional yeast

Toast the rice in a dry pan over medium heat, stirring until well browned. Grind in the blender, then toast the powder again briefly, in a dry pan, stirring constantly.

Combine skim milk powder and water with a wire whisk. Put in heavy saucepan; add salt and bring to a boil. Add rice powder, stirring constantly.

Lower heat and simmer, covered, about 10 minutes, or until cereal is thick. Toast sesame meal in dry pan over medium heat, stirring constantly for a minute or so and add along with yeast to cereal. Stir in sesame meal and nutritional yeast. Serve with milk and honey.

Yield: 4-6 servings.

# Relishes

## Apricot Chutney

2 cups dried apricots, cooked and chopped
2-4 tablespoons honey
$\frac{1}{4}$ teaspoon salt
$1\frac{1}{2}$ tablespoons vinegar
1 teaspoon fresh ginger, minced
            or
$\frac{1}{2}$ teaspoon dry ginger (ground)
$\frac{1}{2}$ teaspoon coriander (ground)
cayenne to taste (optional)
$\frac{1}{2}$ cup raw cashew nuts
$\frac{1}{2}$ cup raisins

Add all but last two ingredients to cooked, chopped apricots. The amount of spices, vinegar and honey can be increased or decreased according to taste.

**2**

Add nuts and raisins. Keeps indefinitely. Serve with chicken curry, or any cold meats.

Yield: Approximately 3 cups.

## Corn Relish

6 ears corn on cob, raw
1 green pepper, diced
1 red pepper, diced
2 onions, minced
$1\frac{1}{3}$ tablespoons dry mustard
$\frac{1}{3}$ teaspoon turmeric
$\frac{1}{3}$ cup honey
$\frac{1}{2}$ cup vinegar

**1**

Cut corn off the cob and add diced green and red peppers and onion.

**2**

Combine remaining ingredients in medium-sized saucepan.

**3**

Add corn mixture and simmer slowly for 6-8 minutes.

**4!**

Chill and serve.

Yield: 6 servings.

# *Relishes*

## Fresh Cranberry Relish

4 cups (1 lb.) fresh cranberries
2 medium-sized red apples, unpeeled and
    cored
1 large or 2 medium-sized oranges, quartered,
    pitted
2/3 cup honey

Wash cranberries; drain, and remove stems.
Alternately put cranberries, apples and
orange quarters through coarse blade of food
chopper.

Blend in honey; combine thoroughly.

Refrigerate, covered, several hours or
overnight before serving.

Yield: One quart.

## Red Beet Relish

2 cups cooked beets, grated (5 medium-sized
    beets)
5 tablespoons horseradish
2 teaspoons honey
1½ teaspoons salt
3-4 teaspoons cider vinegar

Combine grated beets, horseradish, honey,
salt and vinegar; mix thoroughly. Taste and
adjust seasoning.

Place mixture in refrigerator, covered, for
several hours before serving.

Yield: Approximately 2⅓ cups.

# Tomato Catsup

2 cups tomato purée
2 cups tomato juice
1 cup cider vinegar
½ cup honey
1 teaspoon salt
1 teaspoon dry mustard
1 two-inch piece cinnamon stick
½ teaspoon whole allspice (or ½ teaspoon
     ground allspice)
2 stalks celery and leaves
2 onions

In a large, heavy saucepan, combine tomato
purée, tomato juice, cider vinegar, honey, salt,
and mustard. Place over medium heat
and bring to a boil.

Put cinnamon and allspice in a spice bag;
add to catsup mixture; then add celery and
onions. When mixture reaches boiling point,
reduce heat and cook, uncovered, until
catsup is thick (about three hours). Stir
occasionally during cooking.

Remove spice bag, celery and onions. Pour
into heated glass container with tight-fitting
lid; cool at room temperature, then store
in refrigerator. Yield: About 1 pint.

# Spanish Tomato Relish

3 ripe, but firm tomatoes, finely chopped
½ cup green pepper, finely chopped
½ cup celery, finely chopped
⅓ cup chopped parsley
¼ cup onion, finely chopped
⅓ cup red wine vinegar
½ teaspoon salt
¾ teaspoon whole mustard seed
1 tablespoon honey
1 tablespoon chopped fresh basil or ¼
     teaspoon dried basil
¼ teaspoon dried, crushed red pepper
     (optional)

In medium-sized bowl, combine chopped
tomatoes, green pepper, celery, parsley and
onion. Add wine vinegar, salt, mustard
seed, honey, basil and crushed red pepper.
Mix together thoroughly; taste and correct
seasoning.

Cover bowl and place in refrigerator. Chill
thoroughly to blend flavors.

Yield: About 3½ cups.

# *Beverages*

## Apple Julep

4 cups unsweetened apple juice
2 cups pineapple juice, unsweetened
1 cup orange juice
¼ cup lemon juice
Lemon slices and fresh mint sprigs for garnish

Chill ingredients.

Combine ingredients together, in order given, just before serving.

Pour mixture into punch bowl; garnish with lemon slices and fresh sprigs of mint.

Yield: Approximately 6-8 servings.

## Carrot-Pineapple Cocktail

2 cups unsweetened pineapple juice
2 medium-sized carrots, washed and scraped,
          cut in 1-inch pieces
1 slice of lemon, ¼-inch thick
1 cup crushed ice
honey to taste (optional)
Sliced orange for garnish

In electric blender, combine the unsweetened pineapple juice, carrot pieces and slice of lemon. Cover and blend until carrot is liquefied.

Add the crushed ice, and continue to blend until ice is liquefied. Sweeten with honey, if desired.

Serve in cocktail glasses; garnish with a slice of orange.

Yield: Approximately 4 servings.

# Basic Soy Milk*

⅔ cup dry soybeans
4 cups water
⅓ cup oil
¼ teaspoon salt
¼ cup honey

**1** Soak soybeans in cold water overnight. If the weather is hot, refrigerate them.

**2** Drain soaked soybeans and add enough water to the soaking water to measure four cups.

**3** Put soybeans and 2 cups of the water into container of an electric blender. Blend at medium-low speed for about three minutes.

**4** Put soybean mixture into the top of a double-boiler. Stir in the remaining 2 cups water and cook over rapidly boiling water for thirty minutes.

**5** Strain soybean mixture through a cheesecloth-lined strainer. Rinse out top of double-boiler and return strained soy milk to it. Cook thirty minutes over rapidly boiling water.

**6** Strain soy milk through cheesecloth-lined strainer.

**7** Pour ⅔ cup hot soy milk into container of electric blender, add oil and blend on medium-low speed for five minutes. (The full time is necessary in order to obtain an emulsion.)

**8** Add remaining soy milk, salt and honey and blend about two minutes longer. Cool. Store in a covered jar in the refrigerator. Shake vigorously before using. Keeps well for a week.

*Note: Use as you would milk, over cereal, in cooking and beverages.
Yield: About 1 quart.

# Beverages

## Cashew Milk

1 cup (8 ounces) cashew nuts (raw)
4 cups water
honey to taste (optional)*

Put cashew nuts, water and if desired, honey, into container of electric blender and blend on high speed for 2 minutes.

Refrigerate in a closed container.
  *Note: Cashew milk is naturally sweet. You may want to taste it before adding any honey.

Yield: 4 cups.

## Cranberry Drink

2½ cups apple cider
¾ cup raw cranberries, washed
1 banana, peeled
½ cup sunflower seeds
½ cup red strawberries, fresh or frozen
        (unsweetened)

In an electric blender, combine ingredients in order listed. Blend until smooth.

Yield: 4-6 servings.

# High-Protein Milk

4 eggs
½ cup yogurt
2 tablespoons oil
4 cups water
3 cups skim milk powder
1 cup soy flour or soy milk powder
¼-½ cup nutritional yeast (optional)
½ cup wheat germ (optional)
2 teaspoons pure vanilla (optional)

Combine eggs, yogurt and oil in blender, blending until well-mixed and smooth.

Add remaining ingredients, blending until well-combined.
Yield: Approximately 6-8 cups.

### Banana Shake
2 cups High-Protein milk
2 bananas

Combine in blender and blend until smooth.
Yield: 4-6 servings.

### Orange Shake
4 cups High-Protein milk
1 small can frozen orange juice (undiluted)

Mix together.
Yield: 4-6 servings.

### Carob Shake
2 tablespoons carob
¼ cup oil
6 cups High-Protein milk
4 teaspoons honey
4 teaspoons vanilla (unless already in milk)

Dissolve carob in oil, add a little milk and heat briefly, to cook carob.

Blend carob mixture, milk, honey and vanilla until smooth.
Yield: 4-6 servings.

# Beverages

## Hot, Mulled Apple Juice or Cider

1 quart unsweetened apple juice or cider
1 2-inch piece cinnamon stick
5 whole cloves

Combine ingredients in saucepan. Place over medium heat and bring to boiling; reduce heat and simmer for 20 minutes.

Strain mixture and serve hot in mugs.

Yield: Approximately 4-6 servings.

## Hot, Mulled Pineapple Juice

1 can (46 oz.) unsweetened pineapple juice
1 2-inch piece cinnamon stick
$\frac{1}{8}$ teaspoon ground nutmeg
$\frac{1}{8}$ teaspoon ground allspice
dash of ground cloves

Combine all ingredients in medium-sized saucepan; bring to boiling over medium heat. Reduce heat; cover, and simmer for 20 minutes to blend flavors. Remove from heat and remove cinnamon stick.

Serve warm in individual mugs.

Yield: Approximately 6 servings.

# Melon Cooler
# (Beverage or Cold Soup)

1 small cantaloupe
1 can (20 oz.) crushed pineapple—packed in
      its own juice
1 cup crushed ice
unsweetened pineapple juice
Mint sprigs for garnish

Peel and seed cantaloupe; cut into chunks.

**2**

In an electric blender, combine about
one-third of the cantaloupe cubes, crushed
pineapple and crushed ice. Blend at high
speed, adding the remaining cantaloupe cubes
gradually. Stop blender and push large
pieces of fruit away from sides of blender.
Blend until smooth.

**3**

Thin with unsweetened pineapple juice to
consistency desired.

**4!**

Pour into glasses and serve, garnished with
mint sprigs.

Yield: Approximately 6 servings.

# Beverages

## Pineapple Cocktail

½-1 bunch watercress*
2 cups unsweetened pineapple juice
3 tablespoons honey (optional)
1 tablespoon lemon juice
1 piece lemon peel (½-inch x 3-inch)
1 cup crushed ice

Wash and drain watercress, remove long stems. Reserve 6 sprigs for garnishing.

**2**

In an electric blender, combine watercress, pineapple juice, honey (if desired), lemon juice, lemon peel and crushed ice. Blend until smooth and frothy.

**3**

Serve immediately in cocktail glasses. Garnish with a sprig of watercress or lemon slice.
*The amount of watercress is optional. Experiment to see how much watercress and color you want.

Yield: Approximately 4 servings.

## Sesame Milk

¾ cup sesame seeds
4 cups water
2-4 tablespoons honey (optional)

Put sesame seeds, water and honey into container of electric blender and blend on high speed for 2 minutes.

Strain. Refrigerate in a closed container.

Yield: 4 cups.

# Sesame-Orange Mandalay

6 tablespoons sesame seeds
2 cups water
2 tablespoons honey
4 oranges, squeezed (2 cups juice)
      or
4 tablespoons concentrated frozen orange
      juice

Put sesame seeds, water and honey into container of electric blender and blend on high speed for 2 minutes.

Strain sesame milk, add orange juice or orange concentrate and blend for a few seconds longer. Chill before serving.

Yield: 4 cups.

# Watermelon Drink or Cold Soup

5-6 lbs. watermelon
$1\frac{1}{2}$ cups unsweetened apricot juice
$\frac{1}{3}$ cup lime juice
2-4 tablespoons honey (optional)

Peel and seed watermelon. Cut into pieces.

**2**

In electric blender, at high speed, liquefy 2 cups of pieces at a time.

**3**

Add juices and honey to watermelon juice and pulp. Chill and float a lime slice on top, if you wish.

Yield: 6-8 servings.

Soups

2.

?

broth broth broth

MINESTRONE

BORSCHT

broth

gaspacho

beef stock

CHOWDER

Soups

MINESTRONE

gaspach

Soups

french onion

# Soups

In these days of canned and packaged soups, many of which taste very good, what argument can be made for old-fashioned soup-making? How can you convince those harried mothers who never stop running all day to try it? When I put myself in their shoes, I can see that it is indeed an accomplishment to prepare any food at all.

Yet nothing out of a can or a package will ever taste like that homemade chicken soup many of us remember.

As we look back on that soup (my mother's specialty was vegetable), somehow it seems that making it was an all-day process. Well, it wasn't. No mother—then or now— could afford that kind of time. Actually, making soup needs to take only a half hour for preparation.

Buy a soup bone or soup meat the next time you are shopping, and store it in your freezer. Then defrost it one day, brown it quickly in a good-sized pot, cover it with water, add some chunks of onion, some celery tops, put the lid on the pot and move the whole thing to the back of the stove where it can simmer while you do your other work. After an hour or two, add whatever vegetables you want to add and seasonings, and let it all simmer another hour or so. Now you have your complete lunch or supper. It actually took less of your time than if you had prepared a meat, potatoes and vegetable meal and hardly any more time than it would take you to cook a few hamburgers. It also costs a lot less.

It isn't necessary to have meat in your soup to make a meal of it. A hearty potato or bean soup is very satisfying. For more protein, serve the soup with cheese or peanut butter and crackers.

There is one piece of equipment—an electric blender—which is a real boon to a busy mother when she's making soups. Suppose your children have an aversion to eating vegetables; try puréeing them in the blender and adding them to the soup that way. The children won't even know they've eaten vegetables! And of course a puréed soup is also a ready-made baby food—safe and nutritious, without the salt and chemicals added to commercial products for flavor or long shelf life.

Because soup is one of the easiest, most delicious and economical things in the world to make, it is on the menu at Fitness House almost every day. Sometimes it's a new concoction dreamed up by the cooks, sometimes an old favorite returning to the menu by popular request. On a cold blustery winter's day, diners welcome the warmth of a hearty soup. And in summer's heat, one of Fitness House's cold soups is a fitting beginning for lunch.

The role of "soup chef" for the day is a coveted one. All the Fitness House cooks enjoy making soup, probably because it can be a creative and aesthetic experience. There must be a steady supply of stock, so whenever a turkey or chicken is cooked for a chicken salad or turkey a la king, the meat is removed and the carcass, wing tips, extra skin or bits, along with an onion and some celery tops, are put into a large pot, covered with cold water and simmered for a few hours. The same is true for any roast—beef, veal or lamb. Whatever is left of the roast, if it can't be used in any other way, automatically goes into the stock pot.

However, each stock should be distinctive. Beef and veal may be combined if desired but ham or lamb, of course, has its own flavor and lends itself in stock to a specific type of soup. For example, a ham stock is good for any kind of bean soup—split pea, lentil or soybean, while a lamb stock is traditional for Scotch broth.

When a cook doesn't have any leftover bones for making stock, she can always buy beef shin bones, chicken or turkey necks, wings and backs, or even an oxtail, very inexpensively. The butcher will crack the bones on request, so that the minerals will migrate into the stock more quickly. An oxtail, browned and simmered, produces especially good stock. The meat actually falls off the bones and when the broth is refrigerated, it becomes gelatin-like.

Since the kind of soup the stock will be used for is not always decided in advance, it is best to keep it simple. Salt, added to extract the nutrition-rich juices from the meat and vegetables, should be the only seasoning in the stock. Vinegar, if added to stock, will dissolve the calcium in the bones and let it pass into the liquid. (The smell and taste of vinegar cook away as the stock slowly simmers.) In the process of unhurried cooking, the connective tissues in the bones break down and their rich minerals are released into the broth. After it has simmered for a couple of hours, the stock is strained, and the marrow is removed from the bones and stirred back into the liquid.

←Soup stock is strained after it has simmered for a couple of hours.

Marrow is removed from the bone and stirred back in stock.

Stock should always be chilled before using, because as the fat in it cools, it rises to the top of the broth and congeals. This makes it easy to skim off. To allow time for this, stock should be made at least a day in advance of its planned use. Fat that is scooped off the top of chicken stock can be saved and used in chicken dishes, for sautéeing, or as part of the roux (or thickening) in the sauce. Although it is an animal fat, it is largely an unsaturated one.

At Fitness House, the stock that is not used immediately is tucked away in the freezer for future use. We freeze it in a bread pan, then dip the pan in hot water, remove the frozen block and wrap it for return to the freezer. When a recipe calls for stock, we have it on hand.

Stock should be chilled before fat is skimmed off the top of it.

Frozen soup stock is removed from bread pans, wrapped and then returned to freezer for future use.

When vegetables are added to soups, they are usually sautéed first in oil or chicken fat. This helps to seal in the flavor of the vegetables and keep them firm when they are added to the soup. Leftover grain dishes such as cooked bulgur, buckwheat groats, and brown rice give soup flavor and texture.

Vegetables are sautéed in oil . . .                     . . . then they are added to soup.

Cream soups are made with skim milk powder. We have learned, however, that the best method of combining skim milk powder and water is by using a wire whisk instead of a blender. The blender breaks down the particles of protein and the result may be a curdled soup, when the milk is added to the hot liquid. The secret of the nice, smooth consistency of Fitness House cream soups is really a simple one. Half of the vegetables are put in a blender with some of the stock. The rest are sautéed and added later. The blended vegetables help to thicken the soup, and give a more concentrated flavor. Occasionally, when a very thick soup is desired, a combination of soy and rice flour or potato flour is used.

Some of the best soups served at Fitness House have been "born" out of "spur of the moment" ingenuity. One day when the meal needed filling out, and there were a few parsnips and some leeks which needed to be used, a Parsnip-Leek soup made its debut in the dining room, just in time to be included in this cook book.

The Rodale Cookbook

# Soups

## Beef Stock

1 beef shin or soup bone (Have butcher
  saw through it so marrow is exposed)
2 carrots, cut in chunks
2 stalks celery with leaves, cut in chunks
2 onions, cut in chunks
2 quarts cold water
salt to taste

Make stock at least one day before you plan
to use it. In heavy bottom soup pot (4-quart)
brown beef bones well, then carrots, celery
and onions.

Add 2 quarts cold water and salt; cover
with a tight fitting lid. Keep it on a very low
heat, barely simmering, for 3 hours. Strain
the stock, discard the bones and vegetables,
cool the broth, then refrigerate. Before using
stock, remove fat from top of it and discard.

Yield: Approximately 6 cups.

## Chicken or Turkey Stock

3 lbs. chicken backs, necks, or wings
  (or 1 or 2 turkey backs)
cold water to cover
salt to taste
1 medium-sized onion, peeled and quartered
1 stalk celery, with leaves

In six-quart container place chicken or
turkey pieces and bones, water, salt, onion,
celery and slowly bring to a boil. Reduce heat
and simmer, covered with a lid, slowly
for 2 hours.

Remove from heat, strain, cool, and
refrigerate. When the stock is cool, remove
the hardened fat.

Yield: Approximately 5 cups.

# Barley Soup

1 tablespoon oil
½ lb. lean chuck roast of beef cut into
       one-inch cubes
1 lb. soup bone
1½ quarts cold water
2 tablespoons chopped parsley
salt to taste
2 tablespoons paprika
2 peppercorns
1½ whole allspice
¼ cup whole barley
½ cup chopped celery, with leaves
¼ cup chopped onion
½ cup diced carrots
1 cup fresh or home-canned tomatoes
Parsley for garnish

Put one tablespoon oil in a heavy six-quart container with cover. Place container over medium heat and lightly brown beef cubes and soup bone. Add water and bring to a boil, skimming surface. Add parsley, salt, paprika, peppercorns and allspice. Reduce heat to low, cover and simmer for 30 minutes.

Meanwhile, check barley and remove any foreign particles. Add to soup. Stir in chopped celery, onion and carrots. Cover and simmer over low heat for one hour.

Add stewed tomatoes to soup and continue to simmer for 15 minutes longer. Remove soup bone.

Serve in individual dishes or soup tureen, garnished with freshly chopped parsley.

Yield: 8 cups.

# Soups

## Bean Soup

1½ cups dried white beans, water to cover
1 medium-sized meaty beef bone
6 cups cold water
1 cup coarsely-chopped celery
1 large carrot, chopped
1 medium-sized onion, chopped
1 clove garlic, minced
1 tablespoon oil
salt to taste
¼ teaspoon freshly-ground pepper
1 tablespoon coarsely-chopped parsley

Wash beans and cover with cold water; refrigerate, covered, overnight.

Next day, using a 4-quart container, combine beans and liquid along with beef bone and 6 cups water. Place container over medium heat and bring to boiling; reduce heat, cover, and simmer.

Meanwhile, prepare celery and carrot; add to soup. Sauté chopped onion and minced garlic in one tablespoon oil and add to soup mixture. Stir and simmer, covered, for one and one-half hours or until beans are very tender. (Season with salt and pepper to taste during last hour of cooking.)

Remove beef bone and cut off meat and return it to soup.

Garnish soup with freshly-chopped parsley and serve in soup bowls.

Yield: Approximately 8 cups.

# Cream of Celery Soup

2 cups celery, diced
2 tablespoons oil for sautéeing
½ medium-sized onion, diced
4 cups chicken or turkey stock (see recipe
      in this section)
¾ cup skim milk powder
¾ cup water
½ teaspoon kelp powder
salt to taste
Chopped parsley for garnish

Sauté celery in oil until almost tender. Remove ½ cup of celery and set aside—to add to the soup at the end.

After removing the ½ cup celery, add onions to the pan and continue to sauté until they and the celery are tender.

Blend or purée, sautéed celery and onions until the purée is as fine as you wish it to be for the base of your soup. Pour purée into top of a double boiler and start it heating.

**4!**

Add stock to celery purée.

**5**

Combine skim milk powder and water (with a wire whisk, not blender), and add it near the end, just giving it time to heat sufficiently for serving.

**6**

Add reserved diced celery, kelp powder and salt to taste. Garnish with chopped parsley.

Yield: Approximately 6 cups.

# Soups

## Borscht

1 lb. raw (or cooked) beets, peeled and
      shredded
4 cups beet water, vegetable or meat stock
2 tablespoons honey
¼ cup vinegar
tamari soy sauce to taste
salt to taste
½ lb. (or ¼ of a medium-sized head)
      cabbage, shredded
½ cup tomato purée or juice
Yogurt (served separately)

Combine shredded beets and beet water (or
stock) in large pot and cook covered on
medium heat until beets are tender.

Add honey, vinegar, soy sauce and salt to
taste.

Add shredded cabbage and cook until cabbage
begins to soften.

**4!**

Add tomato purée or juice and cook an
additional 10 to 15 minutes. Serve yogurt
with soup.

Yield: Approximately 6 cups.

# Swiss Cherry Soup

½ cup seedless raisins
¼ cup lemon juice
1 stick cinnamon (about 2″ length)
6 thin slices navel orange
5 thin slices lemon
3 cups water
2 cups pitted, dark, sweet cherries (fresh
    or frozen)
2 cups sliced, fresh peaches, peeled
⅓ cup honey
salt to taste
2 tablespoons cornstarch
¼ cup cold water
Yogurt (served separately)

Wash fruit thoroughly before using.

**2**

In medium-sized saucepan, combine raisins,
lemon juice, cinnamon stick, orange and
lemon slices. Add three cups water. Place
over medium heat and bring to boil; reduce
heat, cover, and simmer for 15 minutes.
Remove cinnamon stick.

**3**

Add pitted cherries, sliced peaches, honey and
salt to soup mixture; bring to boil.

**4**

Blend together 2 tablespoons cornstarch
with ¼ cup cold water. Slowly add to the hot
fruit mixture. Cook, stirring until soup is
clear—about 2 to 3 minutes.

**5**

Remove saucepan from heat and immediately
pour hot fruit soup into a bowl; cool. Place
fruit soup in refrigerator, covered, several
hours or overnight before serving.

**6**

Serve fruit soup chilled, accompanied with
yogurt.

Yield: Approximately 8 cups.

# Soups

## Cream of Carrot Soup

1 onion, diced
3 tablespoons oil
1 lb. carrots (5-6 large) unpeeled,
    thinly-sliced
4 cups vegetable stock or water
1 cup skim milk powder
2 cups cool stock or water
salt, white pepper, to taste
Chopped fresh dill or parsley for garnish

Sauté onion in oil until transparent. Lift out of pan and put into blender.

In same pan, sauté carrots until tender. Set aside ⅓ of the carrots. Put ⅔ of sautéed carrots in blender. Add some of the stock or water and purée. Heat in the top of a double boiler.

Combine skim milk powder with cool stock, using a wire whisk. Add to purée. Add salt and pepper to taste.

**4!**

Add the reserved ⅓ sautéed carrots to the soup. Garnish with dill or parsley.

Yield: Approximately 6-8 cups.

# Chicken-Rice Soup

6 cups chicken stock (see recipe in this
       section)
½ cup brown rice (raw)
⅓ cup onion, diced
⅓ cup celery, diced
2 tablespoons oil
1 cup cooked chicken, diced
salt, kelp, tamari soy sauce to taste
2 tablespoons chopped parsley

Heat chicken stock to boiling. Add rice and
simmer 35 minutes.

Sauté onion and celery in oil for about 5
minutes and add to soup. Add chicken, correct
seasoning and just before serving, add
parsley.

Yield: Approximately 6 servings.

# Egg Drop Soup

4 cups chicken stock
salt to taste
1 tablespoon cornstarch
2 tablespoons chicken stock or water
1 egg, lightly-beaten
1 scallion (including green top),
       finely-chopped

In a 2-quart saucepan over high heat, bring
the stock to a boil; add salt.

Dissolve cornstarch in the 2 tablespoons
stock or water; add to the pan, stirring
constantly until stock thickens and becomes
clear.

Slowly pour in the egg; stir once;
immediately turn off heat. Correct seasonings.

Pour into soup tureen or individual bowls;
garnish with the scallion; serve at once.
Yield: Approximately 4 cups.

# Soups

## Old-Fashioned Chicken Rice Soup

1 3½ lb. ready-to-cook roasting chicken
3 quarts water
salt to taste
3 peppercorns
¼ bay leaf
2 sprigs parsley
4 medium-sized carrots, washed (unpared) and cut in cubes
1 stalk celery, with leaves
1 medium-sized onion, peeled
2 whole cloves
½ cup raw brown rice
Chopped parsley for garnish

Rinse chicken well in cold water. Place in large pot along with three quarts of water, salt, peppercorns, bay leaf and parsley. Bring to a boil and skim to remove any foam from surface.

**2**

Reduce heat; add cubed carrots, celery and onion (press cloves into onion). Cover and simmer for one hour or until chicken is tender. Skim off fat.

Lift out chicken; let cool slightly. Remove celery, onion with cloves, and bay leaf; discard. Add rice to broth and simmer slowly until tender.

**4!**

Meanwhile, remove chicken from bones; cut into bite-size pieces.

**5**

Return chicken to broth and heat thoroughly (allow about 20 minutes).

**6**

Garnish with parsley before serving.

Yield: About 2 quarts.

# Fish Chowder

1½ lbs. (about 3 cups) potatoes, diced
4 oz. salt pork, slivered
4 tablespoons oil
2 tablespoons onion, diced
½ cup diced celery
1½ lbs. raw fish—flounder, haddock, etc.
2 cups potato water
2 cups fish stock or water
½ cup skim milk powder
2 cups water
salt, kelp, dill to taste
Chopped parsley to garnish

Cook potatoes until tender. Drain and reserve potato water.

Sauté salt pork until crisp. Drain and discard fat.

In oil, sauté onion and celery until tender.

**4**

Cook fish in potato water for about 10 minutes. Remove bones and skin.

**5**

Combine fish, salt pork, onions, celery, potatoes and stocks in the top of a double boiler. Combine skim milk powder and water, using a wire whisk and add to chowder. Heat to piping hot, season to taste. Garnish with chopped parsley.

Yield: About 6-8 cups.

# Soups

## Einlauf Soup

6 cups chicken stock
1 tablespoon cornstarch
2 tablespoons skim milk powder
½ cup water
6 eggs, beaten
Chopped chives or parsley for garnish

Make chicken stock and keep hot. (See recipe in this section.)

Combine cornstarch and skim milk powder and, using a wire whisk, dissolve in water. Add to beaten eggs, combining with whisk.

Just before serving time, remove chicken stock from heat. Beat egg mixture into hot stock, using whisk, add chopped chives or parsley and serve at once. (Do not heat soup after adding egg mixture.)

Yield: Approximately 8 cups.

## French Onion Soup

2½ cups thinly sliced onions
4 tablespoons oil
6 cups beef stock (see recipe in this section)
salt and pepper to taste
cumin (optional) to taste
Parmesan cheese for garnish or served
    separately

In a heavy iron skillet, or heavy-bottom pot, brown onions in oil until a golden-brown.

Combine onions and beef stock in soup pot, tightly covered, simmering for about an hour.

Season with salt, pepper and cumin to taste.

Sprinkle Parmesan cheese over the top or serve it separately.

Yield: About 6 cups.

# Norwegian Fruit Soup

1 cup large dried prunes
1 cup dried apricots
¾ cup seedless raisins
½ cup dried currants
3 cups cold water
1 one-inch piece cinnamon stick
1 partially-squeezed lemon
4 whole cloves
1 large apple, chopped (core removed)
½ orange, chopped (pulp and skin)
4 slices unsweetened pineapple, cut into
        pieces, or one-half cup crushed
        pineapple
2 tablespoons honey
⅓ cup lemon juice
salt to taste
4 cups cold water
1½ tablespoons cornstarch
2 tablespoons cold water
Yogurt (served separately)

In large, heavy saucepan or kettle, combine
the dried fruits and three cups of cold
water. Add cinnamon stick and stud
partially-squeezed lemon (used for juice in
recipe) with whole cloves and add to dried
fruits in kettle. Place over medium heat and
simmer for 20 minutes.

Add chopped apple, orange, and pineapple
to cooked fruits. Stir in honey, lemon
juice and salt. Add remaining four cups cold
water and continue to simmer for 15
minutes longer.

Dissolve cornstarch in two tablespoons cold
water; add to fruit mixture and cook until
slightly thickened, stirring constantly.
Note: This is a versatile dish and can be
served hot or cold as a soup or as a dessert.
Serve with yogurt.

Yield: Approximately 8 cups.

# Soups

## Gaspacho

3 cups ripe tomatoes, peeled* and chopped
      (about 6 medium-sized tomatoes)
1/2 cup onion, finely-chopped
1 cucumber, diced, peeled and seeded
1/2 cup green pepper, finely-chopped
1 small clove garlic, minced
3 tablespoons chopped parsley
2 tablespoons chopped chives
2 cups tomato juice
1/3 cup red wine vinegar
1/4 cup olive oil
salt to taste
1/4 teaspoon cayenne pepper
Thin slices of cucumber for garnish

In a large bowl, combine the chopped
tomatoes, chopped onion, cucumber, green
pepper, minced garlic, chopped parsley and
chives. Add tomato juice, wine vinegar,
olive oil, salt, cayenne; mix together. Taste
and correct seasoning.

Cover bowl and place in the refrigerator for
at least two hours to chill and blend flavors.

Serve soup "ice cold." Garnish with thin
slices of cucumber.

*To loosen the tomato skins for peeling:
insert fork into tomato and plunge into
boiling water for a few seconds. Peel
immediately.

Yield: Approximately 6 cups.

# Leek and Potato Soup

4 cups potatoes, coarsely-chopped
3 cups leeks, thinly-sliced
6 cups chicken stock, or water
salt to taste
½ cup skim milk powder
1 cup water
1 tablespoon oil
kelp powder, tamari soy sauce, to taste
Chopped parsley for garnish

Scrub potatoes well, do not peel, and cut into chunks.

**2**

Wash leeks thoroughly and slice thin. Reserve about a third of the amount of leeks. for sautéeing and adding to the soup at the end.

**3**

Cover potatoes with stock or water, bring to a boil. Add salt. Add leeks (except for reserved amount), and simmer until potatoes are tender. Put potatoes, leeks and liquid through a food mill.

**4**

Combine skim milk powder and water with a wire whisk. Add to soup. Season to taste.

**5**

Sauté reserve leeks in oil until tender, and add with chopped parsley to the soup just before serving.

Yield: 6-8 cups.

# Soups

## Greek Lemon Soup (Avgalemono)

6 cups concentrated chicken stock (see recipe
      in this section)
½ cup raw, brown rice
salt to taste
1 egg
2 egg yolks
¼ cup lemon juice
2 tablespoons freshly-snipped parsley
⅛ teaspoon cayenne
Fresh dill to garnish

Put 6 cups chicken broth into heavy saucepan
or soup kettle and bring to a boil. Add
brown rice to soup, season with salt and cook
until rice is tender—15 to 20 minutes.

Put whole egg and two egg yolks into
medium-sized bowl; beat with rotary beater
or wire whisk until light and frothy.
Slowly add the lemon juice, beating together
thoroughly.

Just before serving: dilute the egg-lemon
mixture with one cup hot broth, beating
constantly with wire whisk until well blended.
Gradually add the diluted mixture to the
remaining hot soup, stirring constantly. Bring
almost to the boiling point—*do not boil
or the soup will curdle.* Stir in the parsley
and cayenne; adjust seasoning.

**4!**

Remove from heat and serve immediately,
garnished with freshly chopped dill.

Yield: Approximately 6 cups.

# German Lentil Soup

1 lb. lentils (3 cups)
2 quarts cold water
1 beef bone
2 medium-sized onions, diced
2 medium-sized carrots, diced
1/2 cup celery, diced
1 medium-sized potato, peeled and grated
2 bay leaves
salt to taste
1/4 teaspoon dried thyme
1/2 teaspoon pepper (optional)
2 teaspoons lemon juice

Put lentils into large pot with two quarts cold water. Add the beef bone, vegetables, bay leaves, salt, thyme and pepper.

Place over medium heat and bring gently to a boil; lower heat and simmer until lentils and vegetables are soft.

**3**

Remove beef bone and bay leaves from soup. Skim off excess fat from soup and remove meat from beef bone. Add diced meat to soup and correct seasonings.

**4**

Slowly stir in 2 teaspoons lemon juice and serve immediately.

Yield: Approximately 8 cups.

# Soups

## Cold Melon Soup

1 large, ripe cantaloupe
1/4 teaspoon cinnamon (optional)
1/2 cup orange juice (fresh or frozen)
2 cups orange juice
3 tablespoons lime juice
fresh mint sprigs for garnish

**1**

Remove seeds from melon, peel and cut the pulp into cubes.

**2**

Place pulp, cinnamon, and one-half cup orange juice in a blender and purée.

**3**

Combine remaining 2 cups orange juice and three tablespoons lime juice; stir into the purée. Pour mixture into a bowl, cover, and refrigerate at least one hour before serving.

**4!**

Remove melon soup from the refrigerator; stir mixture and pour into soup tureen or individual soup bowls. Serve garnished with sprigs of fresh mint.
Yield: Approximately 6 cups.

## Vichyssoise (French Potato Soup)

3 medium-sized leeks, sliced
1 medium-sized onion, sliced
2 tablespoons oil
4 medium-sized potatoes, peeled and
    sliced fine
4 cups chicken stock
1 cup skim milk powder
1 cup water
salt, pepper to taste
Chopped chives or parsley for garnish

**1**

Sauté leeks and onion in oil until soft. Add potatoes, then chicken stock. Simmer, covered, until the vegetables are very tender. Drain and put them through a food mill.

**2**

Combine skim milk powder and water with a wire whisk; add to puréed soup. Return soup to low heat and adjust seasoning. Then either serve hot or chill overnight and serve very cold. Garnish with chopped chives or parsley.

Yield: About 6 cups.

# Minestrone Genovese

2 large eggplants, peeled and diced
1 head cabbage, coarsely-shredded and
    chopped
2 small acorn squash, peeled, seeded,
    and cubed
1 cup cauliflower flowerets
1 cup lima beans, fresh or frozen
½ lb. mushrooms, quartered or sliced
¼ cup olive oil, for sautéeing
6 cups beef stock
2 tomatoes, peeled, seeded, and
    coarsely-chopped
salt and pepper to taste
chopped parsley for garnish
Parmesan cheese served separately

Sauté the vegetables, (except tomatoes), in olive oil separately until they are slightly softened.

In a large soup kettle, heat 6 cups beef stock and add the vegetables (except tomatoes and mushrooms). Cook slowly till they are tender but not mushy.

Add tomatoes and mushrooms during the last five minutes, just long enough to heat through but not lose their color and texture. Correct seasoning.

![4!]

Garnish with chopped parsley and serve with parmesan cheese.

Yield: Approximately 10 cups.

# Soups

## Split Pea Soup

2 cups split peas
1 medium-sized, meaty beef bone
10 cups cold water
½ cup onions, chopped
1 cup celery, diced
2 cups carrots, diced fine
2 tablespoons oil
salt to taste
freshly-ground black pepper to taste
1 tablespoon chopped parsley

**1**

Into a 4-quart container, with a heavy bottom, put split peas, beef bone and 10 cups water. Place container over medium heat and bring to boiling point. Reduce heat, cover and simmer.

**2**

Meanwhile, sauté vegetables (onions, celery, and carrots) in oil and add to soup mixture. Stir and simmer, covered, for one and one-half hours or until peas are very tender. (Season with salt and pepper during last hour of cooking.)

**3**

Remove beef bone and cut up meat. Return meat to soup. Correct seasoning.

**4**

Garnish soup with freshly-chopped parsley.

Yield: Approximately 8 cups.

# Cream of Mushroom Soup

1½ lb. fresh mushrooms
3-4 tablespoons oil for sautéeing
2 green onions (including tops) finely-sliced
6 cups chicken stock (see recipe in this
      section)
1 cup skim milk powder
1 cup water
3 tablespoons cornstarch
3 tablespoons water
salt to taste
2 egg yolks (optional)

Wash mushrooms; separate caps and stems;
then slice half the mushroom caps about ⅛
of an inch thick and coarsely-chop the
remaining caps and all the stems.

In a stainless steel skillet, or enameled,
(iron will discolor the mushrooms), sauté
the sliced mushroom caps for 2 minutes or
until they are lightly colored. With a slotted
spoon, transfer them to a bowl and set
aside.

Now in the same skillet, sauté the remaining
mushroom caps and all the stems and the
green onions for 2 minutes. Set them aside
in the skillet.

Put sautéed mushrooms and green onions
through a food mill or blend them in a
blender until you have a smooth purée.

**5**

Put purée and chicken stock together in the
top of a double boiler. Combine skim milk
powder and 1 cup water with a wire whisk,
not in a blender, and add to purée and stock
mixture. Heat over medium high heat.

**6**

Dissolve cornstarch in 3 tablespoons water
and stir into soup. Cook until cornstarch is
thickened and has lost its raw taste. Add
salt to taste.

**7**

Beat the egg yolks, and add a little of the
hot soup to them, whisking as you combine,
so as not to cook the egg yolk too quickly.
Then when the egg yolk mixture is warm,
gradually beat it into the hot soup with a
whisk and turn heat off. Add reserved
mushroom caps. Serve immediately.
Yield: About 8 cups.

# Soups

## Cream of Parsnip-Leek Soup

1 lb. parsnips, scrubbed and diced
2 leeks, washed and sliced into chunks
5 cups chicken or turkey stock (see recipes
      in this section)
salt to taste
1/4 cup skim milk powder
1 cup water
tamari soy sauce
Chopped parsley for garnish

Cook parsnips and leeks in well-seasoned stock to cover, until tender. Purée in a blender.

Add remaining stock and heat in the top of a double boiler.

Combine skim milk powder with water, using a wire whisk; add to soup about ten minutes before serving. Add tamari soy sauce and correct seasonings. Garnish with chopped parsley.

Yield: Approximately 6-8 cups.

## Cream of Spinach Soup

2 lbs. fresh spinach or 1 10 oz. package frozen
      spinach
1 cup water
1 1/2 cups skim milk powder
2 tablespoons potato flour or brown rice flour
1 cup stock (beef or chicken—see recipes
      in this section)
4 cups water
grated onion to taste
salt, pepper to taste

Wash fresh spinach and cook in 1 cup of water until just tender, (about 8-10 minutes) stirring occasionally. Blend in electric blender until coarsely-ground, not puréed.

Make white sauce by combining skim milk powder, potato or brown rice flour, stock and 4 cups of water, using a wire whisk. Then cook in double boiler, over hot water, until sauce is thick.

Add spinach mixture to white sauce, then add grated onion, salt and pepper to taste. Keep hot in double boiler until ready to serve.
Yield: Approximately 6 cups.

# Cream of Green Pea Soup

1½ cups shelled, fresh peas or 1 10 oz.
    package frozen peas
1 medium-sized onion, diced
1 stalk celery, sliced
2 tablespoons parsley, chopped
1 sprig fresh basil or ¼ teaspoon dried basil
2 cups chicken stock (see recipe in this
    section)
½ cup skim milk powder
1 tablespoon potato flour or brown rice flour
⅔ cup water
salt, white pepper to taste

Cook peas, onion, celery, parsley and basil
in one cup stock until peas are tender—
about 10 minutes.

**2**

Purée vegetables, herbs and liquid through
a food mill, not in a blender, in order to
remove the skins of the peas. Put into the top
of a double boiler. Add remaining stock
and heat.

**3**

Combine skim milk powder and potato or
brown rice flour, in a bowl and stir in the ⅔
cup water with a wire whisk, until mixture
is smooth. Stir this mixture into puréed
peas. Heat long enough to cook the flour and
thicken the soup, about 15 minutes. Add
salt and white pepper to taste.

Yield: Approximately 4 cups.

# Soups

## Potato Soup

5 cups potatoes, peeled and diced
½ cup celery, diced
⅓ cup onion, diced
salt to taste
2 quarts water
white pepper to taste
1 cup skim milk powder
1 cup cold water
Chopped parsley for garnish

In a heavy six-quart saucepan, place the diced potatoes, celery, onion, salt and water. Place over medium heat and bring to a boil (keep saucepan partially covered); turn heat down to low and simmer for 40 to 50 minutes, or until vegetables are tender.

Season with a few grindings of fresh pepper and additional salt if necessary.

**3**

Combine skim milk powder with one cup water, using a wire whisk. Stir into soup mixture and simmer over low heat for about 5 minutes, stirring constantly. (Do not boil.)

**4!**

Ladle the soup into a tureen or individual soup bowls. Garnish with finely-chopped fresh parsley.

Yield: Approximately 8 cups.

see color photograph

## Pumpkin Soup

½ cup onions, minced
2 tablespoons chicken fat or oil
3 cups chicken stock
3 cups pumpkin purée (see method of
       cooking pumpkin in vegetable section)
salt to taste
nutmeg to taste
toasted whole grain croutons for garnish

Sauté onions in chicken fat or oil until
golden but not brown. Put in blender container
with a little of the chicken stock and blend
until puréed.

Combine onion mixture, remaining stock
and pumpkin purée in a heavy-bottom
saucepan. Heat, add salt and nutmeg to taste
and serve with toasted croutons.

Yield: Approximately 6 cups.

# Soups

## Cream of Pumpkin Soup

1½ tablespoons onion, finely-diced
3 tablespoons oil
2 tablespoons rye flour
4½ cups chicken stock (see recipe in
    this section)
1½ tablespoons cornstarch
½ cup water
2¼ cups pumpkin purée
¾ teaspoon ginger
¼ teaspoon nutmeg
1 cup skim milk powder
1 cup water
salt, white pepper, to taste
3 egg yolks, lightly-beaten
Chopped parsley for garnish

Sauté onion in oil until tender.

Stir in the rye flour and cook over low heat, stirring constantly.

Gradually add the chicken stock, stirring with wire whisk until mixture is smooth and boils.

Mix cornstarch with water and add to mixture, stirring until it begins to thicken and boils again.

**5**

Add pumpkin purée and spices.

**6**

Transfer to the top of a double boiler at this point.

**7**

Combine skim milk powder with water, using a wire whisk. Add to soup and heat thoroughly. Add salt and pepper, to taste.

**8**

Shortly before serving time, add some of the hot soup slowly to the beaten egg yolks, stirring constantly. Then add this mixture to the hot soup gradually.

**9**

Keep soup warm but do not overcook or the soup will curdle. Garnish with chopped parsley.

Yield: Approximately 8 cups.

## Tomato Bouillon

4 cups tomato juice
1 bay leaf
1 small onion, studded with two whole cloves
1 stalk celery, with leaves
3 peppercorns
salt to taste
4 cups chicken or beef broth
1 tablespoon honey (optional)
Chopped parsley for garnish
Yogurt (served separately)

In large pot combine tomato juice, bay leaf, onion with cloves, celery, peppercorns, salt. Slowly bring to a boil; reduce heat and simmer for one-half hour.

Remove soup from heat and strain. Add chicken or beef broth and honey; place over medium heat; simmer for 15 minutes longer.

Serve with chopped parsley and plain yogurt.

Yield: Approximately 8 cups.

# Soups

## Scotch Broth

1 lb. stewing beef or neck of mutton, with
        fat trimmed off
1 shin bone
3 quarts water
4 peppercorns
1 bay leaf
salt to taste
½ cup barley
3 carrots, diced
1 turnip, diced
1 medium-sized onion, diced
Chopped parsley for garnish

Wipe the meat and shin bone and put into
large pot with three quarts cold water. Bring
to boil; add peppercorns, bay leaf, salt and
barley; reduce heat and simmer without
boiling for one hour.

After meat stock has simmered for an hour,
add vegetables and simmer until vegetables
are tender (about 1 hour).

When broth is ready, the meat can be
taken out, cut into small pieces and returned
to the soup.

Serve with parsley as a garnish.

Yield: About 12 cups.

# Swedish Soybean Soup

2 cups dried soybeans
water to cover
1 medium-sized, meaty beef bone
3 quarts cold water
salt to taste
½ teaspoon paprika
1 cup chopped celery, with leaves
1 cup chopped onions
3 medium-sized turnips, diced
¼ cup chopped parsley
⅛ teaspoon cayenne pepper
1 cup tomato purée or canned tomatoes
Chopped parsley for garnish

Wash soybeans and discard beans with imperfections. Cover soybeans with water and place in refrigerator, covered, overnight.

The following day, place soaked soybeans in a large, heavy soup kettle. (Be sure to use a large enough pot and leave partially-uncovered, so as to avoid soybeans cooking over. This can happen very easily.) Add beef bone and three quarts of cold water. Place over medium heat and bring to a boil, uncovered, removing any foam from surface as it accumulates. Reduce heat; add salt and paprika. Cover partially and allow to simmer for three hours, stirring occasionally.

Add the chopped celery, onions, turnips, parsley, cayenne, and tomato purée or canned tomatoes. Cover partially and allow to simmer for another hour or until soybeans are tender. Continue to stir occasionally while cooking. Taste and correct seasoning. Garnish with chopped parsley.

Yield: Approximately 3 quarts.

# Soups

## Tomato, Leek & Onion Soup

2 onions, diced
2 leeks, washed well, sliced thin (if leeks
      are not available, use more onions)
1 clove garlic, minced
¼ cup olive oil
2 tablespoons parsley, chopped
1 teaspoon thyme, crushed
1 bay leaf
2 cups tomatoes, fresh (peeled & diced)
      or canned
3 cups chicken or beef stock (see recipes in
      this section)
salt to taste
tamari soy sauce to taste
1-2 teaspoons honey
Chopped parsley for garnish
Chopped green onion tops for garnish

Sauté onion, leeks and garlic in olive oil
until transparent, but not brown.

Combine sautéed vegetables, parsley, thyme,
bay leaf, tomatoes and stock in two-quart
saucepan. Simmer over medium heat until
tomatoes (if fresh) are cooked and flavors are
well-combined. Remove bay leaf.

Season with salt, tamari soy sauce and
honey to taste. Garnish with chopped parsley
and green onion tops.

Yield: Approximately 6 cups.

# Watercress Soup

1 quart chicken stock
½-1 tablespoon honey
salt to taste
1 bunch watercress
water to cover stems

Heat stock and season with honey and salt to taste.

Before untying the bunch of watercress, cut off stems. Wash stems and boil for about 10 minutes. Drain and add the cooking water to the stock. (Cooked stems may be eaten. They are good, seasoned with a bit of tamari soy sauce.)

Wash tops of watercress (flowers) and add to boiling stock just before serving. Boil soup 3 minutes, no longer, as you don't want to lose the emerald green color. Be sure to cook uncovered after you add the watercress or it will darken.

Yield: 4 cups.

# SALADS AND SALAD DRESSINGS

Is there anything more beautiful or appetizing than a salad—in all its crisp, green glory? What a picture with its varying shades of green, its tomato and radish—reds, its cauliflower—whites! And where could you find a more "natural food" than salad? Composed mostly of raw vegetables or fruits, salad provides our bodies with precious nutrients which we cannot get in the same quantity from any cooked food.

At Fitness House our salads sometimes feature one vegetable primarily, such as coleslaw or carrot salad using raisins, dates, apples, or pineapple as a contrast; some use several raw vegetables arranged decoratively in separate clumps—such as grated cucumbers, carrots, beets, turnips, or cabbage—or these same vegetables may be tossed together.

The only limit to variety in salads is the imagination of the cook. However, it does help to have some talent for deciding which textures, tastes and colors harmonize with or accentuate each other. We serve salads of meat, fish, egg, rice and bean; vegetable or fruit salads, and gelatins, aspics and relishes.

Marinated, cooked vegetables have a distinctive and delicious flavor. This is a very good way to use leftover vegetables because they don't have to be reheated. Contrasting colors and shapes, such as corn, sliced beets, whole green beans, carrots in sticks, asparagus or broccoli spears add interest. Before making this salad, we marinate each vegetable, for at least an hour, in an oil and vinegar dressing. Then we sometimes experiment with new taste combinations, by adding an herb to one or two of the vegetables. A border of raw salad greens around the edge of the platter provides the finishing touch.

The ordinary chicken or turkey salad becomes "exotic" with the addition of pineapple, green grapes, water chestnuts and almonds—with a touch of curry powder. And the unlikely combination of beef and beets in a salad is surprisingly delicious.

Our arranged fruit salad brings everyone back for seconds; it consists of fresh orange slices, pineapple slices, halves of bananas, with dates or prunes added for accent if it is winter time, or strawberries, grapes or cantaloupe in summer. Any fruit can be used—dried or fresh. Cottage cheese and peanut butter are very good accompaniments and a hot muffin just tops off the meal.

To qualify for the time-honored Queen of Salads— Tossed Green Salad—a vegetable must be young, fresh and crisp. This word "crisp" is another way of saying "dry" and "cold" when describing a salad. All greens must be well-washed by being immersed in water, then quickly drained, dried and refrigerated.

The most effective and quickest way to dry the salad greens is to shake or swing them in a wire drying basket for salads (most specialty stores sell them)

To dry lettuce, first put it in a wire drying basket . . .

. . . then twirl or shake the basket vigorously.

or, as we do at Fitness House, in a large towel, holding the four corners firmly and winding up as for a baseball pitch. It is amazing how the centrifugal force draws off the excess water in a few "swings." Ideally, this should be done the day before you are going to serve the greens. One reason for this is that the salad dressing will coat the cold, dry leaves of the salad so much better and not end up, diluted, in a pool at the bottom of the salad bowl.

Leafy vegetables, kept in the light at room temperature, can lose half of their vitamin $B_2$ and C in a day, so get them into the cold dark of the refrigerator at the first opportunity. The greatest concentration of minerals and vitamins of any fresh foods is found in dark green leaves, so use endive (sometimes called chicory), escarole, spinach, romaine, Swiss chard, turnip tops, green cabbage and the darker varieties of lettuce.

Parsley deserves a paragraph of its own. It is loaded with nutrients and should be added generously to salads. We store chopped parsley, covered, in the refrigerator for quite a while. There is little loss of nutrients and it's readily available to use in a salad or as a garnish for many dishes.

The unappetizing, reddish-brown discoloration lettuce has when it's been cut with a knife, is evidence of escaping vitamins. This can be avoided by breaking the lettuce. The core can be easily twisted out by hand, after you bring the head down firmly on the table, core-side down.

To break lettuce, bring head down firmly on a table . . .

. . . then remove core by twisting it.

One of the best additions to a salad is fresh sprouts. They might be radish, mung bean, soybean, lentils, wheat, rye or alfalfa. You can easily grow them yourself in 3-5 days. And when organically grown vegetables are hard to get, you have a home-grown ready supply of vitamin C in these crunchy, fascinating little sprouts. We grow 3 different kinds at a time and serve them daily in our green salads.

Of course, salad dressings rate top billing too, because no matter how beautiful a salad, much of its flavor depends on the dressing. In our opinion the best dressing for a green salad is the basic vinegar and oil combination. We use herbs, spices, garlic, lemon juice and wine vinegar along with a choice of salad oil (see General Introduction for information about oils) to change its character from time to time. This kind of salad dressing provides the most practical way to consume your daily requirements of the essential fatty acids. A salad with a vinegar and oil dressing should be tossed as close to the serving time as possible. Never let a tossed salad wait.

We vary our salads, serving them tossed in an herb or lemon and oil dressing one day and with separate dressings the next. Green onion dressing, a great favorite, has a foundation of yogurt and mayonnaise, both of which we make ourselves. The yogurt is thick and creamy, though it is made with skim milk powder. We make the mayonnaise in the blender; it is the fastest method and we like the results. The combination of yogurt and mayonnaise is a good base for a number of different dressings. It has the consistency of sour cream but instead of the high content of butterfat, it has the extra protein of the yogurt and egg, plus the nutrients of the oil.

A salad can be a meal in itself. It can whet the appetite by preceeding the meal, or it can accompany it. Whatever the salad's role in the menu, its appearance in at least one meal a day is an absolute must.

110

# SALADS

## Apple-Gelatin Salad

4 cups unsweetened apple juice
3 tablespoons honey
$\frac{1}{4}$ teaspoon salt
2 envelopes unflavored gelatin
3 cups red eating apples, (unpeeled)
4 tablespoons lemon juice
1 teaspoon grated lemon rind
1 cup celery, finely-chopped
$\frac{2}{3}$ cup walnuts or pecans, chopped
salad greens for garnish

In medium-sized saucepan, combine apple juice, honey, salt and gelatin. Stir mixture until blended. Place over medium heat and stir until gelatin is dissolved.

Remove from heat and cool mixture. Refrigerate until mixture thickens to consistency of unbeaten egg whites.

**3**

Meanwhile, wash apples. Reserve enough apple slices, dipped in lemon juice for garnish. Core and shred remaining apples. Stir in lemon juice to keep apples from turning dark color. Add lemon rind.

**4!**

Add celery and nuts to apples and stir into thickened gelatin. Rinse a six-cup mold with cold water; turn mixture into mold and refrigerate until set (preferably overnight or 4 to 6 hours).

**5**

Unmold and serve; garnish with salad greens and reserved apple slices.

Yield: 10-12 servings.

# SALADS

## Avocado Salad

2 envelopes unflavored gelatin
$\frac{1}{4}$ cup cold water
1 cup boiling water
2 teaspoons honey
$\frac{1}{2}$ teaspoon salt
2 avocados, peeled and with pit removed
3 tablespoons lemon juice
$\frac{3}{4}$ cup yogurt (see recipe this section)
$\frac{1}{2}$ cup Blender Mayonnaise (see recipe
      this section)
1 teaspoon grated lemon rind
Romaine lettuce for garnish
Tomato wedges, orange and grapefruit
      sections for garnish

Soften gelatin in $\frac{1}{4}$ cup cold water for
about 2 minutes. Add boiling water and stir
until gelatin is dissolved. Stir in honey
and salt. Refrigerate until consistency of
unbeaten egg whites—about 1 hour.

Meanwhile, cut peeled avocados into pieces
and put into blender along with 3
tablespoons lemon juice; purée until creamy

and smooth. (If blender is not available,
mash with fork until smooth.) Stir in yogurt
and mayonnaise; mix well. Add lemon rind.

Remove gelatin from refrigerator and
combine with avocado mixture. Blend
together thoroughly. Turn mixture into a
5-cup ring-mold that has been rinsed in cold
water, cover, and refrigerate until set—
about 3 hours.

**4!**

Unmold on romaine or other lettuce leaves
and garnish with tomato wedges, or
orange and grapefruit sections.

Yield: 6 servings.

## Garbanzo Bean (Chickpea) Salad

2 tablespoons olive oil
3 tablespoons oil (sesame or safflower)
3-4 tablespoons cider vinegar
2 teaspoons salt
1 cup garbanzo beans, cooked (see method
      of cooking garbanzo beans in
      vegetable section)
2 tablespoons parsley, chopped
1 cup celery, chopped
2 tablespoons green onion, sliced
1/4 cup pimiento, chopped for garnish
lettuce, green pepper rings and pimiento
      for garnish

Combine oils, vinegar and salt in a small
bowl; mix well with fork to make marinade.

In large bowl, combine garbanzo beans,
parsley, celery and green onion. Pour
marinade over mixture and toss lightly. Stir
in chopped pimiento and refrigerate for
at least two hours before serving.

3

Serve in lettuce lined bowl, garnish with
additional pimiento and green pepper rings.
Yield: Approximately 4-5 servings.

## Swedish Beef and Beet Salad

2 cups cooked beef, cut in 1/2 inch cubes
2 green onions, thinly-sliced
1 apple, diced
2 stalks celery, diced
1 tablespoon pickled beets, minced
2 teaspoons liquid from beets
1/2 cup mayonnaise
salt to taste
Chopped parsley for garnish

Mix all ingredients a few hours before
serving. Chill. Garnish with chopped parsley
and a border of crisp salad greens.

Yield: 4-6 servings.

# SALADS

## Marinated Kidney Beans and Garbanzos

⅓ cup cider vinegar
⅓ cup olive oil
3 tablespoons chopped parsley
1 teaspoon honey
1½ teaspoons salt
¼ teaspoon crushed oregano
¼ teaspoon kelp (optional)
¼ teaspoon freshly-ground pepper
⅓ cup sliced onion, including tender
     green tops
2 cups garbanzo beans (chickpeas) cooked,
     drained (see method of cooking
     garbanzo beans in vegetable section)
2 cups kidney beans, cooked, drained
romaine or iceberg lettuce leaves for garnish

Prepare marinade: combine vinegar, oil, parsley, honey, seasonings and sliced green onions. Blend together thoroughly.

In medium-sized bowl, combine garbanzo and kidney beans. Pour marinade over beans and toss lightly but thoroughly.

Place in refrigerator, covered, and marinate several hours or overnight, stirring occasionally.

**4!**

Serve in bowl lined with outer leaves of iceberg or romaine lettuce.

Yield: 8-10 servings.

# Brain Salad

1 calf brain (about 1 lb.)
1 pint water
2 teaspoons vinegar
⅓ cup mayonnaise
1 teaspoon lemon juice
salt and pepper to taste
salad greens for garnish
Chopped parsley for garnish
Hard-cooked egg (sliced) for garnish

Remove all membrane from brain while holding under cold, running water. In saucepan, bring water to a boil, adding vinegar. Add brain and simmer for 15 minutes.

Remove brain and rinse in cold water. Pat dry and chop into half-inch pieces.

Place chopped brain in mixing bowl, add mayonnaise, lemon juice, and salt and pepper. Arrange on salad greens and garnish with chopped parsley and egg slices.
Yield: 4 servings.

# Pickled Beets

½ cup cider vinegar
½ cup beet juice
1 tablespoon honey
2 cloves
½ teaspoon salt
3 peppercorns
¼ bay leaf
2 small green onions, sliced
2½ cups cooked beets, sliced

Boil together  vinegar and beet juice for a few minutes.

Add honey, cloves, salt, peppercorns and bay leaf. Heat to boiling. Pour over onions and beets and allow to cool.

Yield: 6-8 servings.

# SALADS

## Coleslaw

1 head green cabbage (medium-sized)
¼ cup lemon juice
½ teaspoon salt
¼ teaspoon pepper
1 tablespoon honey
1 cup yogurt
1 tablespoon mayonnaise

Slice cabbage very fine.

Make dressing by combining lemon juice, salt, pepper, honey, yogurt and mayonnaise.

Pour dressing over cabbage, mix well.

Yield: 6 servings.

## Cabbage, Apple, and Date Salad

½ lb. cabbage (¼ of a medium-sized head)
2 medium-sized apples
1 cup dates, pitted and sliced
¼ cup mayonnaise
½ lemon, juiced
2 tablespoons yogurt
2 tablespoons honey
salt to taste

Remove core from cabbage and shred.

Remove core from apples and grate.

Combine cabbage, apples and dates.

In a bowl, combine mayonnaise, yogurt, honey, lemon juice. Toss salad in the dressing. Add salt to taste.

Yield: 4-6 servings.

# Carrot-Raisin Salad

3 cups raw carrots, shredded
½ cup raisins
¼ cup Blender Mayonnaise (see recipe
      in this section)
¼ cup yogurt
2 tablespoons lemon juice
1 tablespoon honey (optional)
⅛ teaspoon salt
salad greens for garnish
⅓ cup chopped soy nuts or chopped peanuts
      for garnish

**1**

In medium-sized bowl, combine shredded carrots and raisins.

**2**

In a small bowl, combine mayonnaise, yogurt, lemon juice, honey and salt; blend together.

**3**

Pour dressing over carrot-raisin mixture and mix together thoroughly. Chill before serving.

**4**

Line a serving dish with greens; spoon salad in center and sprinkle soy nuts or chopped peanuts over top and serve.

Note: One-half cup pitted dates may be substituted for raisins.

Yield: 6 servings.

# SALADS

## Chicken Salad Oriental

4 cups cooked chicken, diced (white meat or a combination of white and dark)
1 cup drained, unsweetened pineapple chunks
2/3 cup water chestnuts, drained and thinly-sliced (one 5-oz. can)
2 green onions, sliced thin
1/2 cup yogurt
1/2 cup mayonnaise
2 teaspoons lemon juice
1 tablespoon honey
1 teaspoon ginger
1/2 teaspoon salt
1/4 teaspoon paprika
1/3 cup slivered almonds (toasted)
salad greens for garnish

In a mixing bowl, combine chicken, pineapple, water chestnuts, and green onions. Toss together lightly.

In a small mixing bowl, combine yogurt, mayonnaise, lemon juice, honey, ginger, salt and paprika. Blend together. Pour over chicken mixture and toss gently, but thoroughly. Chill in refrigerator, covered, for at least one hour before serving.

Serve chicken salad on crisp greens. Sprinkle with toasted almonds.

Note: If desired, one-half cup chopped celery may be added to the above recipe.

Yield: 6 servings.

# Chicken-Rice Salad with Cashews

3 cups chicken, cooked and coarsely-diced
        (see recipe in poultry section)
½ cup celery, diced
2 green onions, sliced thin
3 cups cooked brown rice
½ cup mayonnaise
½ cup yogurt
1 tablespoon lemon juice
1 teaspoon honey
1 teaspoon salt
½ cup raw, unsalted cashew nuts (whole)
Salad greens for garnish

Combine chicken, celery, onion and rice in large bowl.

In small bowl, combine mayonnaise, yogurt, lemon juice, honey and salt; mix well.

Pour dressing over mixture and toss lightly but thoroughly.

**4!**

Adjust seasonings; mix lightly. Place in refrigerator, covered, for about two hours before serving to blend flavors. (Cashew nuts should be added just before serving—to retain crispness.) Serve on crisp salad greens.

Yield: 6 servings.

# SALADS

## Cranberry Salad

1⅓ cups honey
1 cup water
4 cups fresh cranberries, washed
2 tablespoons unflavored gelatin
¼ cup cold water
2 tablespoons lemon juice
1 cup celery, diced
1 cup walnuts, chopped
yogurt served separately

In saucepan, combine honey and water. Place over medium heat and simmer for about five minutes.

**2**

Add cranberries and cook slowly, without stirring until all the skins pop open (about 5 minutes).

Soften gelatin in ¼ cup cold water; dissolve in hot cranberry mixture. Add lemon juice and cool.

**4!**

When mixture begins to thicken, fold in celery and nuts; transfer to mold and chill until firm.

**5**

Unmold and serve with yogurt.

Yield: 6-8 servings.

# Pickled Cucumbers

4 medium-sized cucumbers
⅔ cup white vinegar
4 tablespoons water
5 tablespoons honey
1 teaspoon salt
pepper to taste
4 tablespoons parsley, chopped

Select fresh, crisp cucumbers, score the skin and slice thin.

**2**

Combine vinegar, water, honey and salt and pepper to taste. Mix well.

**3**

Combine parsley and cucumbers and pour vinegar mixture over them. Correct seasoning.

**4!**

Weigh down with plate and refrigerate three hours.

Yield: 6 to 8 servings.

# Greek Salad

1 cup goat cheese (feta), cubed
½ medium-sized cauliflower, separated
          into flowerets
1 carrot, cubed
1 cucumber, cubed
1 medium-sized onion, diced
1 green pepper, cut in strips
2 tomatoes, diced
½ cup dried lima beans, soaked, cooked
          and drained
1 stalk celery, diced
1 head lettuce, cut in chunks
10 radishes, sliced

Toss all ingredients in Greek salad dressing (see recipe in this section).

Note: Other raw vegetables may be substituted or added, such as: summer squash, zucchini, chopped parsley, etc.

Yield: About 10 servings.

# SALADS

## Golden Salad

2 tablespoons unflavored gelatin
⅓ cup cold water
1 cup hot pineapple juice (unsweetened)
⅓ cup honey
¾ cup orange juice (fresh or frozen)
¼ cup lemon juice
¼ teaspoon salt
1 cup raw carrot (grated on coarse grater)
1 cup orange segments, cut in small pieces
1½ cups unsweetened, crushed pineapple
      (drained)
lettuce for garnish
yogurt served separately

Soften gelatin in ⅓ cup cold water.

**2**

Dissolve gelatin mixture in hot pineapple juice. Stir in honey and blend well. Add orange juice, lemon juice and salt; cool mixture.

**3**

When mixture begins to thicken, fold in other ingredients.

**4!**

Transfer gelatin mixture to a mold and chill until firm. Unmold on iceberg or romaine lettuce and serve plain or with yogurt.

Note: ⅔ cup chopped pecans or walnuts or 1 cup sliced bananas may be used in place of (or in addition to) orange segments.

Yield: About 6 servings.

# Green Salad

½ head iceberg lettuce, washed well,
      dried, crisped and broken into
      bite-sized pieces
¼ head curly endive, washed well, dried,
      crisped and broken into bite-sized
      pieces
¼ pound fresh spinach, washed well, dried,
      crisped and broken into bite-sized
      pieces
½ bunch radishes, washed well, cut in
      slices, or small wedges
½ medium-sized cucumber, washed well,
      sliced, peeled if necessary
3 tomatoes, washed, cut in wedges

Substitute for spinach and radishes, any of
the following:
      Watercress
      Raw, grated carrots
      Raw, grated turnips
      Raw cauliflower, separated into tiny
          flowerets, or slice flowerets
          cross-wise
      Red or green cabbage sliced thin
      Celery cabbage cut cross-wise into
          silces as you would cut celery

Combine ingredients, except for tomatoes,
just before serving time. Either toss in a
dressing and decorate with tomatoes, or
arrange with tomatoes on top and serve
dressing separately.
Yield: 6-8 servings.

# Spinach and Yogurt Salad

1 cup fresh spinach, drained and chopped
1 tablespoon lemon juice
1 teaspoon onion, finely-grated
½ teaspoon salt
1 cup yogurt (beat with wire whisk to remove
      any lumps)

In a deep bowl combine the spinach, lemon
juice, onion and salt. Toss the mixture with
a spoon. Then stir in the yogurt and mix
thoroughly. Refrigerate for at least one
hour before serving.

Yield: 4 to 6 servings.

see color photograph

## Sprouted Lentils, Bean and Rice Salad

½ lb. pinto beans or kidney beans
1 lb. fresh green beans, cooked
2 cups cooked brown rice
1 cup celery, diced
½ green pepper, diced
¼ cup pimiento, chopped
¼ cup lentils, sprouted*
½ cup oil
½ cup wine vinegar
1 tablespoon honey
1 teaspoon salt
1 teaspoon pepper
1 medium-sized red onion sliced thin—
        for garnish

Soak pinto or kidney beans overnight in water to cover. Do not drain. Using soaking water, cook the beans until just tender. Don't overcook. Drain. Save broth for soup.

Combine green and pinto or kidney beans, rice, celery, pepper, pimiento and lentil sprouts.

Combine oil, vinegar, honey and seasonings. Toss salad in dressing with the onion rings.

*(See "Growing Your Own Sprouts" in this section.)

Yield: 10 servings.

# SALADS

## Fresh Mushroom Salad

1 lb. raw mushrooms
5 tablespoons olive oil
2 tablespoons wine vinegar
1/4 cup chopped parsley
1 teaspoon dried tarragon or 1 1/2 tablespoons
       chopped fresh tarragon
1/2 teaspoon salt
1/2 teaspoon kelp powder
1/8 teaspoon freshly-ground pepper
Watercress for garnish

Rinse mushrooms quickly, but thoroughly in cold water. Remove the stems and reserve for another use.

Slice large mushroom caps crosswise about one-fourth inch thick, small ones may be halved.

Place sliced mushrooms in a mixing bowl. Add olive oil, wine vinegar, chopped parsley, tarragon (dried or fresh), salt, kelp powder, and freshly-ground pepper. Toss the salad well. Cover and allow to stand in the refrigerator for one hour to blend flavors.

**4!**

Remove from refrigerator, correct seasonings. Spoon salad into serving dish lined with fresh watercress.

Note: For variation, substitute fresh, chopped dill instead of the tarragon.

Yield: 6 servings.

# SALADS

## Spanish Paella Salad

¾ cup raw brown rice
2½ cups chicken stock (see recipe in soup
    section)
½ teaspoon saffron, crumbled
1¼ teaspoons salt
4 tablespoons tarragon vinegar*
⅛ teaspoon dry mustard
2½ cups diced, cooked chicken (see recipe
    in meat section)
1 medium-sized green pepper, chopped
1 medium-sized tomato, peeled and chopped
½ cup cooked green peas
¼ cup minced onion
⅓ cup finely-sliced celery
1 tablespoon chopped pimiento
⅓ cup oil
Salad greens, tomatoes and watercress
    for garnish

Remove any foreign particles from brown rice. Set aside.

Bring 2½ cups chicken broth to a boil in a medium-sized saucepan. Add saffron, and ¼ teaspoon salt to broth, unless it is salty enough. Stir in brown rice, reduce heat,

cover, and simmer for about 40 minutes, or until rice is tender and liquid is absorbed. Stir rice occasionally.

Remove from heat and put cooked rice into mixing bowl. Combine tarragon vinegar, dry mustard and ½ teaspoon salt; pour mixture over rice and toss lightly. Allow to stand at room temperature until cool.

**4!**

Add diced chicken, chopped green pepper, chopped tomato, green peas, minced onion, sliced celery and chopped pimiento. Pour ⅓ cup oil over ingredients and toss together lightly. Add remaining ½ teaspoon salt. Adjust seasoning—if desired, more vinegar and salt may be added.

**5**

Cover and refrigerate two or three hours before serving.

Serve on crisp salad greens and garnish with cherry tomatoes or tomato quarters and watercress.

*If tarragon vinegar is not available, cider or wine vinegar may be substituted. Use $\frac{1}{2}$ teaspoon dried tarragon leaves or 1 tablespoon fresh chopped tarragon with cider or wine vinegar.

Yield: 6-8 servings.

# Spinach Salad

$\frac{1}{2}$ lb. fresh spinach
1 small head Boston lettuce
$\frac{1}{4}$ cup scallions, finely-chopped
3 tablespoons oil
$\frac{1}{2}$ teaspoon vinegar or lemon juice
salt to taste

Wash spinach and lettuce well, then drain and break into pieces of desired size.

Crisp in refrigerator.

Combine spinach, lettuce, scallions, oil, vinegar and salt. Toss until all the greens are lightly-coated with the dressing. Serve immediately.

Yield: 4 servings.

# SALADS

## Potato Salad

2 lbs. potatoes, unpeeled
3 slices bacon
½ stalk celery, diced
1 small onion, diced
3 tablespoons oil
¼ cup skim milk powder
¾ cup water
¼ cup vinegar (cider or white)
½ teaspoon salt
2 tablespoons honey
1 tablespoon cornstarch
2 tablespoons water
1 egg, beaten
1 teaspoon prepared mustard
¼ teaspoon basil
2 hard-boiled eggs, chopped
2 teaspoons parsley, chopped

Cook unpeeled potatoes in lightly-salted boiling water to cover. When cooked, drain and cool. Peel and dice in one-inch pieces.

Dice and sauté bacon. Drain on paper towels. Discard bacon fat.

Sauté celery and onion in oil.

**4!**

Mix skim milk powder and water together (with a wire whisk, not in blender) and add vinegar, salt and honey.

**5**

Dissolve cornstarch in water, add egg and mustard. Combine with milk mixture, add to sautéed vegetables and cook over low heat, stirring frequently, until thickened.

**6**

Remove from heat, add basil, and pour over potatoes. Add chopped eggs and half of bacon. Mix lightly.

Sprinkle chopped parsley and remaining bacon over the top for garnish.
Yield: 6-8 servings.

# Summer Rice Salad

3 cups cooked brown rice
5 tablespoons olive oil
7 tablespoons wine vinegar
1 teaspoon freshly snipped tarragon or
      ½ teaspoon dried tarragon
½ teaspoon salt
½ cup green pepper, chopped
½ cup celery, finely-chopped
¼ cup parsley, chopped
¼ cup green onion, finely-chopped
3 tablespoons chives, chopped
½ cup cucumber, cubed
3 tablespoons pimiento, chopped
iceberg or romaine lettuce leaves and
      hardcooked eggs and tomatoes for
      garnish

Place cooked brown rice in a large mixing bowl. Add olive oil, half of the wine vinegar, and the tarragon to the rice. Toss together lightly. Stir in salt. Cool at room temperature.

Add green pepper, celery, parsley, green onion, chives and cucumber to marinated rice. Add rest of wine vinegar, one tablespoon at a time. Reduce the amount of vinegar

if a less tart salad is desired. Correct seasoning at this point. Stir in chopped pimiento.

Refrigerate rice salad, covered, until ready to serve; or, if desired, this salad may be served at room temperature.

Heap rice salad onto serving dish surrounded with greens, garnish with hard-cooked egg quarters and tomato slices or quarters.

Yield: 6 servings.

# SALADS

## German Potato Salad

2 lbs. potatoes
6 strips bacon, slivered (optional)
       bacon fat rendered from bacon
           or
        1/3 cup oil
1/2 cup onions, minced
1/3 cup vinegar
1/3 cup water
1/4 cup parsley, chopped
salt, pepper to taste
1 tablespoon parsley, chopped for garnish

Scrub but do not peel potatoes. Cook just until tender but still firm. Drain. Slice while hot into shallow ovenproof dish.

**2**

If using bacon, sauté bacon slivers in skillet, over medium-low heat, and add onions, sautéing them in the bacon fat. If not using bacon, heat oil in skillet and sauté onions until golden but not brown.

Add vinegar, water and parsley to skillet, stirring to combine ingredients. Salt and pepper to taste. Pour dressing over hot potatoes and keep warm in oven until ready to serve. Garnish with fresh chopped parsley.

Yield: 6-8 servings.

# Tomato Aspic

3 cups tomato juice
1 stalk celery with leaves
1 small onion, quartered
3 sprigs parsley
1/4 teaspoon salt
1/4 teaspoon crushed bay leaf
dash of cayenne pepper
4 teaspoons unflavored gelatin
1/2 teaspoon kelp powder
1 teaspoon honey
1/2 teaspoon tamari soy sauce
2 tablespoons lemon juice
1/2 teaspoon horseradish
Salad greens or watercress to garnish

In a one-quart saucepan, combine two cups tomato juice, celery stalk, cut into 3-inch pieces, onion quarters, parsley sprigs, salt, crushed bay leaf and cayenne.

Place saucepan over medium heat and bring to boil; reduce heat and simmer, uncovered, for 15 minutes. Remove from heat and strain mixture; set aside.

Meanwhile, put one cup of tomato juice in a small bowl. Sprinkle gelatin over top and allow to stand until softened (about 5 minutes). Add softened gelatin to hot tomato mixture, from step two, and stir until gelatin is dissolved. Stir in kelp powder, honey, soy sauce, lemon juice and horseradish. Cool slightly.

Pour cooled tomato mixture into a one-quart ring mold, which has been rinsed in cold water, and place in refrigerator for several hours to chill, until firm.

Remove tomato aspic from refrigerator and run a spatula around the edge of mold to loosen it; invert over a serving dish; shake gently to release. If necessary, place a hot, damp dishtowel over inverted mold, and shake again to release.

Surround aspic with salad greens or watercress. Center may be filled with coleslaw, chicken, potato or egg salad or cottage cheese as desired.
Yield: 6 servings.

# SALADS

## Sauerkraut Salad

4 cups sauerkraut
1 cup celery, chopped
1/2 cup green pepper, chopped
1/3 cup onion, chopped
1 small pimiento chopped or one small jar
      (2 oz. size) pimiento cut into one-half
      inch slivers
1/4 cup cider vinegar
1/3 cup oil
1/4 teaspoon celery seed
1/8 teaspoon kelp powder
1/2 cup honey
1/8 teaspoon cayenne
salad greens for garnish

Drain sauerkraut in strainer. Place in medium-sized bowl and add celery, green pepper, onion and pimiento.

In small bowl combine vinegar, oil, celery seed, kelp powder, honey, and cayenne. Blend together thoroughly and pour over sauerkraut and vegetables. Mix together; cover container and place in refrigerator to marinate overnight.

To serve, line salad bowl with greens and place salad in center.

Yield: 8 to 10 servings.

# Sweetbread Salad

2 pair sweetbreads (about 1 lb.)
4 tablespoons water
1 tablespoon vinegar
$\frac{1}{3}$ cup mayonnaise
$\frac{1}{3}$ cup yogurt
$\frac{1}{2}$ teaspoon dry mustard
$\frac{1}{8}$ teaspoon curry powder (optional)
$\frac{1}{2}$ teaspoon kelp powder
$\frac{1}{8}$ teaspoon paprika
1 medium-sized cucumber, peeled and diced
$\frac{1}{3}$ cup celery, chopped fine
3 tablespoons parsley, chopped
1 tablespoon chives or onion, chopped
salt to taste
Salad greens, pimiento strips for garnish

Wash sweetbreads under cold, running water. Remove as much of the connective tissue as possible. Place in saucepan with a tight-fitting lid. Add 4 tablespoons water and 1 tablespoon vinegar. Steam over low heat for 15 minutes.

**2**

Drain sweetbreads. Remove any remaining connective tissue. Dice them and chill while preparing dressing.

**3**

In a small bowl, combine mayonnaise, yogurt, dry mustard, curry powder, kelp powder and paprika. Blend together.

**4**

Remove sweetbreads from refrigerator. Add cucumber, celery, parsley and chives or onion. Pour dressing over sweetbread mixture and toss ingredients together lightly but thoroughly. Season with salt to taste. Cover and place in refrigerator to chill.

**5**

Serve on salad greens. Decorate with pimiento strips, if desired.

Yield: 6 servings.

133

# SALADS

## Tomato-Bulgur Salad

½ cup coarsely-ground bulgur (crushed
      wheat)
cold water to cover
⅓ cup onion, finely-chopped
½ cup parsley, chopped
3 medium-sized fresh, ripe tomatoes,
      chopped
⅓ cup lemon juice
1 teaspoon kelp powder or salt
¼ cup olive oil
2 tablespoons finely-cut fresh mint or 1
      tablespoon dried-crumbled mint
Romaine lettuce and fresh mint or parsley
      for garnish

Place the bulgur in a bowl and pour enough
cold water over bulgur to cover completely.
Allow it to soak for about 10 to 15 minutes.

Drain bulgur in a sieve or colander lined
with a double thickness of dampened
cheesecloth. Wrap the bulgur in the
cheesecloth and squeeze it vigorously until
completely dry.

Place the drained bulgur in a deep bowl and
add the chopped onion, parsley, tomatoes,
lemon juice and kelp powder or salt. Toss
the mixture gently but thoroughly. Place in
refrigerator, covered for about one hour
to blend flavors.

**4!**

Just before serving, stir in the olive oil
and chopped mint; adjust seasoning. Mound
the salad in a serving dish surrounded by
romaine lettuce leaves. Garnish with
additional mint or fresh parsley, if desired.

Yield: 4-6 servings.

# Exotic Turkey Salad

2½ cups cooked turkey, cubed
2 cups celery, diced
1 can (1 lb. 4 oz.) unsweetened pineapple
      chunks, drained
¾ cup almonds, blanched and slivered
      (save a few and toast them for
      garnish)
½ lb. seedless grapes, cut in half
1½ cups mayonnaise
2 teaspoons curry powder
1 tablespoon tamari soy sauce
1 tablespoon lemon juice
salt to taste
Salad greens, watercress and toasted
      almonds for garnish

Combine first five ingredients.

Make dressing by combining mayonnaise,
curry powder, tamari soy sauce, lemon juice
and salt.

Pour over turkey mixture; toss lightly until
well-mixed; correct seasonings.

**4!**

Serve on crisp salad greens, garnished with
watercress, and sprinkle a few toasted
almonds over the top.

Yield: 6 servings.

# SALADS

## Macedoine of Vegetables

2 cups (4 or 5 medium-sized) cooked,
    cubed potatoes
2 cups cooked peas
2 cups cooked green beans, cut into
    one-inch pieces
2 cups cooked lima beans
2 cups cooked carrots, cubed
$1\frac{1}{2}$ tablespoons wine vinegar
$\frac{1}{2}$ teaspoon kelp powder
$\frac{1}{4}$ teaspoon dry mustard
1 teaspoon salt
$\frac{1}{2}$ teaspoon freshly-ground pepper
1 tablespoon lemon juice
1 cup mayonnaise (approximately)
$\frac{1}{2}$ cup pignolia nuts or sunflower seed
    kernels
3 hard-cooked eggs, sliced
2 medium-sized tomatoes, cut in wedges
salad greens, hard-cooked eggs, tomato
    wedges for garnish

Place cooked vegetables in large mixing bowl.

**2**

Combine wine vinegar, kelp powder, dry mustard, salt and pepper in a small bowl. Blend together and pour over cooked vegetables; toss gently.

**3**

Sprinkle one tablespoon of lemon juice over top and stir in enough mayonnaise to moisten the vegetables well. Add pignolia nuts or sunflower kernels. Taste and correct seasoning.

**4!**

Cover and place in refrigerator and chill for several hours before serving.

**5**

Pile macedoine of vegetables on a serving plate lined with salad greens. Garnish with hard-cooked eggs and tomato wedges.

Note: Tomato aspic ring is an excellent accompaniment with this vegetable combination—omit tomato wedges.

Yield: 8-10 servings.

# Marinated, Cooked Vegetable Salad

*Vegetables which lend themselves well are:*
Cauliflower
Carrots
Beets
Green beans
Corn
Peas
Broccoli
Asparagus

This salad gives wide scope to the creative cook. It can be as pretty as a painting, if you choose your colors and textures with imagination. You can use a round or rectangular platter; you can decide to use a combination of 2, 3, 4, or 5 vegetables. If you use cauliflower, for example, you can put the whole head in the center of a round platter, and surround it with clumps or "hills" of 2 or 3 other vegetables, such as carrots, corn or green beans. You might want two "hills" of each arranged opposite each other, with colors alternating (the green between the orange and yellow).

Simply cut the vegetable in whatever shape you desire, cook it just until tender, drain and cool it.

Once the vegetable is completely cooked and cooled, marinate it in the following oil and vinegar dressing (preferably for an hour, stirring every 15 minutes). Then arrange your platter. Mayonnaise or yogurt may be served separately.

As to amounts, you will have to plan to make more than you would ordinarily need to serve one vegetable, as your guests will want to try each vegetable on the platter. So plan a 4-ounce portion of each vegetable for each person, unless, of course, you use a very large variety of vegetables (5 or 6) and your vegetable platter is just one of a number of dishes on a buffet for a larger group of people.

MARINADE:
1 cup vinegar (cider)
1 cup safflower oil
3 teaspoons honey
2 teaspoons salt
$1\frac{1}{2}$ teaspoons oregano
$\frac{3}{4}$ teaspoon kelp powder
$\frac{3}{4}$ teaspoon pepper

# SALADS

## Vegetable Mold

2 cups tomatoes (fresh or canned), diced
1 envelope unflavored gelatin
½ teaspoon salt
3 tablespoons honey
2 teaspoons lemon juice
½ teaspoon grated lemon rind
½ cup celery, diced
¾ cup carrots, shredded
Lettuce leaves for garnish
Yogurt or cottage cheese (served separately)

Place tomatoes in small saucepan; sprinkle gelatin over tomatoes, mix together with wooden spoon.

Place saucepan on burner over medium heat and bring to a boil. Remove from heat and add salt and honey; cool mixture. Stir in lemon juice and rind.

**3**

Meanwhile, prepare vegetables. Add to tomato-gelatin mixture. Turn into a one-quart mold and place in refrigerator for three to four hours or overnight to set.

**4!**

Unmold salad on serving plate lined with romaine or iceberg lettuce leaves. Serve with yogurt or cottage cheese.

Yield: 4-5 servings.

## Raw Vegetable Pinwheel Salad

2 cups carrots, coarsely-grated
2 cups green or white cabbage, finely-shredded
2 cups raw beets, peeled and finely-grated
2 cups cucumber, peeled, seeded and
    coarsely-grated
1-2 cups fresh sprouts from wheat, soybeans,
    radishes, etc. (optional)
Salad greens for garnish

Prepare vegetables. Keep each one separate.

**2**

Arrange in clumps or "hills" on a platter which has first been lined with crisp salad greens. Either keep the sprouts in a clump in the center, or sprinkle them on top of the white cabbage or cucumbers for color.

**3**

Serve either a yogurt—mayonnaise, or oil-and-vinegar dressing (see recipes in this section) separately; or, if you prefer, lightly toss each vegetable in a dressing before you arrange it.

Yield: 6-8 servings.

## Tossed Raw Vegetable Salad

½ lb. (¼ of a medium-sized) green
    cabbage, finely-shredded
½ lb. carrots, finely-grated
½ lb. red cabbage, finely-shredded
¼ green pepper, slivered
1 fresh pimiento or red pepper, slivered
¼ head cauliflower, separated into flowerets,
    and sliced crosswise

Prepare vegetables and combine in layers or at random in a large salad bowl.

Just before serving, toss in oil-and-vinegar dressing (see recipes in this section) or serve separate dressings.

Yield: 6-8 servings.

# SALADS

## Waldorf Salad

4 medium-sized tart, eating apples, cored
      and cubed (leave red skin on for
      color)
$\frac{1}{4}$ cup celery, chopped
$\frac{1}{4}$ cup raisins
$\frac{1}{2}$ cup walnuts, chopped
1 tablespoon lemon juice
2 tablespoons yogurt
2 tablespoons mayonnaise
2 teaspoons honey
pinch of salt
Lettuce leaves for garnish

Combine apples, celery, raisins and walnuts.

Mix together lemon juice, yogurt, mayonnaise, honey and salt. Stir until well blended.

Add dressing to apple mixture, mix well, and serve on crisp lettuce leaves.

Yield: 4-6 servings.

Carrot-Pineapple Cocktail

Pineapple Cocktail

High-Protein Banana Shake

Sesame-Orange Mandalay

Melon Cooler

Apple Julep

Watermelon Drink

for recipes see chapter on Appetizers, Snacks, Nuts, Seeds, Relishes and Beverages

for recipes see chapter on
Appetizers, Snacks, Nuts,
Seeds, Relishes and Beverages

Christmas
Confetti
Dip

Mexican
Bean
Dip

Guacamole

Caraway Corn Crackers

## Almond Crunch Cereal

for recipe see chapter on
Appetizers, Snacks, Nuts, Seeds,
Relishes and Beverages

# Pumpkin Soup

for recipe
see chapter on Soups

# Growing Your Own Sprouts

Obtain any of the following seeds or beans which have not been treated with chemicals.

mung beans
soybeans
lentils
alfalfa
wheat
rye
radish
watercress

Put ¼-½ cup seeds in a quart jar and soak them for 8 hours or overnight. Cover the jar with cheesecloth or nylon netting, securing the cloth with a rubber band around the neck of the bottle. Put jar in a dark place or cover with paper bag to preserve vitamins.

After the seeds have soaked the proper amount of time, pour off the soaking water, saving it to use in soups because of its nutrients. Rinse the seeds and drain them, leaving the jar tilted top-side down, so that any excess moisture will drain off.

At the end of the day, rinse sprouts again in order to remove any fungus which may have started to grow.

Repeat this rinsing process twice a day for at least 3 days, until the sprouts are as long as desired.* Then refrigerate in a closed container. Sprouts keep well in the refrigerator 8-10 days. The vitamin C content is actually increased after 3-4 days of refrigeration. Sprouts may be frozen but after being thawed they do not retain their crispness, so should be used for soup or in a hot dish instead of for salad.

*Mung, soy and lentil sprouts are most palatable when the sprout is ½-1 inch in length; alfalfa, wheat, rye, radish and watercress when the sprout is no longer than the seed.

# SALAD DRESSINGS

## Basic Mayonnaise

1 egg
1 tablespoon lemon juice
1 teaspoon honey
¼ teaspoon salt
1 cup oil
1 tablespoon lemon juice

Have all ingredients at room temperature.

**2**

In small mixing bowl, with electric beater set at medium speed, beat egg, 1 tablespoon lemon juice, honey and salt.

**3**

Add ¼ cup oil, one drop at a time, beating constantly.

**4!**

Slowly add remaining oil, a tablespoon at a time in the beginning, beating well after each addition, then adding oil in a steady stream, beating continuously until mixture reaches a thick consistency.

**5**

Gradually add remaining 1 tablespoon lemon juice and continue beating until thoroughly combined.

**6**

Refrigerate, covered, in glass container until ready to use. Mayonnaise will thicken during refrigeration.

Yield: Approximately 1 cup.

# Blender Mayonnaise

1 egg or 2 egg yolks
2 tablespoons lemon juice or cider vinegar
1/4 teaspoon salt
1/2 teaspoon dry mustard
1 1/3 cups oil

Combine egg or egg yolks, lemon juice or vinegar, salt and dry mustard in blender. Blend together for about one minute.

**2**

Gradually add oil, slowly but continuously, blending until all of the oil is incorporated. Stop blender and scrape down sides with rubber scraper periodically.

**3**

Spoon mayonnaise into a glass container, cover and store in refrigerator.

Yield: About 1 1/2 cups.

# Fruit Dressing

1 cup yogurt
2 tablespoons fresh orange juice
1 teaspoon orange rind
1 teaspoon lemon juice
1/2 teaspoon lemon rind
1 tablespoon honey
1/4 teaspoon nutmeg
1/8 teaspoon mace

Blend all ingredients together in order given.

Pour into a container with cover and place in refrigerator.

Serve with fruit salads or gelatin salads.

Yield: Approximately 1 1/4 cups.

# SALAD DRESSINGS

## Chive Dressing

1 cup yogurt
1/2 cup mayonnaise
1/2 cup snipped chives
1 tablespoon lemon juice
1 teaspoon salt
1 tablespoon horseradish

In small bowl, combine all ingredients, mixing well. Refrigerate, covered, until ready to use.

Yield: 1 1/2 cups.

## Spicy French Dressing

1 cup oil
1/3 cup red wine vinegar
2 tablespoons catsup
1 tablespoon lemon juice
1/2 teaspoon salt
1/4 teaspoon paprika
1/4 teaspoon cayenne

In a screw top jar, combine oil, vinegar, catsup, lemon juice, salt, paprika and cayenne. Cover and shake vigorously to blend. Store in refrigerator, covered, until ready to serve.

Yield: About 1 1/2 cups.

# Green Herb Dressing

¾ cup mayonnaise
⅔ cup yogurt
1 teaspoon freshly-snipped dill weed
2 tablespoons chopped parsley
2 tablespoons snipped chives
2 teaspoons freshly-chopped tarragon leaves
1 teaspoon freshly-snipped thyme leaves or
        marjoram leaves
1½ teaspoons freshly-snipped basil leaves
¼ teaspoon paprika
½ teaspoon kelp powder
¼ teaspoon salt

In small bowl, combine ingredients in order given. Mix together thoroughly. Adjust seasoning.

Cover and place in refrigerator several hours or overnight to blend flavors.

Serve with green salad; or combine wedges of fresh tomatoes and thinly sliced cucumbers and toss lightly with dressing.
Note: Substitute whatever fresh herbs you have on hand for the ones above.
Yield: Approximately 1½ cups.

# Greek Salad Dressing

6 tablespoons safflower oil
6 tablespoons olive oil
2 tablespoons lemon juice
2 tablespoons wine vinegar
2 cloves garlic
1½ tablespoons yogurt
1 tablespoon prepared mustard
½ teaspoon salt
¼ teaspoon sage
¼ teaspoon thyme
¼ teaspoon basil
¼ teaspoon oregano

Combine all ingredients in blender; blend five minutes.

Store in covered jar in refrigerator.

Yield: Approximately 1 cup.

# SALAD DRESSINGS

## Herb Dressing

½ cup oil
3 tablespoons wine vinegar
¼ teaspoon dried crushed thyme
¼ teaspoon dried crushed marjoram
¼ teaspoon crushed tarragon or 1 teaspoon
     freshly chopped
1 tablespoon freshly-chopped basil or ½
     teaspoon dried crushed
1 tablespoon freshly-snipped parsley
½ teaspoon salt

Combine all ingredients in a jar with a tight-fitting lid and shake vigorously. Allow to stand for 15 minutes before serving.

Shake well before adding to crisp salad greens.

Yield: ⅔ cup.

## Herb French Dressing

½ teaspoon summer savory
½ teaspoon rosemary
½ teaspoon chives or basil
½ cup oil
2 tablespoons wine vinegar
2 tablespoons cider vinegar
½ teaspoon salt
¼ teaspoon dry mustard

Crush herbs by mortar and pestle or by rolling with a rolling pin.

Put all ingredients together in bowl and whisk.

Store in covered glass container in refrigerator.

Yield: ¾ cup.

# Lemon Dressing

⅔ cup oil
⅓ cup lemon juice
1 clove garlic, minced
½ teaspoon prepared mustard
1½ teaspoons salt
¼ teaspoon pepper

Combine all ingredients in blender, blend 5 minutes.

Store in covered jar in refrigerator.

Yield: 1 cup.

# Lime Sesame Dressing

½ cup oil
½ teaspoon grated lime rind
3 tablespoons lime juice
½ teaspoon dry mustard
½ teaspoon honey
¼ teaspoon salt
⅛ teaspoon paprika
3 teaspoons toasted sesame seed*

Combine all ingredients in a jar with a tight-fitting lid. Shake vigorously to combine well.

Chill in refrigerator before serving.

Delicious on a fresh fruit salad.

* Note: To toast sesame seeds, place in a shallow pan in a 325°F. preheated oven and bake for 15 minutes or until lightly browned.

Lemon juice and rind may be substituted for lime in the above recipe, if desired.

Yield: ¾ cup.

## Mock Green Goddess Dressing or Dip

1 cup mayonnaise
½ cup yogurt
2 green spring onions (use green part also)
      cut in one-inch pieces
1 tablespoon tarragon vinegar
1½ teaspoons lemon juice
1 clove garlic, halved
½ cup watercress leaves
⅛ teaspoon cayenne pepper
½ teaspoon salt

Add ingredients to blender container in order given. Cover and run on high speed until onions are finely-chopped and dressing is smooth in texture.

Pour into a small serving dish. Cover and refrigerate to allow flavors to blend.

Yield: 1½ cups.

## Green Onion Dressing

1 cup yogurt
2½ cups mayonnaise
2 tablespoons lemon juice
½ teaspoon salt
¾ cup thinly-sliced green onions (including
      tops)

Combine yogurt and mayonnaise with wire whisk.

Add lemon juice, salt and onions.

Store in glass, quart container in refrigerator, covered.

Yield: About 4 cups.

# Orange-Honey Dressing

1 teaspoon salt
½ teaspoon dry mustard
½ teaspoon paprika
1 cup oil
⅓ cup honey
¼ cup lemon juice
½ cup fresh orange juice or frozen
       orange concentrate
1 teaspoon lemon rind

Combine salt, mustard and paprika. Add remaining ingredients and beat until well combined. Chill in refrigerator until ready to serve.

Yield: 2 cups.

# Russian Dressing

1 cup yogurt
2 cups mayonnaise
1 cup catsup
2 teaspoons horseradish

Combine yogurt and mayonnaise with wire whisk.

Stir in catsup and horseradish.

Store in covered quart glass jar in refrigerator.

Yield: About 4 cups.

# SALAD DRESSINGS

## Yogurt

1½ cups skim milk powder
3¾ cups water
2 tablespoons plain commercial yogurt for
      "starter" (or use 2 tablespoons of
      your homemade yogurt from a
      previous batch)

Combine skim milk powder and water with a wire whisk. Add yogurt "starter" and mix thoroughly.

**2**

Strain into a crockery, glass or stainless steel bowl, cover with a dry dish towel and wrap bowl in a blanket. Keep in a warm place (about 90 degrees) overnight. (If you have an oven with a pilot light, it is an ideal place.)

**3**

Next morning, with paper toweling, blot off the liquid which has formed on top of the yogurt. Remove 2 tablespoons of yogurt and keep in a jar in the refrigerator for your next "starter."

**4!**

Place yogurt in small glass jars, cover tightly and store in refrigerator until ready to use. Yogurt will keep well for at least a week.

Yield: 1 quart.

# Yogurt-Roquefort Dressing

⅓ cup mayonnaise
1½ cups yogurt
2 tablespoons onion or chives, minced
1 tablespoon lemon juice
½ teaspoon salt
4 tablespoons crumbled roquefort or blue
      cheese

Combine all ingredients, except cheese, and
mix well to blend flavors. Fold in cheese,
broken into small chunks (not too fine). Store
covered in refrigerator until ready to serve.

Yield: Approximately 2¼ cups.

halupkis

Mackerel

Mediterranean

LAMB
STEW

sauce

pot roast

Sukiyaki

4.

4.

beef

stew

Meat

Mediterranean

Sauce

Plen

Sukiyaki

MEAT
LOAF

stroganoff

Sauce

Sauerbrate

# Meats, Poultry, Fish & Sauces

The most important part of any meal is the protein. Usually this means the meat course. Though meat is not the only source of high quality protein, it is complete in the most concentrated form.

Why is protein so important? It is a necessary raw material in building young, growing bodies, and it is equally necessary for maintaining bones, muscles, hair, skin and nails, at any age. About 20 percent of the human body is protein.

In the five lunch-time meals we serve weekly we try to include one meal each of beef, chicken or turkey, and fish. The remaining two luncheons might feature a cheese dish, an egg dish or one using soybeans or some organ meat. The beef meal could be a stew, a meat loaf, occasionally a roast, or the beef may be the mainstay of a hearty vegetable soup. The poultry might appear in a chicken-and-rice pilaf or a turkey-cashew salad. The fish is usually broiled and served with a sauce. Sometimes we offer a fish chowder or casserole for variety. Occasionally veal or lamb is on the menu instead of beef, but, delicious as they are, these meats (organically grown) are not easy to come by and are quite expensive, so we don't have them as often as we'd like.

Our most popular meal by far, is sautéed liver. People at the Press stand in line to sign up for that meal a week ahead of time. In order to keep peace in the Rodale Press "family," we must schedule liver at least every other week.

I have puzzled about what it is that makes our method of cooking the liver produce such "raves." We simply dredge the slices in salted rye flour, sauté them quickly in corn or peanut oil in a skillet over medium high heat. I can only conclude that it is the fast cooking and brief time between the cooking and eating that makes the liver taste especially good.

In general, organ meats are the most nutritious meats you can eat. This stands to reason because these organs in the animal carry on the vital life processes, and therefore they must contain more protein, vitamins and minerals of a superior quality than the muscle meats do. Liver contains from 20 to 50 times as much $B_{12}$ as the muscle meats, for example, and kidneys contain 10 times as much.

It is unfortunate that, in America, most of the kidneys sold over the counter go to pets. Although kidneys have less of a following than liver at Fitness House, our more adventurous guests do seem to enjoy the Kidney Creole and Beef-and-Kidney Casserole.

Of all the edible kidneys, those from veal and lamb have the least distinctive flavor. Those from beef have more of the "kidney" taste, but some people (especially the British) like this. Pork kidneys and livers are stronger still.

Kidneys should also be cooked as little as possible, except for pork kidneys, which must always be cooked thoroughly to eliminate the danger of trichinosis. One important point to remember about preparing kidneys is to cut the white tissue out of the center of the kidney even before washing it.

Cut white tissues from the centers of kidneys before washing them.

Enzymes convert the nitrogen in this white tissue into ammonia, which is soluble in water and can penetrate the meat. Bathing the kidneys in a little vinegar after washing them will help neutralize any remaining ammonia. Heat speeds up the ammonia production and causes it to evaporate, so cook kidneys at a low heat and for a short time, if this odor is offensive to you.

We have served Brain Salad and Creamed Sweetbreads, (the thymus gland of young calves) experimentally, and they have been received surprisingly well.

Brains and sweetbreads take very little cooking. First remove the membrane as you hold the meat under running cool water. Then steam briefly if they are intended for a salad. If they are to be sautéed or added to a sauce, no pre-cooking is necessary. To insure against masking the delicate flavor of sweetbreads, many cooks prefer to broil them. Brains and sweetbreads usually must be ordered from the butcher in advance.

Organ meats are perishable and must be used at once, or frozen. Liver and kidneys are readily available in all supermarkets.

Beef heart is nutritionally superior to other meats which we sometimes grind up to include in our meat loaf. Another good way to use heart is in making vegetable soup. We cook it in the stock, whole, then remove it, cut it up and add it along with the vegetables toward the end of the cooking time.

The meat we serve at Fitness House is almost always organically raised. We are fortunate to have several farm sources available to us. It is not easy for those who live in a metropolitan area. But if you have a freezer, it's worth a drive into the country to search out a farmer who raises meat organically, or at least naturally, without antibiotic, or hormone injections. Such meats bought by the quarter or side, are reasonably priced.

Chicken and turkey can be used in a variety of delicious dishes. They are the most inexpensive of meats and provide a good source of high quality protein with little fat.

We find that the most practical way to serve chicken at Fitness House is oven-baked. If you prefer this method, you may want to save money and buy a whole chicken. It is a simple, quick process to cut a chicken into serving pieces and you can make soup out of the back, wing tips and giblets—thus cooking two meals in one. The trick is to cut through the cartilage in each joint instead of the bone. You can locate the cartilage by stretching, twisting or bending the legs and wings away from the body as you cut through the skin.

The one essential tool for this operation is a sharp knife. Sharpen your knife using a steel or whetstone, by drawing the blade of the knife firmly over the top and bottom of it.

First, cut off both legs. Slit the skin between the leg and the breast, sever leg from back and if desired, separate drumstick from thigh. Then cut the wings off, stretching out and cutting through the cartilage where they join the breastbone. Cut off the tips and use for soup. Separate the front from the back by cutting through the ribs on each side, and pulling front and back apart, severing them between breastbone and back. Divide the breast in two, by cutting as far as possible through center of breastbone at top and bottom. Lay breast, meat side up, on board and press hard to flatten it. The small bones will break and you can cut through the meat dividing the breast in half.

When cutting up a chicken, first separate the legs from the body.

The trick is to cut through the cartilage instead of the bone.

The cartilage is easy to locate if you bend the joint as you cut.

A sharp knife is essential.

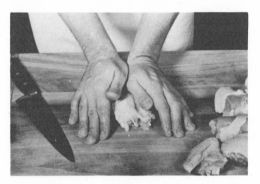

A chicken breast is flattened in order to break the small bones.

Then it is cut in half.

The simplest way to cook a chicken at home is to roast a whole frying or roasting chicken for an hour and a half in a medium-hot oven, or longer in a slower oven. It can be steamed in a covered roasting pan or, if you prefer the skin crisp and golden, roast it uncovered. Add salt if you wish and put a piece of onion and some celery tops in the cavity, brush the bird with a little oil, and that is all there is to it.

All meats are best if cooked very slowly, at a low temperature, because of the basic principle that protein toughens at a high temperature.

Avoid boiling meat. The only time we cook meat in water on top of the stove is when we use beef shin to make a soup stock. We keep the liquid at a simmer, never letting it boil. We often simmer a whole chicken to be used in Chicken a la King, for example, which calls for sauce made of chicken stock.

Potassium nitrate (saltpeter) is used in curing hams. Because of this we leave the use of ham to your discretion. At Fitness House we use both ham and bacon sparingly, just for flavor. Perhaps we ham lovers can do something to change this method of preparation by protesting to the meat producers.

Deep-fat-frying or frying in very hot oil is definitely out at Fitness House, and we believe it should be abandoned altogether as a cooking practice. Oil heated to the smoking point releases carcinogenic carbons. The same principle causes our concern about charcoal broiling meats at home. It is fat dripping into the fire that causes it to flare up and char the meat. If you like to barbecue or broil your meats, place the meat under the heat for cooking, so the fat can drain off harmlessly.

Fish is another fine source of protein and it contains practically no fat, but it does have plenty of B vitamins and minerals. Choose ocean fish of the smaller varieties and inland fish caught in lakes or streams which have not been polluted by industrial wastes such as methyl mercury. The large, predatory fish which eat smaller fish may accumulate pollutants from them, so it is safest to eat the smaller ocean fish such as mackerel, herring, sardines and flounder.

Every cook should know how to clean or fillet a fish. It is necessary to clean a fish if you plan to cook it whole or in steaks. If you plan to cook fish fillets, the filleting process makes cleaning the fish unnecessary. In either case a sharp knife is essential.

HOW TO CLEAN A FISH (For baked whole fish or fish steaks)

First, scale the fish with a knife or fish scaler. Then remove the head by cutting behind the pectoral fins through the backbone and down through the neck of the fish.

Insert knife into cavity, slit belly down to anal vent, removing entrails.

Dorsal and ventral fins may be removed by cutting about ½ inch into the flesh along both sides of the fins. Do not cut off fins with a pair of scissors as this will leave numerous small bones in the fish.

Rinse fish in cold, salted water.

## HOW TO FILLET A FISH (For broiled fish or baked fillet of fish)

**First, cut above the tail, just to (not through) the bone. Then place the tip of the knife in incision and cut along dorsal fin.**

Lift up edge of fillet and cut along backbone, loosening fillet from bone.

Place fillet, skin side down on board, and cut to (not through) skin above tail.

Hold knife at 45° angle and, using a sawing motion, cut between the skin and flesh.

Repeat same process on the other side, this time starting at the head and working toward the tail.

Rinse fillets with cold water and pat dry with a towel.

Broiling is the best method of cooking fish fillets. If you plan to stuff a whole fish, baking is best. Whatever way you prepare it, fish needs very little cooking. Heat penetrates the fish very quickly since there is so little fat. (Fat is a poor conductor of heat and retards cooking.) Cooking time can vary from 10 minutes to half an hour, depending on the thickness of the fish. Properly cooked fish is flaky but not dry.

Buy fresh fish whenever possible. If you don't live near enough to the ocean, or close to a safe source of inland water fish, look for fish that has been quickly frozen soon after it was caught. It will probably be fresher when you thaw it than unfrozen fish which has been shipped a long way.

Unfortunately, shellfish are usually found at the mouths of polluted rivers which are contaminated by raw sewage. They should certainly never be eaten raw and even when they are cooked, may carry disease.

Few of us would be willing to give up our meat-eating altogether, but I believe we would do well to eat less of it, especially less meat that has not been organically raised. This saves money, helps preserve our land resources and guards against excessive intake of chemicals from grasses and feed. With a little planning, protein needs can be met in spite of a cut in meat consumption. One way to do that is to try some of the recipes we use at Fitness House that combine meat with grains or legumes. Depending on the kind of meat, poultry or fish we eat, as little as $3\frac{1}{2}$ ounces can supply anywhere from 30 to 61 percent of our daily protein needs (according to recent research and experiments reported in *Diet For A Small Planet* by Frances Moore Lappe published by Ballantine Books).

A meal without meat used to be unthinkable at Fitness House but gradually, over the last few months, we have begun to introduce a variety of new dishes which are not only delicious, but so interesting that the meat is not missed. With the added daily protein we take in from foods such as eggs, milk and cheese, it is clear that meat is not a daily necessity. This realization may be a major factor in future meal planning throughout America, as we learn more about how to nourish our bodies and feed a hungry world.

## SAUCES

Many a hum-drum dish becomes elegant with the addition of a sauce, and although the French are credited with making this worthy contribution to culture, they do not have a patent on new sauce creations. Like soups, sauces reflect the genius of the cook.

Starting with a basic "roux" (flour and fat), and adding stock, vegetable broth or milk, one can invent any number of variations by adding eggs, cheese, tomatoes, spices and herbs—depending on what will best augment the dish which is planned.

We offer several basic sauces, (some flourless) as well as some Fitness House favorites which originated in our kitchen.

Cicero reputedly said: "Hunger is the best sauce." We Americans could be accused of saying: "Catsup is the only sauce." A good cook will dispute both statements and produce a sauce to prove it.

# *Beef*

## Broiled Hamburgers

1½ lbs. ground beef (lean chuck or round)
5-6 tablespoons tomato juice
⅛ teaspoon freshly-ground black pepper
     (optional)
kelp powder to taste

Mix tomato juice and pepper into meat
lightly with hands, just until it is absorbed.
Form into patties.

Broil 4 inches under the broiler unit for 5-7
minutes on each side or until desired
doneness is acquired. Sprinkle lightly with
kelp powder before serving.

Yield: 4-6 servings.

## Chili Con Carne

2 lbs. ground beef (chuck or round)
1 medium-sized onion, chopped
1 cup celery, chopped
½ cup green pepper, chopped
1 clove garlic, minced
2 tablespoons soy or corn oil
2 cups fresh or canned tomatoes
1 cup tomato purée
2 teaspoons cumin, ground
2 teaspoons chili powder
1½ teaspoons salt
2 cups cooked kidney beans

In heavy skillet, brown ground beef, onion,
celery, green pepper, and garlic in oil.

Stir in tomatoes and tomato purée. Add
seasonings and cover; simmer for 45 minutes
to one hour.

Add kidney beans and adjust seasoning.
Continue to simmer 30 minutes longer.

Yield: 6-8 servings.

# Ground Beef Stuffed Peppers

Preheat oven to 350°F.
6 medium-sized green peppers
½ cup onion, chopped
1 clove garlic, minced
¼ cup olive oil
1 lb. ground beef
½ cup soy grits
1 cup cooked brown rice
1 teaspoon tamari soy sauce
½ teaspoon salt
½ teaspoon kelp powder
1½ cups tomato juice
¼ cup chopped parsley
3 tablespoons wheat germ
3 tablespoons Parmesan cheese, grated

Wash and drain green peppers. Remove stem ends from peppers and carefully remove seeds and ribs. Set aside.

Sauté onion and garlic in olive oil until tender. Stir in the ground beef and continue to sauté only until it is no longer red. Add the soy grits, cooked rice, tamari soy sauce, salt and kelp powder. Mix together to blend ingredients. Stir in one-half cup tomato juice and the chopped parsley. Cook for five minutes.

Remove from heat and allow mixture to cool slightly. Stuff the peppers with the meat mixture. Place in a baking dish and pour one cup of tomato juice around the stuffed peppers. Cover and place in a preheated oven and bake 45 to 50 minutes or until peppers are tender. Baste occasionally with pan liquid. Remove cover after first thirty minutes of baking. Top peppers with wheat germ combined with cheese, and brown slightly.

Yield: 6 servings.

# *Beef*

## Halupkis or Cabbage Rolls

Preheat oven to 325°F.
1 large head green cabbage, enough to
       yield 12 good-sized cabbage leaves
1 small onion, minced
1 clove garlic, minced
1½ tablespoons oil
1½ lbs. ground beef*
1 egg, beaten
1 cup cooked brown rice
¼ teaspoon summer savory
¼ teaspoon pepper
1 teaspoon salt
¼ cup raw wheat germ
3 tablespoons nutritional yeast (optional)

SAUCE:
4 teaspoons potato flour or brown rice flour
2 cups tomato juice
4 tablespoons catsup
1 teaspoon salt

With sharp knife, cut core from large head
of cabbage.

Par-boil cabbage in boiling salted water
about 8 to 10 minutes. Remove and allow to
cool before handling. Then remove a few
leaves at a time and trim away thick
ridge on back of leaf, to make it easier to roll.

**3**

Sauté minced onion and garlic in oil.

**4!**

Mix ground beef and beaten egg, rice and
sautéed onion and garlic. Add seasonings,
wheat germ and nutritional yeast (if desired).

**5**

Spread each leaf (on thick end) with meat
mixture, fold the two sides over and roll,
starting with the thick end. Fasten with
toothpicks, if necessary. Place rolls in
oiled pan.

**6**

Make sauce: Using a small saucepan, slowly
add potato or brown rice flour to tomato
juice, stirring constantly with wire whisk or
wooden spoon. Then add catsup and salt.
Cook over low heat until thickened, stirring
constantly. Correct seasonings and pour
sauce over cabbage rolls.

Cover pan and bake at 325°F. for 1 hour. Then remove cover and bake another 20 minutes or until the rolls are tender and lightly browned.

*Note: 1 lb. of left-over, cooked, ground meat may be substituted for 1½ lbs. raw meat.

Yield: 6 servings.

## Italian Meat Balls with Sauce

⅓ cup minced onion
1 clove garlic, minced (optional)
1 tablespoon olive oil
¼ cup potato flour or brown rice flour
1½ tablespoons cornstarch
½ cup water
2 eggs, slightly-beaten
1½ lbs. beef (ground round) (or ½ lb. ground veal may be used with 1 lb. ground round)
⅓ cup raw wheat germ
2 tablespoons fresh parsley (chopped fine)
1 teaspoon salt
¼ teaspoon ground pepper
⅓ cup Romano or Parmesan cheese (grated)

Sauté minced onion and garlic in one tablespoon oil until golden but not brown.

In a small mixing bowl, combine potato or brown rice flour, cornstarch and water, making a smooth paste. Add beaten eggs and mix thoroughly.

please turn page

# *Beef*

**3**

In a large mixing bowl, combine meat, sautéed onion and garlic. Next add beaten eggs and starch mixture, then wheat germ, minced parsley, salt, pepper and grated cheese. Mix ingredients thoroughly. Form meat mixture into balls about two inches in diameter.

**4!**

Brown meat balls under broiler, turning them as they brown. Remove and set aside.

Yield: 4-6 servings or approximately 24 meat balls.

SAUCE:
1 onion, chopped (approximately ⅔ cup)
1 clove garlic, minced
2 tablespoons olive oil
3 cups fresh or canned tomatoes
2 cups tomato purée
1 teaspoon crushed oregano
¼ teaspoon crushed basil
1½ teaspoons salt
2 teaspoons honey

In a 4-quart container, sauté onion and garlic in olive oil until golden but not brown. Stir in tomatoes, tomato purée, oregano, basil, salt and honey.

**2**

Simmer sauce, uncovered for thirty minutes. Add browned meat balls and continue to simmer forty-five minutes longer; adjust seasonings.

Note: This dish may be served with spaetzle, polenta or brown rice (see recipes in grain section).

Yield: Approximately 4 cups.

# Molded Meat Loaf with Oatmeal

Preheat oven to 350°F.
2 lbs. lean ground beef (chuck or round)
1/3 cup wheat germ
1/2 cup oatmeal
2 tablespoons freshly chopped parsley
1/2 teaspoon freshly ground pepper
1 teaspoon salt
1/2 cup chopped onion
2 tablespoons oil
2 eggs
1/4 cup skim milk powder
1/2 cup water
1/2 cup tomato juice

In a large mixing bowl, combine ground beef, wheat germ, oatmeal, chopped parsley, pepper, and salt; set aside.

Sauté onion in oil until tender but not brown; add to meat mixture.

Beat eggs lightly. Combine skim milk powder and water, with a wire whisk, and add to eggs. Blend together and add to meat mixture; then add tomato juice. Mix thoroughly.

**4!**

Oil a 9 x 5 x 3-inch loaf pan. Turn meat mixture into pan, packing down well. Allow to rest 10 to 15 minutes in refrigerator.

**5**

Run spatula around edge of meat loaf to loosen. Carefully turn out into a lightly oiled shallow baking pan, keeping original shape as much as possible. Brush surface with oil.

**6**

Place meat loaf on middle rack of a preheated oven and bake for one hour and fifteen minutes. Remove from oven when nicely-browned and allow to rest 10 minutes before serving.

Yield: 6-8 servings.

# Beef

## Porcupine Balls

Preheat oven to 325°F.
1 tablespoon soy grits
¼ cup tomato juice
1 cup cooked brown rice
1 lb. ground beef (raw)
1 egg, slightly-beaten
2 teaspoons grated onion
1 teaspoon salt
⅛ teaspoon marjoram
1 teaspoon paprika
dash of pepper
1½ cups tomato juice
½ teaspoon honey
¼ cup soy sauce

Soak soy grits in ¼ cup tomato juice for 15 minutes.

Combine cooked rice with beef, egg, onion, salt, marjoram, paprika, pepper and soy grits-tomato mixture. Mix lightly.

Shape mixture into balls about 2 inches in diameter. Place in shallow baking dish. Combine 1½ cups tomato juice, honey and soy sauce. Pour mixture over meatballs and bake about 35 minutes in preheated oven.

Yield: 6 servings. Approximately 18 meatballs.

# Vegetable-Beef Loaf

Preheat oven to 350°F.
1 onion, chopped (⅓ cup)
1 clove garlic, minced
⅓ cup green pepper, chopped
⅓ cup celery, chopped
½ cup carrot, shredded
1 tablespoon oil
3 tablespoons soy grits
⅔ cup tomato juice
1 lb. ground beef (chuck or round)
⅔ lb. ground beef heart (if heart is not
       available, substitute ½ lb. ground
       beef)
1 egg, beaten
¼ cup wheat germ
2 tablespoons nutritional yeast
2 tablespoons soy flour (sifted)
3 tablespoons chopped parsley
2 tablespoons catsup
⅓ teaspoon salt
⅓ teaspoon pepper
⅓ teaspoon thyme
⅓ teaspoon basil

Sauté onion, garlic, green pepper, celery and carrot in oil.

Soak soy grits in tomato juice for about 15 minutes.

**3**

Combine meat, egg, wheat germ, nutritional yeast, soy flour, parsley, catsup and seasonings. Add sautéed vegetable mixture and the soy grits and tomato mixture.
Mix well.

**4!**

Oil 9 x 5 x 3-inch loaf pan, bottom and sides, and press meat mixture into pan.

**5**

Bake at 350°F. for 1 hour or until meat is cooked at center. Turn out of loaf pan, slice, serve.

Yield: 6-8 servings.

# *Beef*

## Swedish Meatballs

$\frac{1}{3}$ cup skim milk powder
$\frac{2}{3}$ cup water
$1\frac{1}{2}$ lbs. ground beef (round)—ground twice
1 medium-sized onion, grated
$\frac{1}{8}$ teaspoon allspice (ground)
$\frac{1}{8}$ teaspoon ginger (ground)
1 teaspoon salt
$\frac{1}{4}$ teaspoon freshly-ground pepper
$\frac{2}{3}$ cup potato flour or brown rice flour
$1\frac{1}{2}$ tablespoons cornstarch
2 eggs, slightly-beaten

Combine skim milk powder and water, using a wire whisk, and heat (do not boil).

Combine ground beef, grated onion, allspice, ginger, salt and pepper in a large bowl; set aside.

In a small bowl, combine potato or brown rice flour and cornstarch. Slowly stir potato flour-cornstarch mixture into ground meat mixture; combine thoroughly.

**4!**

Using electric beater set at low speed (or with spoon), gradually mix warm milk into meat mixture. Add slightly-beaten eggs and beat until mixture looks puffy and light— about 5 minutes.

**5**

Cover meatball mixture and allow to rest (in refrigerator) for about one-half hour before forming into balls. Using a teaspoon, shape mixture into balls, about one inch in diameter, rolling them between palms of hands. (For easy handling, wet hands with water or oil, when necessary.)

**6**

Brown meatballs under broiler, turning to brown on all sides. Remove to shallow baking dish; set aside.

GRAVY:
4 tablespoons rye flour
2 cups beef stock (see recipe in soup
    section)
salt and pepper to taste
Chopped parsley for garnish

Add rye flour to drippings from broiler pan
and stir until smooth. (Do not use more than
3 tablespoons of drippings.)

**2**

Gradually stir in the broth or stock; bring
to boil, stirring constantly. Season sauce
with salt and pepper to taste; simmer about 5
minutes; add meatballs to sauce; simmer
gently, covered, for 15 minutes.

**3**

Turn meatballs and sauce into serving dish.
Garnish with chopped parsley.

Yield: 6-8 servings (Approximately 65
meatballs).

# Beef Stew

3 lbs. beef stew (chuck, round, brisket
    or shin)
oil for browning
2 medium-sized onions, diced
water to cover meat
4 medium-sized carrots, cut in chunks
4 medium-sized potatoes, cut in chunks
    (optional)
salt, kelp powder to taste
3-4 tablespoons potato flour or rye flour
½ cup cold water
chopped parsley for garnish

Cut stew meat into 1½-inch cubes, trimming
off any fat.

Brown stew meat in oil, using just a little
to start with and adding more as it is needed.
Lift meat out and put in heavy-bottom pot.

**3**

Brown onions in same pan used for browning
meat. The onions absorb the browned-meat
juices, adding to the flavor of the stew. Add
onions and juice to stew.

please turn page

# *Beef*

**4!**

Put enough cool water in the pot to cover the meat, cover with a lid and bring slowly to a boil. Then turn down heat and simmer for 1-2 hours or until meat is almost tender.

**5**

Add carrots and potatoes (if desired) to stew. Add salt and kelp powder to taste. Continue to simmer for $\frac{1}{2}$ hour longer or until vegetables and meat are tender.

**6**

Thicken the stew before serving by dissolving the potato or rye flour in cold water, then adding the hot gravy carefully to the flour mixture, stirring constantly, until it is a smooth sauce. Pour sauce into the stew, stirring carefully. Heat until flour is cooked (about 5 minutes). Garnish with chopped parsley.

Yield: 6-8 servings.

## Sauerbraten

1 beef roast (round or rump), boneless (3-3$\frac{1}{2}$ lbs.)
1 tablespoon salt
$\frac{1}{2}$ teaspoon freshly-ground pepper
2 medium-sized onions, sliced
1 large carrot, shredded or sliced
1 stalk celery, chopped
6 whole cloves
2 whole bay leaves
4 whole allspice
$\frac{1}{2}$ teaspoon peppercorns
1$\frac{3}{4}$ cups red wine vinegar
1$\frac{1}{2}$ cups cold water
2 tablespoons oil

Wipe meat with moist paper towels. Rub meat with salt and pepper, and place in a large glass bowl or deep earthenware crock. Add onions, carrot slices, celery, cloves, bay leaves, allspice and peppercorns.

Heat vinegar and water in saucepan until boiling; cool slightly and pour over meat, vegetables and spices. Allow to cool; cover and place in refrigerator. Marinate for 48 hours or more, turning several times a day.

When ready to cook, remove meat from marinade (reserve marinade), wipe dry with paper towels. Heat oil (in heavy-bottom pan or skillet) to medium-high temperature. Brown roast on all sides. Pour reserved marinade over meat (liquid should not come more than halfway up the meat); cover tightly and simmer slowly for about three hours or until fork-tender.

Remove roast to a warm platter and keep hot while preparing gravy.

*Sauerbraten Gravy:*
2 cups marinade
2 tablespoons oil
2½ tablespoons potato flour or rye flour
½ teaspoon salt
½ cup cold water
½ cup yogurt (optional)
Chopped parsley to garnish

Strain hot marinade, measure 2 cups and set aside. Heat oil in saucepan, then stir in potato or rye flour and salt, stirring constantly until mixture bubbles.

Gradually blend in ½ cup cold water and the marinade, stirring constantly. Cook until mixture thickens. Adjust seasoning. Add yogurt if desired.

Slice sauerbraten and ladle some hot gravy over meat. Garnish with chopped parsley. Pour remaining gravy into sauceboat; serve sauerbraten with potato dumplings or potato pancakes.
Yield: 6 servings.

# Beef

## African Beef and Ground-Nut Stew*

2 lbs. stew beef (chuck or round)
4 tablespoons peanut oil
3 cups water
1½ cups peanut butter
2 tomatoes (fresh) or 1 small (1 lb.)
      can tomatoes, diced
2 onions, sliced thin
1 lb. okra (fresh) or 1-10 oz. package frozen,
      sliced
⅛ teaspoon crushed red pepper (optional)
½ teaspoon allspice
1 tablespoon cornstarch
¼ cup water
salt to taste

Brown stew beef in oil over medium-high heat.

**2**

Add 1½ cups water. Cover and simmer over low heat until meat is tender (45 minutes-1 hour).

**3**

Add remaining 1½ cups water and gradually stir in peanut butter.

**4!**

Add tomatoes, onions, okra, crushed red pepper (if desired), allspice, and bring to a boil. Cover and reduce heat, stirring occasionally. Simmer 25 minutes or until onions and okra are tender.

**5**

Dissolve cornstarch in ¼ cup water and stir into stew. Bring to a boil and cook briefly, stirring until stew is thickened (about 5 minutes). Salt to taste.

*Note: In Africa, peanuts are called "ground-nuts."

Yield: 8-10 servings.

# Beef Stroganoff

1½ lbs. round steak, 1 inch thick
3 tablespoons oil
1 cup onion, chopped or thinly-sliced
1 clove garlic, minced
½ lb. fresh mushrooms, sliced ¼-inch thick
2 tablespoons potato flour or rye flour
1 teaspoon salt
½ teaspoon pepper
1½ cups beef stock
2 tablespoons tomato purée
¼ cup dry sherry (optional)
1 teaspoon freshly-snipped dill (optional)
2 teaspoons potato starch
1 cup yogurt
Fresh dill or parsley for garnish

Trim fat from round steak; cut across grain to make strips 1-inch wide, ¼-inch thick and about 2 inches long.

**2**

In a large, heavy skillet heat two tablespoons oil to a medium heat. Add just enough beef strips to cover bottom of pan. Sear quickly on all sides, removing beef as it browns. Brown rest of beef; set aside.

Add remaining one tablespoon oil to same skillet and sauté onion, garlic and mushrooms until barely tender—about 5 minutes. Remove from heat; add browned beef strips. Sprinkle potato flour over mixture, tossing lightly. Season with salt and pepper. Place skillet over medium heat; add stock slowly, stirring until smooth. Add tomato purée. Bring mixture to a boil; reduce heat and simmer about 45 minutes or until steak is fork-tender. Stir in dry sherry and snipped dill.

**4!**

In a small bowl, blend potato starch with yogurt, and stir slowly into meat mixture. Simmer (do not boil) for about two minutes longer.

**5**

Serve Stroganoff with rice, noodles (spaetzle) or buckwheat groats. Sprinkle two tablespoons of dill or parsley over top.

Yield: 6 servings.

# *Beef*

## Brazilian Pot Roast

Preheat oven to 325°F.
1 beef roast (chuck or rump—3 or 4 lbs.)
1 clove garlic, minced
½ teaspoon salt
¼ teaspoon freshly-ground black pepper
   (optional)
1 teaspoon cumin
½ cup cider vinegar
½ cup water
2 tablespoons oil
1 onion
1 carrot
1 bay leaf

With wide-pronged cooking fork, poke holes
in roast over all the surface.

**2**

Combine garlic, salt, spices, vinegar and
water. Pour over meat, taking care that
marinade seeps into holes in meat. Let stand
30 minutes to 1 hour.

**3**

Brown all surfaces of roast in oil, over
medium-high heat.

**4!**

Cook in preheated 325°F. oven in a covered
pan or on top of stove in a covered,
heavy-bottom pot over low heat, using
marinade liquid and adding more water, if
desired. Add onion, carrot and bay leaf
to the pot. Simmer slowly for 2-3 hours or
until meat is fork tender.

**5**

Thicken remaining liquid in pot, if desired,
and pour over sliced meat before serving.

Yield: 6-8 servings.

# Chinese Pepper Steak

1½ lbs. flank steak (or sirloin) 1 inch thick
2 cups green pepper, cut into ½-inch-wide
    strips
5 tablespoons oil
½ cup coarsely-chopped onion
3 teaspoons grated fresh ginger (or ½
    teaspoon ground ginger)
2 tablespoons cornstarch
4 tablespoons tamari soy sauce
3 tablespoons dry sherry
½ cup beef stock (or water)

Trim excess fat from flank or sirloin steak.
Cut diagonally across the grain into thin
slices, then cut strips about 3 inches long. If
using sirloin, thinly slice. To make beef
easier to slice, store in freezer until partially
frozen. Thaw slices completely before
sautéeing.

**2**

In a large skillet, over medium heat, stir-fry
green peppers in 2 tablespoons oil for
about one minute. Cover skillet and simmer
for about one more minute. Remove cover
and stir again.

Add chopped onion and grated ginger or
ground ginger. Sauté until transparent. Push
sautéed vegetables to one side, add strips
of meat and additional oil as needed, one
tablespoon at a time. Stir-fry quickly just
until no pink shows. Sauté in this manner
until all meat has been browned. Toss
together with vegetables.

**4!**

In a small bowl, combine cornstarch, soy
sauce and sherry. Blend together thoroughly,
slowly adding beef stock or water. Add
mixture to cooked steak and vegetables,
stirring constantly, to coat well. Cook over
low heat for 2 or 3 minutes, adding
additional water or stock if a thinner sauce
is desired.

**5**

Remove from heat and transfer to a heated
serving dish. Serve immediately.

Yield: 4-6 servings.

# Beef

## Fruited Pot Roast

3 tablespoons oil
1 rump or chuck roast weighing 4 or 5 lbs.
3 medium-sized onions, peeled and chopped
¼ teaspoon cloves (ground)
2 cups apple juice or apple cider
1½ cups dried prunes (uncooked)
1½ cups dried apricots (uncooked)
2-4 tablespoons cornstarch
¼ cup cold water

In heavy-bottom pot or skillet*, heat oil to medium-high temperature. Brown meat on all sides.

Add onions, cloves, and apple juice or cider, and cover tightly. Turn heat down, and simmer for two hours or until nearly tender.

Add prunes and apricots and continue to cook ½ hour longer.

**4!**

If desired, thicken liquid in pot with cornstarch dissolved in cold water.

*Note: Roast can also be cooked in a 350°F. oven. After browning meat, transfer to roasting pan with close-fitting lid. Add onions, cloves and liquid. Cover tightly; cook for 2½ hours; then add prunes and apricots, and cook ½ hour longer.

Yield: 10 servings.

# Sukiyaki

1½ lbs. flank steak, thinly cut on the slant
     across the grain; or beef tenderloin
     or sirloin steak, sliced as thin as
     possible
3 tablespoons oil
1 cup tamari soy sauce
1 tablespoon honey
½ cup beef stock (see recipe in soup section)
1 cup green onions, cut in diagonal slices,
     ½ inch wide
1 cup celery, cut in diagonal slices, 1
     inch wide
1 cup fresh mushrooms, thinly-sliced
5 cups torn fresh spinach leaves, or shredded
     Chinese cabbage
1 5-oz. can (⅔ cup) water chestnuts, drained
     and thinly-sliced
1 5-oz. can bamboo shoots, drained
1½ cups fresh bean sprouts (see growing
     your own sprouts in salad section)

Partially freeze beef before slicing for best results.

**2**

Just before cooking, arrange sliced meat and vegetables neatly on a large platter or tray.

The ideal utensil to use for sukiyaki is (of course) a Chinese wok, but if you do not have one, use a large 12-inch electric skillet or an ordinary skillet. Heat oil to medium-high temperature, add beef strips and cook quickly, turning them over and over, one or two minutes or just until browned. Combine soy sauce, honey and beef stock; pour over sautéed beef. Cook until soy mixture bubbles. Push meat to one side.

**4!**

Keeping separate, add onions, then celery, then mushrooms. Stir-fry each vegetable over medium high heat about one or two minutes and push to one side before adding next vegetable.

**5**

Again keeping separate, add spinach or Chinese cabbage, then water chestnuts, bamboo shoots, and bean sprouts. Stir-fry each food until just heated through. Serve immediately.
Yield: 6 servings.

# *Beef*

## Stuffed Eggplant

Preheat over to 350°F.
2 eggplants, split in half lengthwise
1 medium-sized onion, chopped
1/2 clove garlic, minced
2 tablespoons oil
1/2 lb. cooked beef, cut in small cubes
2 cups tomatoes (fresh or canned)
salt to taste
1/2 teaspoon basil
3 tablespoons wheat germ
3 tablespoons Parmesan cheese

Scoop pulp from eggplant halves, leaving
1/2-inch shell. Dice pulp.

Sauté onion, garlic and eggplant pulp in oil.

Add cubed, cooked meat, tomatoes, salt (to
taste) and basil.

**4!**

Fill eggplant shells with mixture; top with
wheat germ combined with cheese.

**5**

Put water 1/2 inch deep in bottom of baking
pan. Add filled eggplant halves, cover with
foil and bake at 350°F. for 1/2 hour. Then
uncover and continue baking until shell
is tender enough to eat (about 20 minutes).

Yield: 6-8 servings.

# Lamb

## Broiled Lamb, Cantonese Style

2 lbs. shoulder of lamb
2 cloves garlic, minced
4 tablespoons tamari soy sauce
1 tablespoon honey

Cut lamb into pieces 1/4-inch thick, 2 inches long and 1 inch wide.

Combine garlic, soy sauce and honey. Mix well.

Marinate lamb in mixture for 30 minutes, turning frequently.

Remove meat from marinade and place under very hot broiler for about 5 minutes, turning once or twice. Serve immediately.

Yield: 4-6 servings.

## Irish Lamb Stew

Preheat oven to 300°F.
4 1/2-5 lbs. lamb neck chops
6 onions, sliced 1/4-inch thick
6 potatoes, sliced 1/4-inch thick
salt and pepper to taste
water to cover

In a 3-quart casserole, put a layer of neck chops, seasoning them lightly to taste, then put a layer of onions, then a layer of potatoes, seasoning again to taste.

Add enough water to almost cover the potatoes. Cover casserole with a tight-fitting lid and bake slowly in a preheated oven for 3-4 hours, or until the lamb is tender.

Serve with carrots and turnips.

Yield: 4-6 servings.

# *Lamb*

## Greek Lamb Pilau

2½ lbs. lamb stew cut from a shoulder or leg
6 cups lamb stock (strained) or water
2 cloves garlic, minced
1 teaspoon oregano
1 teaspoon rosemary
1 teaspoon basil
salt to taste
¼ teaspoon fresh-ground black pepper
      (optional)
¼ cup onions, minced
3 tablespoons oil
1½ cups uncooked brown rice
4 cups lamb stock
⅓ cup blanched almonds, slivered or halved
3 tablespoons oil
⅔ cup raisins
1 green pepper sliced in rings

Cut lamb into 1½-inch cubes, trimming fat away. Simmer bones for 1-2 hours to make lamb stock.

**2**

Put lamb, 6 cups strained stock or water, garlic, herbs, salt and pepper into a pot and simmer until lamb is tender (about 1 hour). Lift out lamb and set aside. Strain stock.

**3**

Sauté minced onions in oil until tender. Add brown rice and stir. Add 4 cups strained stock, stir and cover tightly. Simmer over medium heat until stock is absorbed and rice is tender (about 35-40 minutes). Do not stir during cooking.

**4**

Toss lamb and rice together gently and heap onto serving platter.

**5**

Prepare garnish: Sauté almonds lightly in oil until golden; lift out with slotted spoon; then sauté raisins in same pan with more oil, if necessary, until raisins are puffy. Lift out. Scatter almonds and raisins over lamb and rice. Top with thin slices of raw green pepper.

This dish should be accompanied by Greek salad (see recipe in salad section).

Yield: 6-8 servings.

# Lamb Curry

½ cup yogurt
1 teaspoon turmeric
1 teaspoon cumin
½ teaspoon cardamom
2½ lbs. boneless lamb (from leg or
        shoulder) cut in one-inch cubes
¼-½ cup oil
2 large onions, sliced
2 cloves garlic, minced
1 teaspoon ginger
1 teaspoon dry mustard
½ teaspoon cinnamon
¼ teaspoon whole cloves
1½ cups stock (lamb or chicken) or water
cayenne pepper and salt to taste
2 teaspoons lemon juice
2 tablespoons unsweetened coconut shreds

Combine yogurt, turmeric, cumin and cardomom for marinade. Add lamb cubes and marinate for one hour, turning the meat well in the mixture.

In a heavy bottom pot sauté marinated lamb cubes in oil until brown. Lift out and set aside.

**3**

Sauté onions, garlic and other spices in same pan.

**4!**

Add the lamb and the stock or water to the onions and spice mixture, and simmer, covered, for 45 minutes to an hour or until lamb is tender. Be careful not to overcook it.

**5**

Correct seasonings, add lemon juice and coconut shreds just before serving.

Yield: 6 servings.

# Lamb

## Lamb Haricot

Preheat oven to 350°F.
1½ cups (about 12 oz.) dried baby lima
      beans
4 tablespoons oil
2 lbs. lamb shoulder, cut into pieces 2 inches
      x 4 inches, about ¼ inch thick
salt and pepper to taste
1 cup chopped onions
1 tablespoon potato flour or brown rice flour
3-4 cups water
2 tablespoons chopped parsley
1 bay leaf
½ teaspoon thyme (fresh or dried)
chopped parsley to garnish

Cook beans in salted water for 30 minutes;
drain.

**2**

Put oil in heavy-bottom skillet; brown the
lamb on all sides; season with salt and pepper.
Add onions and cook for 10 minutes. Skim
off extra fat.

**3**

Dissolve flour in a little cold water. Add to
meat along with remaining water & herbs;
then add cooked beans. Combine thoroughly.
Place in casserole, cover, and bake in
preheated 350°F. oven for 1½ hours.

**4**

Discard bay leaf. Sprinkle with chopped
parsley and serve.

Note: Pork may be used in this recipe in
place of lamb.

Yield: 6 servings.

# Lamb Patties

2 lbs. ground lamb
½ cup wheat germ
3 eggs, slightly-beaten
1 teaspoon dry mustard
½ teaspoon thyme (fresh or dried)
salt and pepper to taste

Combine ground lamb, wheat germ, eggs, mustard and thyme. Mix thoroughly.

**2**

Form into patties about three inches in diameter. Broil for 8 minutes on first side; turn and broil 5 minutes. Salt and pepper lightly before serving.

Yield: 6-8 servings.

# Stuffed Lamb

Preheat oven to 350°F.
4 lbs. shoulder of lamb (with shoulder blade removed)
2 tablespoons oil
½ cup onion, chopped
2 tablespoons chives, chopped
2 lamb kidneys, chopped
2 cups cooked bulgur
½ cup parsley, chopped
½ teaspoon thyme (fresh or dried)
salt and pepper to taste

Trim all excess fat from lamb shoulder. Set aside.

Put oil in heavy-bottom skillet and sauté onions and chives until golden. Remove and in the same pan, sauté chopped lamb kidneys until tender and slightly brown; then add sautéed onions and chives, bulgur, parsley, thyme, salt and pepper to taste. Toss until well-combined.

Put filling into pocket of lamb shoulder (formed by removing the blade); secure with cord or skewers; roast in preheated oven for 1 hour or until lamb is tender.
Yield: 4-6 servings.

# *Lamb*

## Lamb Stew

2½ lbs. leg or shoulder of lamb
4 tablespoons oil
1 onion, chopped
1 clove garlic, minced
2 large carrots cut in chunks
2 potatoes cut in chunks
4 cups lamb stock or water
1 small can tomato purée
1 tablespoon dry cooking sherry
1 teaspoon tamari soy sauce
½ teaspoon salt
⅛ teaspoon kelp powder
2-4 tablespoons cornstarch (optional)
½ cup cold water (optional)
2 tablespoons chopped parsley

Cut meat into 1-inch cubes, trimming off excess fat. Simmer bones for 1-2 hours to make lamb stock.

In heavy-bottom pot, lightly brown lamb cubes on all sides, using oil only as needed.

Add onions and garlic and sauté briefly.

Add carrots, potatoes, lamb stock or water, tomato purée, sherry and seasonings. Cover, bring to a boil, then turn down heat and simmer for about 45 minutes or until lamb is tender.

Correct seasonings, thicken with cornstarch dissolved in water, if desired. Garnish with chopped parsley and serve.

Yield: 6-8 servings.

# Moussaka

Preheat oven to 375°F.
1 large or 2 small eggplants
5 tablespoons olive oil
½ cup green pepper, chopped
½ cup onion, chopped
1 lb. ground beef or ground lamb
2 cups fresh tomatoes, peeled and chopped,
      or one cup canned tomatoes
⅔ cup tomato purée
1 teaspoon fresh, chopped basil or ¼
      teaspoon dried
½ teaspoon fresh, chopped thyme or ¼
      teaspoon dried
1½ teaspoons salt
¼ teaspoon freshly-grated black pepper
4 tablespoons wheat germ
½ cup grated Parmesan cheese

Lightly oil a two-quart casserole; set aside.

**2**

Wash and peel the eggplant. Cut into slices, cross-wise, about one-half inch thick.

**3**

Add two tablespoons oil to a large skillet and place over medium heat. Add eggplant slices, a few at a time, and brown quickly on both sides. Remove to a platter as eggplant slices brown, adding more oil to skillet as needed.

**4**

Using the same skillet, add 1 tablespoon oil. Stir in chopped green pepper and onion; sauté over low heat, stirring constantly, until tender, about 5 minutes. Stir in ground beef or lamb and cook over medium heat, stirring constantly, until lightly-browned; or just until no pink shows.

**5**

Pour excess fat from meat and vegetable mixture. Return skillet to low heat and add tomatoes and tomato purée. Stir in basil, thyme, salt, and pepper. Simmer mixture for about 10 to 15 minutes, uncovered. Remove from heat.

please turn page

In small bowl, combine wheat germ and Parmesan cheese. Arrange alternate layers of meat sauce and eggplant slices in prepared casserole; beginning and ending with meat sauce. Sprinkle mixture of wheat germ and Parmesan cheese over each layer of meat sauce, except bottom.

**7**

Bake in preheated oven, on middle rack, uncovered for 45 minutes; or until eggplant is tender. Remove casserole from oven and allow to stand for 10 minutes before serving.

Yield: 6-8 servings.

# Veal

## Veal Paprika

Preheat oven to 350°F.
2 lbs. veal cutlets, $\frac{1}{4}$ inch thick
    (approximately 6 cutlets)
1 cup lemon juice
$\frac{1}{2}$ teaspoon salt
1 cup rye flour
$\frac{1}{2}$ cup oil
1 cup onions, diced
$1\frac{1}{2}$ tablespoons paprika
$\frac{1}{2}$ cup chicken stock
1 tablespoon rye flour
1 tablespoon cornstarch
1 cup yogurt
chopped parsley for garnish

**1**

Marinate veal cutlets in lemon juice for an hour turning them after 30 minutes. Mix salt and flour together. Pat cutlets dry, dip them in salted flour and shake off excess.

**2**

In a skillet, sauté cutlets in oil over medium high heat, lightly-browning them—about 3 or 4 minutes on each side. Lift out of pan, place in baking dish and set aside.

**3**

Using the same skillet, sauté the onions until they are a light-golden color. Stir in paprika, coating the onions, then add the chicken stock and bring it to a boil, stirring in any brown bits left in the pan from the meat.

**4**

Pour onion-stock mixture over cutlets, cover and bake in a preheated oven for 1 hour, or until tender when pierced with a fork.

**5**

Meanwhile, combine flour and cornstarch and stir it gradually into the yogurt. Place yogurt mixture in skillet and set aside.

**6**

When cutlets are tender, pour the liquid off into the yogurt mixture, stirring to prevent lumps. Simmer for 5 minutes or so, until the sauce is thickened. Pour sauce over cutlets. Garnish with chopped parsley and serve immediately.

Yield: 4-6 servings.

# *Veal*

## Raisin-Rice-Stuffed Veal Breast

Preheat oven to 300°F.
1 veal breast (about 4 lbs.)
1 teaspoon salt
1 medium-sized onion, chopped fine
2-4 tablespoons oil
3 cups cooked brown rice
2 tablespoons chopped parsley
1/3 cup seedless raisins
grated rind of one-half orange
1 egg, beaten
1/2 teaspoon poultry seasoning (or a
      combination of 1/8 teaspoon powdered
      thyme, 1/4 teaspoon sage, and 1/4
      teaspoon marjoram, blended together)

Have butcher cut a large pocket in the side of the veal breast. Wipe veal with moist paper towels. Sprinkle 1/2 teaspoon salt over veal and inside of pocket; set aside.

Sauté onion in two tablespoons oil until tender but not brown.

In mixing bowl, combine rice, sautéed onion, chopped parsley, raisins, orange rind, 1/2 teaspoon salt, beaten egg, and poultry seasoning. Mix together thoroughly.

**4!**

Fill pocket in veal with stuffing and skewer or use heavy, rounded wooden toothpicks to close opening. Place veal breast, rib side down, in an open shallow roasting pan. Cover veal breast generously with oil. Place in a preheated oven for two and one-half hours. Baste occasionally with accumulated liquid. (Do not cover—veal should turn brown while baking.)

**5**

Remove from oven 10 minutes before serving.

Yield: 6-7 servings.

# Veal Loaf

Preheat oven to 325° F.
1/3 cup soybean grits
1/2 cup beef or chicken stock (see recipes
      in soup section)
1/2 cup onion, chopped
1/2 cup green pepper, chopped
2 tablespoons oil
1/2 cup carrots, grated
2 lbs. veal, ground
2 eggs, slightly-beaten
2 tablespoons parsley, chopped
1/2 teaspoon salt
1/2 teaspoon freshly-snipped thyme (1/4
      teaspoon dried thyme)
1/4 teaspoon freshly-ground pepper
1/2 teaspoon powdered kelp

**1**

Lightly oil a 9 x 5 x 3-inch loaf pan.

**2**

Combine soybean grits with one-half cup
stock and allow to stand for five minutes.

**3**

In a skillet, sauté onion and green pepper in
the 2 tablespoons oil until tender, then
add grated carrot and sauté for five minutes
longer.

**4**

In a large mixing bowl, combine ground veal,
soybean grits-stock mixture, slightly-beaten
eggs, chopped parsley, salt, thyme, pepper
and powdered kelp. Add sautéed vegetables
and mix together thoroughly.

**5**

Turn mixture into prepared loaf pan or
baking dish and brush top surface of veal loaf
with oil. Place on middle rack of preheated
oven and bake, uncovered, for one hour
or until loaf is nicely-browned. Baste veal
loaf occasionally with accumulated liquid
from pan.

**6**

Remove veal loaf from oven about 10 minutes
before cutting and serving. This is also
very good served cold.

Yield: 6 servings.

# Organ Meats

## Sautéed Brains

2 calves' brains (about 2 lbs.)
1 quart boiling water
1 tablespoon vinegar
corn meal for dusting
2 tablespoons oil
few drops of lemon juice
salt and pepper to taste
Chopped parsley for garnish

Remove all membrane from brains while
holding under cold, running water. Then drop
into boiling water to which vinegar has
been added. Simmer for five minutes, then
remove and pat dry. Dust with corn meal.

Heat oil in heavy-bottom skillet and sauté
brains for five minutes on each side. Drizzle
a few drops of lemon juice over each
piece and add salt and pepper to taste.
Garnish with chopped parsley.

Yield: 6-8 servings.

## Creamed Sweetbreads with Mushrooms

3 pairs sweetbreads (2 lbs.)
1 lb. fresh mushrooms, sliced
4½ tablespoons oil
½ cup skim milk powder
1 cup water
2 tablespoons cornstarch
3 tablespoons soy flour
¼ teaspoon paprika
½ teaspoon salt
1½ cups chicken stock (see recipe in soup
  section)
2 egg yolks
2 tablespoons dry sherry (optional)
Chopped parsley for garnish

**1**

Snip connective tissue from sweetbreads with kitchen scissors. Wash and pull small pieces of sweetbread free from the elastic tissue. Set aside.

**2**

In a small skillet, sauté mushrooms in two tablespoons oil, over medium heat, for 5 minutes.

**3**

Combine the skim milk powder with one cup water in a small bowl. Blend with a wire whisk until mixture is smooth and free from lumps.

**4**

In a heavy saucepan, combine $2\frac{1}{2}$ tablespoons oil, cornstarch, soy flour, paprika and salt; blend together. Place over medium heat and cook until mixture bubbles. Remove from heat. Gradually blend in the milk mixture and chicken stock until mixture appears smooth. Return saucepan to medium heat and cook, stirring constantly, until the sauce is thickened and smooth. Drop small pieces of sweetbreads into boiling sauce and cook for about 8 minutes or until sweetbreads are tender.

**5**

Beat two egg yolks; spoon a little of the hot sauce into beaten yolks and blend together. Turn mixture into hot sauce and blend, stirring constantly. Return to heat and add dry sherry (if desired) and sautéed mushrooms. Garnish with chopped parsley.

Yield: 6 servings.

197

# *Organ Meats*

## Beef and Kidney Stew

1½ lbs. beef cubes (round or chuck)
2-3 tablespoons oil
4 small leeks, chopped, or 1 onion, diced
2 large carrots, cut in chunks
2-3 cups beef stock or water
1 beef kidney
2 teaspoons vinegar
⅛ teaspoon each of thyme, marjoram, savory
salt to taste
¼ teaspoon crushed black peppercorns
3-4 tablespoons cornstarch
½ cup cold water
2 tablespoons chopped parsley (use for
       garnish on top)

In a heavy-bottom pot, brown beef cubes well on all sides in hot oil. Add leeks (or onions) and carrots and continue to sauté for about five minutes. Add enough beef stock (or water) to cover meat and vegetables. Simmer, covered with a lid, for 2 hours or until beef is tender and easily cut with a knife.

(If preferred, beef and vegetables can be sautéed in a skillet, then transferred to a casserole with added liquid, and cooked (covered) in a 350°F. oven for 2 hours or until tender.)

Meanwhile, prepare kidney. Before washing it, carefully snip white tissue out of kidney with kitchen scissors. Then wash with cold water, cut into ¾-inch cubes, and mix with vinegar.

When beef is tender, add herbs, salt and pepper; thicken with cornstarch which has been dissolved in water.

**4!**

Add kidney last, mix in well and continue to simmer on low heat (covered) for 10-15 minutes or until as tender as desired. Garnish with chopped parsley.

Note: Turnips and/or potatoes may also be added to stew along with the onions and carrots.

Yield: 4-6 servings.

# Creamed Veal Kidneys

3-4 veal kidneys (about 1 lb.)
4 teaspoons vinegar
3 tablespoons oil
3 tablespoons shallots, chopped (or onions, chopped)
1 cup fresh mushrooms, sliced
3 tablespoons potato flour or rye flour
½ cup chicken stock (see recipe in soup section)
⅓ cup skim milk powder
1 cup cold water
1 teaspoon salt
¼ teaspoon paprika
1 teaspoon lemon juice (optional)
3 tablespoons chopped parsley

Cut kidneys lengthwise. Before washing, carefully snip white tissue out of kidneys using kitchen scissors. Then wash with cold water, dice into 1-inch pieces, and mix with 4 teaspoons vinegar.

**2**

Heat 2 tablespoons oil in skillet and sauté pieces of kidney over medium heat, quickly, until they are just cooked through. Remove kidneys (while still pink), with slotted spoon and set aside.

**3**

Prepare sauce: Using the same skillet (no need to wash), add one tablespoon oil and place over medium heat. Add chopped onion or shallots and sliced mushrooms; sauté until tender but not brown—5 to 8 minutes. Sprinkle potato or rye flour over onion and mushroom mixture, mixing thoroughly to blend. Slowly add the chicken stock, stirring thoroughly to prevent lumping. Simmer for 5 minutes or until mixture thickens.

**4!**

Blend skim milk powder with one cup cold water until smooth, using wire whisk. Stir into sauce, blending thoroughly. Season with salt, paprika, and lemon juice (if desired); simmer but do not boil. Add chopped parsley and drained kidney pieces. Serve immediately.

Yield: 4 servings.

# Organ Meats

## Kidney Creole

2 veal kidneys
2 teaspoons vinegar
3 tablespoons rye flour
2 tablespoons skim milk powder
2-4 tablespoons oil
1 onion, chopped
1 green pepper, diced
1 clove garlic, minced
1 stalk celery with leaves, chopped
1 cup tomato purée
salt to taste
1 pinch each of basil, savory, and thyme
1/4 teaspoon black pepper, freshly ground

Cut 2 veal kidneys lengthwise. Before washing, carefully snip white tissue out of kidneys, using a kitchen scissors; then wash with cold water, dice into 3/4 inch cubes and mix with vinegar.

Combine rye flour and skim milk powder. Dredge kidneys in mixture, sauté them in oil for about 5 minutes. Lift out onto paper towel.

Using same pan, sauté onion, green pepper, garlic and celery for about 5 minutes, adding more oil if necessary.

Add tomato purée, seasonings and simmer for 10 minutes. Add kidneys and simmer for another 10 minutes. Serve immediately.

Yield: 4-6 servings.

# Pork Kidney Ragout

Preheat oven to 350°F.
3-4 pork kidneys (or about 1 lb.)
4 teaspoons vinegar
4 tablespoons oil
½ cup onion, chopped
½ cup celery, chopped
1 clove garlic, minced
1 cup carrots, sliced
3 tablespoons potato flour or rye flour
1½ cups chicken or beef broth
2 tablespoons parsley, chopped
salt to taste
¼ teaspoon freshly-ground pepper
1 cup mushrooms, chopped
chopped parsley for garnish

Cut kidneys lengthwise. Before washing, carefully snip white tissue out of kidneys using kitchen scissors. Then wash with cold water, dice and mix with 4 teaspoons vinegar.

**2**

Heat 3 tablespoons oil in skillet and sauté diced kidneys over medium heat, pushing to one side as they brown. Add chopped onion, celery, garlic, and sliced carrots; continue to sauté 10 minutes longer.

**3**

Sprinkle three tablespoons potato or rye flour over kidney-vegetable mixture and mix together to blend. Gradually stir in the stock, mixing constantly to prevent lumping. Add two tablespoons chopped parsley and seasoning; simmer for 15 minutes.

**4!**

Meanwhile, sauté chopped mushrooms in 1 tablespoon oil for 5 minutes. Add to kidney-vegetable mixture.

**5**

Turn mixture into a lightly-oiled, two-quart, oven-proof casserole and bake (covered), in a preheated oven, for one hour or until kidneys are tender. Garnish with chopped parsley before serving.

Yield: 4-5 servings.

# Organ Meats

## Chicken Liver Paté

½ lb. chicken livers
1 cup chicken stock (see recipe in soup
    section)
½ cup onion, chopped
2 tablespoons chicken fat or oil
2 hard-cooked eggs
2 teaspoons freshly-minced parsley
1 teaspoon salt
¼ teaspoon tamari soy sauce
freshly-ground pepper
1-2 tablespoons mayonnaise

Wash chicken livers and place in saucepan.
Add one cup chicken stock, set over
medium heat and bring to a boil. Lower
heat and simmer for 8 to 10 minutes or
until done.

Remove from heat and drain livers; reserve
liquid.

Meanwhile, sauté chopped onion in chicken
fat or oil until golden. Grind chicken livers,
hard-cooked eggs, and onion, using medium
blade of food chopper. Or purée in an
electric blender, using a little of the liquid
in which the livers were cooked.

**4!**

Spoon mixture into a bowl; add seasonings
and enough mayonnaise to moisten. Cover
and refrigerate until ready to serve.

**5**

Serve with crackers or in lettuce cups as an
appetizer. (Whole-grain bread or toast
may be used in place of crackers.)

Yield: Approximately 1½ cups.

# Fitness House Liverwurst

1 medium-sized carrot, sliced
1 onion, sliced
2 tablespoons oil
1 lb. beef liver (with membrane removed)
¼ teaspoon crushed peppercorns
1 clove garlic
¼ teaspoon sage
¼ teaspoon basil
2 tablespoons nutritional yeast
½ cup skim milk powder
2 packages gelatin, unflavored
½ cup cold water
½ cup hot beef stock (see recipe in soup
      section)

Sauté carrot and onion in oil until onion is transparent.

Lay beef liver on top of vegetables, add peppercorns, cover and steam 8 minutes.

**3**

Pass liver, garlic, and vegetables through meat grinder 2 or 3 times, using blades with smallest holes.

**4!**

Stir into mixture, sage, basil, nutritional yeast, skim milk powder.

**5**

Soak gelatin in cold water for five minutes. Then dissolve gelatin mixture in hot stock. Combine this with liver mixture, put into well-oiled loaf tin and chill overnight. Turn out of pan and slice thin.

Yield: Makes one loaf, 9 x 5 x 3-inch.

# Organ Meats

## Liver Loaf

Preheat oven to 350°F.
1 lb. beef liver
½ medium-sized green pepper
1 medium-sized onion
1 bunch parsley
5 slices bacon, cooked crisp
2 eggs, well-beaten
¾ cup wheat germ
¼ teaspoon pepper
½ teaspoon powdered sage
1 teaspoon salt

Remove membrane from liver. Force through meat grinder with green pepper, onion, parsley and cooked bacon.

To liver mixture, add beaten eggs, wheat germ and seasonings; mix well.

Pack firmly in an oiled 9 x 5 x 3-inch loaf pan. Place in preheated oven and bake for 1-1¼ hours, or until done in the center.

Remove from the oven and serve hot; or cool loaf, then chill and serve cold with catsup.

Yield: 6 to 8 servings.

# Liver with Avocado

1 lb. calves (or baby beef) liver
3 tablespoons oil
1 large ripe avocado, peeled, with seed
       removed, and sliced
⅓ cup water
salt to taste
½ teaspoon freshly ground black pepper
2 tablespoons lemon juice

Remove membrane from liver and cut into 1-inch wide strips.

**2**

In skillet, heat oil to medium-high temperature, keeping it below the smoking point. Sauté the liver strips and brown quickly, turning to avoid too much browning. Remove to heated platter while still pink on the inside, as too long sautéing will toughen liver.

**3**

Sauté avocado slices in same skillet, adding more oil if necessary, until lightly-browned. As the slices brown, remove from skillet and arrange over liver.

**4**

Add the ⅓ cup water, salt and pepper to the skillet and bring to a boil, stirring constantly (cook about 5 minutes). Pour mixture over liver and avocado. Sprinkle with lemon juice.

Yield: Approximately 5-6 servings.

# *Organ Meats*

## Liver-Veal Loaf

Preheat oven to 350°F.
½ lb. beef liver
1 cup boiling water
1 medium-sized onion, chopped
2 tablespoons oil
1½ lbs. veal, ground
2 eggs, slightly-beaten
1 teaspoon parsley, chopped
1 teaspoon salt
½ teaspoon freshly-ground pepper
⅛ teaspoon powdered sage
⅔ cup wheat germ
1 cup tomato purée

Remove membrane from liver and place liver in a bowl; pour boiling water over it and allow to stand for 10 minutes.

Meanwhile, sauté chopped onion in oil until tender, but not brown; set aside.

Drain water from liver and pat dry with paper towel. Cut liver coarsely and grind.

Combine ground liver and ground veal. Add sautéed onion, eggs, parsley, salt, pepper and sage. Stir in wheat germ. Gradually stir in the tomato purée, mixing thoroughly.

**5**

Turn mixture into a well-oiled loaf pan (9 x 5 x 3-inch) and place on middle shelf of preheated oven and bake one and one-half hours.

**6**

Remove from oven, turn out onto serving platter and serve immediately.
Note: This loaf is excellent served cold as a luncheon dish.

Yield: 6 servings.

## Sautéed Liver

6 pieces beef liver or calves' liver (about
        1½ lbs.)
½ teaspoon salt
¾ cup rye flour
¼ cup oil

Remove membrane from liver.

**2**

Stir salt into flour.

**3**

In skillet, heat oil to a medium-high
temperature, keeping it below the smoking
point.

**4!**

Dredge liver slices in salted rye flour, one at
a time.

**5**

Sauté liver slices quickly, turning them only
once after the under side is a golden
brown.

**6**

When both sides of liver slices are golden
brown and no more juice is coming out,
transfer to serving platter and serve
immediately.

**7**

Crisp bacon slices or sautéed sliced onions
may be served with the liver.

Yield: 6 servings.

# *Poultry*

## Baked Chicken Supreme

Preheat oven to 425°F.
1 chicken (2½ to 3 lb. broiler-fryer)
1 teaspoon salt
¼ teaspoon paprika
1 teaspoon freshly-chopped tarragon or
        ½ teaspoon dried
freshly-ground pepper to taste
3 tablespoons lemon juice
2 teaspoons tamari soy sauce
¼ cup dry sherry (optional)
2 shallots (or 1 medium onion), diced
½ cup chicken broth or stock (see recipe
        in soup section)
2 teaspoons potato starch or cornstarch
1 cup yogurt
salt to taste
2 tablespoons freshly-chopped parsley

Rinse broiler-fryer; wipe well with paper towels. Cut into serving pieces (see method in introduction to this section). Arrange chicken pieces in a heavy, shallow pan (13 x 9 x 2-inch), lightly oiled.

Season chicken pieces with salt, paprika and fresh or dried tarragon. (If desired, freshly-ground pepper may also be used.) Sprinkle lemon juice, soy sauce and sherry (if desired) over chicken. Place diced shallots or onions around chicken pieces.

**3**

Place pan in preheated 425°F. oven and bake, uncovered, for 20 minutes. Lower oven temperature to 375°F.; cover pan and continue to bake for 30 minutes, basting occasionally with accumulated liquid. (Remove cover after 30 minutes baking and continue to bake 15 or 20 minutes longer, or until chicken is tender and nicely-browned.)

**4!**

Remove from oven and place chicken pieces on heated platter to keep warm.

**5**

In a saucepan, combine ½ cup chicken broth with accumulated liquid from chicken. Simmer over low heat for a minute or two.

**6**

Combine potato starch and yogurt with a wire whisk and stir into sauce until mixture thickens (do not boil); correct seasoning.

**7**

Remove from heat and pour a little of the sauce over chicken. Serve remaining sauce in a separate container. Garnish with two tablespoons chopped parsley and serve.

Yield: 4 servings.

# Roast Chicken

Preheat oven to 350°F.
1 3-4 lb. young roasting chicken
salt and pepper to taste
1 onion, cut in chunks
3 or 4 celery stalks, including leaves
1 tablespoon oil

Wash chicken inside and out and pat dry with paper towels. Rub inside with salt and pepper. Place onions, celery stalks and leaves inside cavity. Brush the skin with oil and dust with salt and pepper.

Place breast side up on a rack in an open roasting pan. Roast in preheated oven until drumstick moves easily when tested gently (about 1½-2 hours).

Yield: 4 servings.

# *Poultry*

## Barbecued Chicken

Preheat oven to 325°F.
2 chickens (2½-3 lbs. each) cut in serving
      pieces—8-10 pieces of chicken (see
      method in introduction to this
      section)
1 cup catsup
½ cup honey
1 cup vinegar
4 tablespoons lemon juice
1 clove garlic
1 medium-sized onion
4 tablespoons tamari soy sauce
¾ teaspoon salt
¼ teaspoon cayenne
1 tablespoon paprika
1 tablespoon crushed bay leaves
2 sprigs parsley
2 teaspoons turmeric
½ teaspoon sage
½ tablespoon thyme
2 teaspoons dry mustard

Wash chicken and lay on oiled baking pan,
skin side up.

Blend all ingredients for barbecue sauce
in blender until thoroughly liquified. Pour
over chicken pieces, coating each one.

Bake uncovered in preheated oven for 1½
hours, basting frequently.

Yield: 6-8 servings.

# Brazilian Chicken

8 chicken quarters or 2/3 lb. chickens, cut
into serving pieces (see method in
introduction to this section)
½ cup lemon juice
6 large cloves garlic
2 teaspoons cumin seed*, or 2 teaspoons
ground cumin
salt, pepper to taste

**1**

Wash chicken, pat dry with paper towels.
Place in baking pan or casserole, skin side up.

**2**

Put lemon juice and garlic cloves into electric
blender container.

**3**

Lightly "toast" whole cumin seed in a
heavy dry skillet over low heat, stirring
constantly, for a few minutes. Do not let it
burn. Add to lemon juice and garlic and
blend until mixture is liquified.

**4**

Brush chicken with cumin marinade, sprinkle
with salt and pepper to taste, and set aside
for at least an hour before cooking time
(to absorb flavor).

**5**

Meanwhile, preheat oven to 350 degrees F.
Cover chicken, bake in preheated oven for an
hour. Remove cover, baste chicken, turn
oven to 400 degrees F. and continue to
bake for ½ hour or until chicken is golden
brown. Serve pan broth with chicken.

*Note: Whole cumin seed is best. Toasting
and freshly grinding improves its flavor, but
if it is not available, use ground cumin.

Yield: 6-8 servings.

# Poultry

## Chicken A La King

½ cup skim milk powder
½ cup cold water
3 tablespoons oil
1 cup fresh mushrooms, thinly-sliced
¼ cup green pepper, chopped
2 tablespoons cornstarch
½ teaspoon salt
2 cups chicken stock (see recipe in soup
     section)
⅛ teaspoon turmeric
2 teaspoons grated onion
2 egg yolks, slightly-beaten
3 cups cooked chicken, cubed (see recipe
     in poultry section)
1 tablespoon lemon juice
¼ teaspoon paprika
2 tablespoons pimiento, chopped

In a small bowl, combine skim milk powder with one-half cup cold water, mixing thoroughly with a whisk. Set aside.

**2**

Heat 3 tablespoons oil in a large 10-inch skillet over medium heat. Sauté mushrooms and green pepper until tender, stirring occasionally (about 5 minutes). Blend in cornstarch and salt.

**3**

Remove from heat. Gradually stir in chicken stock, blending until smooth. Add skim milk and return to low heat. Cook, stirring constantly until mixture thickens and comes to a boil. Boil one minute. Stir in turmeric and grated onion.

**4!**

Stir small amount of hot mixture into two slightly-beaten egg yolks; return to hot mixture. Cook, stirring, over low heat about one minute. Stir in cubed chicken, lemon juice and paprika, heating gently.

**5**

Remove from heat, stir in chopped pimiento and serve over rice or whole grain toast.

Yield: 6-8 servings.

# Chicken Chop Suey

*(Pork may be substituted for chicken)*
½ cup onion, chopped
1 cup celery, chopped
½ cup green pepper, chopped
¼ lb. fresh mushrooms, sliced
2 tablespoons oil
2 cups cooked chicken, cut in one-inch strips
    (see recipe in poultry section)
2 cups chicken stock (see recipe in soup
    section)
2 tablespoons tamari soy sauce
2 tablespoons cornstarch
¼ cup cold water
1 cup fresh sprouts (mung bean or soybeans—
    see "Growing Your Own Sprouts"
    in salad section)

In heavy-bottom pot (or Chinese wok), sauté onion, celery, green pepper and mushrooms in oil until just tender.

Add chicken, chicken stock and tamari soy sauce, and simmer (stirring constantly). Dissolve cornstarch in cold water and add gradually, stirring until cornstarch mixture is cooked and chop suey is thickened.

Add raw bean sprouts just before serving.

Yield: 6 servings.

# *Poultry*

## Chicken Curry

2 onions, sliced
2 chilis, ground (optional)
2 cloves garlic, minced
2 tablespoons oil
1 stick cinnamon
¼ teaspoon whole cloves
1 tablespoon turmeric
1 teaspoon ginger
1 teaspoon cumin
2 tablespoons coriander
1 3-4 lb. chicken, cut into portions (each
      leg into 2, each breast into 4—include
      wings and back, if desired—see
      method in introduction to this section)
1 cup tomato juice
1 cup chicken stock (see recipe in soup
      section)
1-2 tablespoons cornstarch (optional)
¼ cup cold water (optional)
*Serve with:*
   yogurt
   coconut
   peanuts or almonds and raisins, mixed
   apricot chutney

Using a large heavy-bottom pot, sauté onions, chilis (if desired) and garlic in oil. Add cinnamon, cloves, turmeric, ginger, cumin and coriander and sauté together until onion is transparent.

**2**

Add raw chicken pieces and sauté until chicken is well coated with spices and slightly golden in color.

**3**

Add tomato juice and chicken stock to pot, cover with a tight-fitting lid and simmer on very low heat for one to two hours or until chicken is tender, stirring occasionally.

**4**

If desired, thicken sauce with cornstarch dissolved in water just before serving.

**5**

Serve with brown rice and separate small bowls of yogurt, coconut, nuts and raisins, chutney.

Yield: 4 servings.

# Chicken Garbanzo

Preheat oven to 375°F.
3 tablespoons oil (sesame or safflower)
3 tablespoons olive oil
6 portions chicken (either half breasts
     or whole legs)
1 small onion, chopped
½ cup celery, diced
½ cup tomato purée
¼ cup catsup
¼ teaspoon basil (more if desired)
¼ teaspoon oregano (more if desired)
¼ teaspoon black pepper (optional)
1 tablespoon tamari soy sauce
¼ teaspoon salt
1½ cups garbanzo beans (chickpeas),
     cooked (see Method of Cooking
     Garbanzo Beans in vegetable section)

Mix the two oils and brush chicken portions with some of it.

Lay chicken in baking pan, skin-side up, and bake in preheated oven until chicken is nicely browned (30-45 minutes).

Meanwhile, sauté onions and celery in remaining oil until tender. Add tomato purée and catsup, seasonings and herbs. Add cooked garbanzo beans and enough of the water they were cooked in to make a medium-thick sauce.

![4!]

Pour sauce over chicken. Cover tightly with foil. Turn oven down to 350 degrees F. Bake for one-half hour, covered, then remove foil and let chicken brown for one-half hour longer.

Yield: 4-6 servings.

# *Poultry*

## Chicken Teriyaki

Preheat oven to 325°F.
2 chickens (2½-3 lbs. each) or 8-10 pieces
⅔ cup tamari soy sauce
2 tablespoons grated fresh ginger root or
        2½ teaspoons ground ginger
2 tablespoons honey
¼ cup lemon juice
⅔ cup cold water
1 small clove garlic, minced
¼ cup dry sherry (optional)
2 teaspoons cornstarch (optional)
2 tablespoons cold water (optional)

Wash chicken, cut into serving pieces, (see method in introduction to this section), and dry on paper towels. Place in a large mixing bowl.

Combine soy sauce, ginger, honey, lemon juice, water, garlic and dry sherry (if desired) in a small bowl; mix together. Pour over chicken pieces.

Cover bowl and place in refrigerator overnight or for at least 5 hours; turn chicken pieces occasionally to marinate evenly.

Remove chicken pieces from marinade; reserve marinade. Place chicken pieces (skin side up) in a shallow oven proof baking dish and bake, on middle rack, in a preheated oven for 1½ hours or until chicken pieces are fork-tender. Do not cover while baking. Baste chicken with marinade sauce every 15 minutes during baking, using all of sauce in the process.

If desired, liquid in baking dish may be thickened before serving. Slowly add cornstarch-water mixture to hot liquid in baking dish, stirring constantly, and continue to cook until sauce thickens. Remove from heat. Serve in sauce boat.

Yield: 6-8 servings.

# Greek Chicken Pilau

1 chicken (about 3½ lbs.)
1 quart chicken stock (see recipe in soup
     section)
1 teaspoon minced garlic
1 teaspoon oregano
1 teaspoon rosemary
1 teaspoon sweet basil
salt to taste
½ teaspoon black pepper (fresh-ground)

*Rice:*
    ¼ cup onions, minced
    3 tablespoons oil
    1 cup brown rice (raw)
    2¾ cups strained stock (from chicken)

*Garnish:*
    ⅓ cup blanched almonds (slivered or
        halved)
    3 tablespoons oil
    ⅔ cup raisins
    1 green pepper, sliced in rings

Cut raw chicken into 8 pieces—each leg into two, each breast into four, and wings, if desired (see method in introduction to this section).

**2**

Put chicken, stock, garlic, herbs, salt and pepper into pot and simmer until chicken is tender (about 1 hour). Lift chicken out and set aside. Strain stock.

Prepare rice: Sauté minced onions in oil until tender. Add raw brown rice and stir. Add strained stock, stir and cover tightly. Simmer over medium heat until stock is absorbed and rice is tender (about 35-40 minutes). Do not stir during cooking.

**4!**

Toss chicken pieces and rice together gently and heap on serving platter.

**5**

Prepare garnish: Sauté almonds lightly in oil until golden; lift out with slotted spoon; then sauté raisins in same pan with more oil, if necessary, until raisins are puffy. Lift out with slotted spoon. Scatter almonds and raisins over chicken and rice. Top with thin slices of raw green pepper.

This dish should be accompanied by Greek salad (see recipe in salad section).

Yield: 6-8 servings.

# *Poultry*

## Oven-Baked Chicken

Preheat oven to 350°F.
2 chickens (2½-3 lbs.) or 8-10 pieces
¼ cup soy flour
½ cup oat flour
¾ teaspoon salt
⅛ teaspoon pepper
3 tablespoons oil for brushing chicken
1 tablespoon oat flour
1 tablespoon cornstarch
¼ cup water

Wash chicken, cut into serving pieces (see method in introduction to this section). Let drain but do not dry.

Mix next 4 ingredients and put in paper bag.

Put 2 or 3 pieces of chicken in bag and shake to coat chicken. Continue until all pieces are coated.

**4!**

Place chicken, skin side up, in oiled pan. Brush each piece lightly with oil. Bake in preheated oven for one hour or until chicken is nicely-browned and tender.

**5**

If desired, gravy can be made from the liquid in the pan. Strain pan liquid into saucepan; dissolve 1 tablespoon oat flour and 1 tablespoon cornstarch in ¼ cup water; add to pan liquid, stirring; bring to a boil and add more chicken stock or water to make desired consistency.

Yield: 6 servings.

# Simmered Chicken

1 3-lb. roasting chicken, whole, or cut in
      half or quarters (three chicken
      breasts may be used if all white
      meat is desired)
5 cups cold water
1 stalk celery, with leaves
1 medium-sized onion, peeled and quartered
3 sprigs parsley
1½ teaspoons salt
¼ teaspoon paprika
4 whole allspice
4 whole peppercorns

Wash chicken; place in six-quart pot and
add 5 cups cold water. Add remaining
ingredients. Slowly bring to a boil, skimming
foam from surface. Reduce heat, cover
and simmer one hour or until chicken is
tender.

Remove from heat. Lift out chicken, cool
and remove meat from bones. Cut into pieces
of desired size.

Strain broth. Cool and refrigerate. When cold,
skim off fat to use for cooking. Freeze
stock if not planning to use in a few days.

Yield: Approximately 2½ cups diced
chicken.

see color photograph

## Sweet-Sour Chicken

Preheat oven to 350°F.
2 chickens (broiler-fryers, about 1½ lbs.
    each)
1 can (1 lb. 4 oz.) unsweetened pineapple
    chunks and juice
3 tablespoons wine vinegar
1 tablespoon tamari soy sauce
½ teaspoon dry mustard
1 teaspoon salt
⅛ teaspoon cayenne pepper
2 medium-sized green peppers
1 tablespoon cornstarch
2 tablespoons cold water

Rinse broiler-fryers and pat dry with paper towels. Cut into serving pieces. Place chicken parts, skin side up, in a shallow baking dish or pan. Surround with drained pineapple chunks.

**2**

In a medium-sized bowl, combine unsweetened pineapple juice, wine vinegar, soy sauce, dry mustard, salt and cayenne pepper. Mix together thoroughly and pour over chicken pieces.

**3**

Place in a preheated oven on middle rack and bake, uncovered, for 50 minutes. Baste frequently.

**4!**

Meanwhile, wash green peppers. Remove stem, seeds and pulp. Cut into strips (two-inch length by one-half-inch width).

**5**

Add green pepper strips to chicken and continue to bake for 10 minutes. Combine cornstarch with cold water in a small bowl. Stir into liquid in baking dish and bake 20 minutes longer, or until thickened and bubbly.

**6**

Remove from oven and serve immediately.

Yield: 4-6 servings.

# Turkey Newburg

½ lb. fresh mushrooms, thinly-sliced
¼ cup oil or turkey fat
¼ cup oat flour
2 cups turkey stock (see recipe in soup
      section)
½ cup skim milk powder
2 tablespoons cornstarch
1 cup cold water
4 cups turkey meat (approximately 1¼ lbs.)
salt to taste
2 egg yolks
¼ cup sherry (optional)

In heavy-bottom pot, sauté mushrooms in oil or turkey fat until tender. Stir in oat flour. Add turkey stock, stirring constantly; continue to simmer over low heat.

**2**

Meanwhile, combine skim milk powder, cornstarch and cold water, using wire whisk. Stir into sauce and cook until cornstarch has lost its raw taste and sauce is thick (about 10 minutes).

Add turkey. Salt to taste.

**4!**

Beat egg yolks and add some of hot turkey mixture to egg yolks; then add egg yolk mixture to turkey, stirring all the time. Cook one minute longer. Add sherry, if desired. Serve with brown rice.

Yield: 6-8 servings.

# Fish

## Baked, Stuffed Fish

Preheat oven to 350°F.
4 small fish—about ½ lb. each, after head and
    tail are removed. (Porgies, Boston
    mackerel, brook trout or any tasty,
    small fish may be used)
2 tablespoons chopped onion
⅛ teaspoon dill (fresh or dried)
1 tablespoon oil
2 cups cooked brown rice
salt to taste
kelp powder to taste

Wash fish and pat dry with paper towels.

Sauté the onions and dill in oil until just
tender, not brown. Combine with rice and
mix thoroughly. Season to taste.

Put ½ cup of stuffing in each fish cavity;
place in oiled, shallow baking dish; brush fish
lightly with oil and bake in a preheated
oven for 20 minutes.

Yield: 6-8 servings.

## Mackerel Mediterranean

Preheat oven to 350°F.
4 mackerel (about 1½ lbs. each), filleted,
    unskinned
2 onions, medium-sized, sliced thin
3 cups tomatoes (fresh or canned),
    chopped-coarsely and drained
½ teaspoon coriander, ground
½ teaspoon fennel, ground
½ teaspoon basil
½ teaspoon oregano
1 clove garlic, minced
½ teaspoon salt
pepper to taste
1½ tablespoons olive oil

Wash mackerel. In casserole or baking pan,
layer mackerel fillets, skin-side up, with
onions in between.

Combine remaining ingredients. Pour over
mackerel.

Bake, uncovered, in preheated oven for
45 minutes to an hour, until onions are cooked
and fish is tender.
Yield: 6-8 servings.

# Broiled Fish

2 lbs. flounder, sole or haddock
3 tablespoons oil
3 tablespoons lemon juice
salt, pepper to taste
Parsley sprigs and lemon wedges for garnish

Rinse fish in cold water. Pat dry with paper towel and cut into serving pieces.

**2**

Brush broiler rack with a litle oil and arrange pieces of fish on it. Combine oil and lemon juice in small bowl and brush fish with it. Salt, pepper to taste.

Place fish about four inches under the broiler unit and broil for 5-8 minutes (depending on thickness of fish), or until fish flakes easily when tested with fork but is still moist.

**4!**

Remove fish from broiler pan to heated platter. Garnish with parsley and lemon wedges.

Yield: 4-6 servings.

# *Fish*

## Fish Patties

1½ lbs. potatoes (about 4 medium-sized)
½ lb. cooked haddock, cod or flounder, flaked
½ lb. cooked sea trout, bass or bluefish
1 egg
⅓ cup whole-grain, dry bread crumbs
⅓ cup barley flour
3 tablespoons wheat germ
1 onion, grated
1 teaspoon thyme, ground
½ teaspoon salt
pepper to taste
⅔ cup whole grain bread crumbs
½ cup oil

Boil potatoes, peel and mash. Combine mashed potatoes, cooked, flaked fish, egg, ⅓ cup bread crumbs, barley flour, wheat germ, grated onion, thyme, salt and pepper to taste. Form into patties of desired size.

**2**

Dip patties in ⅔ cup bread crumbs. Sauté in oil until golden brown (about 5 minutes for each side).

**3**

Place in paper-towel-lined baking pan in low oven to keep warm until ready to serve. Serve with tomato sauce. (See recipe in meat-sauce section.)

Yield: 6-8 servings.

# Flounder Au Gratin

Preheat oven to 300°F.
1 lb. fresh fillet of flounder
5 tablespoons oil
4 tablespoons brown rice flour
2 tablespoons soy flour
4 teaspoons cornstarch
1 cup skim milk powder
4 cups water
nutmeg, salt, kelp powder, to taste
4 egg yolks
4 egg whites
4 tablespoons wheat germ

Brush flounder with 1 tablespoon oil and
bake in preheated oven for 15-20 minutes, or
until tender.

To make white sauce—sift rice and soy
flours and cornstarch together. Put 4
tablespoons oil into saucepan, stir in flours
and heat until it bubbles. Meanwhile,
combine skim milk powder and water using
a wire whisk and add slowly to oil-flour
mixture, stirring constantly. Cook until sauce
is thickened and flours have lost their raw
taste. Season with nutmeg, salt, kelp
powder to taste.

Beat egg yolks and add a little of the hot
sauce to them slowly, stirring, then stir egg
yolk-mixture into hot sauce, and continue
to stir for one minute longer. Remove from
heat. Meanwhile preheat oven to 350°F.

Break cooked flounder into bite-size pieces
and add to sauce.

Beat egg whites until stiff, and fold them into
fish mixture.

Pour into casserole, top with wheat germ and
bake in preheated oven for about 1/2 hour
or until the au gratin has set. Serve
immediately.

Yield: 4-6 servings.

# Fish

## Flounder Florentine

Preheat oven to 350°F.
1/4 cup onion, chopped
1/8 teaspoon dill (crushed)
2 tablespoons oil
1 1/2 lbs. fresh spinach, chopped
1/2 cup cooked brown rice
1/4 cup toasted almonds (chopped)
1 tablespoon lemon juice
6 fillets of flounder (about 1 1/2 lbs.)

In a saucepan, sauté onion and dill in oil until tender.

Add spinach and sauté just enough to wilt the spinach (about 3 minutes).

**3**

Add rice, almonds and lemon juice. Heat, stirring occasionally.

**4!**

Place 1/4 cup of the mixture on each fish fillet. Roll and press ends securely.

**5**

Arrange in oiled, shallow baking dish (10 x 6 x 2 inches). Bake in preheated oven for 20 minutes.
Note: If desired, fish roll-ups may be served with mushroom sauce or egg sauce (see recipes in meat, poultry, fish-sauce section).

Yield: 6 servings.

# Crusty Oven-Baked Fish

Preheat oven to 400°F.
2 lbs. haddock or flounder fillets
½ cup wheat germ
½ cup peanut flour (raw peanuts ground in
    blender or nut grinder)
¼ cup sesame seeds
½ cup bran flakes or whole grain bread
    crumbs
1 teaspoon salt
½ teaspoon black pepper
½ teaspoon oregano
½ teaspoon marjoram
½ teaspoon paprika
½ teaspoon garlic powder
1 egg, beaten
½ cup oil
½ cup lemon juice

Rinse fish. Cut into portions and leave to drain.

Combine all dry ingredients to make crumb mixture and set aside.

Combine egg, oil and lemon juice in a blender or use an eggbeater to obtain an emulsion.

Dip portions of fish into egg dip and then into crumb mixture.

**5**

Lay on shallow baking pan which has been lightly oiled. Bake in preheated oven approximately 20 minutes, until tender.

Yield: 6-8 servings.

# Sauces

## Basic White or Brown Sauce (Medium-Thick)

**Recipe No. I**
2 tablespoons oil
2 tablespoons soy flour
2 tablespoons brown rice flour
1 cup liquid (milk, soy milk, or stock)
salt, pepper to taste

Put oil into a saucepan. Do not heat.

**2**

Combine soy and brown rice flour in a small bowl and dissolve mixture in the oil.

**3**

Stir the liquid in gradually, smoothing out any lumps.

**4!**

Put saucepan over medium heat. Stir constantly, cooking until mixture boils and is thickened. Season to taste.
Yield: 1 cup.

**Recipe No. II**
2 tablespoons oil
4 tablespoons brown rice flour
1 cup liquid (milk, soy milk, or stock)
salt, pepper to taste

Put oil into a saucepan. Do not heat.

**2**

Dissolve brown rice flour in oil.

**3**

Stir the liquid in gradually, smoothing out any lumps.

**4!**

Put saucepan over medium heat. Stir constantly, cooking until mixture boils and is thickened. Season to taste.

Yield: 1 cup.

**Recipe No. III**
2 tablespoons oil
4 tablespoons rye flour
1 cup liquid (milk, soy milk, or stock)
salt, pepper to taste

Put oil into a saucepan. Do not heat.

**2**

Dissolve rye flour in the oil.

**3**

Stir the liquid in gradually, smoothing out any lumps.

**4!**

Put saucepan over medium heat. Stir constantly, cooking until mixture boils and is thickened. Season to taste.

Yield: 1 cup.

*Note: This medium-thick sauce is good for creamed vegetables, chicken or fish.

# Basic Tomato Sauce (Use for Spanish Omelette, Fish, etc.)

1 medium-sized onion, diced
1 clove garlic, minced
1 stalk celery, diced
1 green pepper, diced
1 carrot, diced
1/4 cup oil
2 cups tomatoes, fresh or canned, drained
            and chopped
1 teaspoon salt
freshly ground pepper to taste
1 teaspoon basil
1 bay leaf
1/4 cup chopped parsley

In heavy-bottom pot, sauté onion, garlic, celery, green pepper, carrot in oil for 5-10 minutes over medium heat.

**2**

Add tomatoes and next 4 ingredients, mixing well. Turn down heat. Cover pot and simmer for 10 minutes longer. Remove bay leaf. Add chopped parsley and serve.

Yield: Approximately 3 cups.

# Sauces

## Basic White or Brown Sauce (Thin)

**Recipe No. I**
2 tablespoons oil
2 tablespoons potato flour
1 cup liquid (milk, soy milk or stock)
salt, pepper to taste

Put oil into saucepan. Do not heat.

Dissolve potato flour in the oil.

Stir the liquid in gradually, smoothing out any lumps.

Put saucepan over medium heat. Stir constantly, cooking until mixture boils and is thickened. Season to taste.

Yield: 1 cup.

**Recipe No. II**
2 tablespoons oil
1½ teaspoons cornstarch
2 tablespoons rye flour
1 cup liquid (milk, soy milk or stock)
salt, pepper to taste

Put oil into a saucepan. Do not heat.

Dissolve cornstarch, then rye flour in oil.

Stir the liquid in gradually, smoothing out any lumps.

Put saucepan over medium heat. Stir constantly, cooking until mixture boils and is thickened. Season to taste.

Yield: 1 cup.

*Note: This thin sauce is good for thickening soups or making gravy.

# Au Gratin Sauce for Fish

2 tablespoons oil
4 tablespoons barley flour
1⅓ cups chicken stock (see recipe in soup
      section)
4 tablespoons tomato juice
1 teaspoon tamari soy sauce
¾ cup cheddar cheese, grated
3 tablespoons skim milk powder
⅓ cup water
1 tablespoon chopped parsley

In the top of a double boiler, heat oil and gradually stir in barley flour.

**2**

Heat stock and add it to oil and flour, a little at a time, blending until smooth. Stir in tomato juice and tamari soy sauce.

Add grated cheese gradually, stirring constantly to blend it in.

**4!**

Combine skim milk powder and water with a wire whisk and add to sauce, mixing until smooth. Add chopped parsley. Spoon some sauce over broiled fish just before serving and broil for 3 minutes or until it is golden brown.

Yield: Approximately 3 cups.

# Sauces

## Curried Yogurt Sauce (For Broiled Fish)

1 cup mayonnaise
½ cup yogurt
2 teaspoons parsley, minced
1½ teaspoons fresh dill, minced
½ teaspoon curry powder
1 teaspoon honey
1 teaspoon tamari soy sauce

Mix ingredients together in order given.

Broil fish until just tender.

Place one tablespoon Curried Yogurt Sauce on top of each serving of fish. Broil one minute longer. Remove fish to serving platter. Serve remaining sauce in separate container.

Yield: Approximately 1½ cups.

## Horseradish Sauce

1 cup yogurt
½ teaspoon salt
⅛ teaspoon cayenne
1 tablespoon grated horseradish

Combine all ingredients in a small bowl.

Refrigerate, covered, until well chilled (about one hour). Serve cold with roast beef.

Yield: One cup.

# Egg Sauce for Broiled Fish

2 tablespoons oil
4 teaspoons potato flour or brown rice flour
1 cup water
⅓ cup skim milk powder
salt and pepper to taste
2 hardboiled eggs, chopped coarsely
1 teaspoon parsley, finely-chopped
1 teaspoon lemon juice

Put oil in top of double boiler but do not heat yet. Add potato or brown rice flour to the oil, whisking slowly.

Combine water and skim milk powder with a wire whisk, and add slowly to the above mixture, stirring constantly. Add salt and pepper to taste.

Cook 10 minutes, or until flour is cooked and sauce is thick.

Just before serving, add the chopped eggs, parsley and lemon juice.

Yield: 4-6 servings.

# Sauces

## Mushroom Sauce

4 tablespoons oil
3/4 lb. mushrooms, washed and sliced
4 tablespoons soy flour
4 tablespoons brown rice flour
1/2 cup skim milk powder
2 cups water
salt, pepper to taste

In heavy-bottom saucepan, sauté mushrooms in oil for about five minutes. Lift out with slotted spoon and set aside.

Combine soy and brown rice flour, stir into juices remaining in the pan used to sauté mushrooms. Smooth out all lumps. Do not heat.

**3**

Combine skim milk powder and water, using a wire whisk. Add milk gradually to flour—oil mixture, stirring until smooth.

**4!**

Heat, stirring constantly, until sauce boils and is thickened. Add cooked mushrooms. Season to taste.

Yield: Approximately 3 cups.

# Peanut Butter Sauce

½ cup peanut butter
1 onion, grated
1 clove garlic, minced
3 tablespoons soy milk powder
½ teaspoon honey
3 tablespoons lemon juice
4 tablespoons tamari soy sauce

Combine all ingredients in electric mixer or blender. If necessary, add about ½ cup hot water to make the sauce the consistency of heavy cream.

Good over hamburgers, or with cooked rice or bulgur.

Yield: About 2 cups.

# Pierre Sauce

1 clove garlic, minced
¼ cup sesame oil (or safflower)
2 tablespoons barley flour
3 tablespoons potato flour (or brown rice flour)
3 cups hot chicken stock (see recipe in soup section)
¼ cup tomato juice
1 tablespoon vinegar
1 teaspoon tamari soy sauce
¼ teaspoon paprika
salt to taste
white pepper to taste

Sauté garlic in oil for about 30 seconds.

Combine barley and potato flours and stir into oil. Heat until foamy.

Add hot chicken stock, stirring with a whisk. Add tomato juice, vinegar, tamari soy sauce, seasonings and cook 15 minutes over medium heat. Set aside over low heat, covered, until ready to serve.
Yield: Approximately 3½ cups.

Soybeans

CURF

omelette

COTTAGE

CHEESE

fondue

EGGS

chili

eggs

eggplant

fondue

5.

eggplant

omelette

eggs florentine

Soybeans

eese fondue

# Soybeans, eggs and cheese

## Soybeans

For us in the Fitness House Kitchen "discovering" the soybean has been a pleasant and surprising adventure. The soybean is one of the most versatile, fascinating and valuable of all plants.

Early Chinese records dated before 2000 B.C. mention soybeans, and some historians credit this humble plant with being the reason for China's survival as a nation. Whether or not this is true, it was just about their sole source of protein for hundreds of years.

As well as being a food of the past, the soybean appears to be a food of the future. From a second-rate meat-substitute during World War II, it has experienced phenomenal growth until today it is our second largest crop in production, a large proportion of it going for stock feed. More and more it is being recognized as important food for people. The soybean is 34 percent high-quality protein, while other dry legumes contain only 20 to 24 percent protein with almost twice as much carbohydrate as soybeans.

Because they are rather bland in flavor, soybeans require distinctive seasonings so we often serve them curried or barbecued. They are also very good in our cheese-stuffed peppers and stuffed-eggplant dishes, adding to the variety of textures and to the protein content.

A 3½ ounce serving of cooked soybeans has approximately 130 calories and costs about five cents. How else can you get important protein for that price? In addition to protein, the soybean is especially rich in calcium, iron and phosphorus and contains large amounts of the B vitamins, vitamin A and D, vitamin E, the unsaturated fatty acids and lecithin. The oil in soybeans is 51.5 percent linoleic acid— believed to be the most effective fatty acid for preventing cholesterol in the blood from forming unhealthful deposits.

Because soy flour is highly concentrated, it has an extremely high protein content—much higher than any other soy product. It is very easy to use in cooking. There are basically two types of soy flour—full (or high fat) and low fat. They are interchangeable in recipes. We use soy flour in our breads, muffins, cookies, for breading and, in combination with other flours, for thickening agents. We also add it, along with skim milk powder, to custards and puddings to raise the protein content.

Soy flour or soy powder, reconstituted with water, can replace milk in custards, puddings, sauces or beverages for those who are allergic to cow's milk. There is surprisingly little change in flavor. You can even make your own soy milk from the soybean—a method preferred by some. We include a recipe for this. The use of soy milk in infant formulas is well-known. When using soy flour for baking, just remember to turn the oven temperature 25 degrees lower than usual as it tends to brown at a lower temperature than other flours.

Soy grits or granules, derived from soybeans, are used at Fitness House to thicken stews, bind meat loaves or as an ingredient, along with other grains, in our Almond Crunch cereal. We have even used them in our Carob-Almond Torte and were delighted with the result—a moist, delicious cake.

Because of the high protein content, soybeans do require longer soaking and cooking than other legumes. They should be soaked at least 8 hours before cooking, and they will cook in less time if they have been frozen first. At Fitness House, we soak them at room temperature for an hour or so and then put them in the freezer overnight. Next morning we boil them for 2-3 hours. They tend to boil over more readily than ordinary beans, so be sure to use a large enough pot and leave the lid slightly to one side until you have the heat adjusted to a simmer.

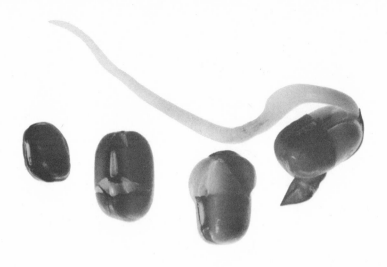

These are soybeans in
various stages of sprouting.

The subject of soybeans should not be left without mentioning soybean sprouts. They can be added to salads, soups, omelets or any dish you fancy for that extra nourishing crunch.

If the soybean is a stranger to you, we hope that by now you are so intrigued you will make it a point to acquaint yourself with this wonderful little bean.

## Eggs

The egg has been called "Nature's pre-packaged masterpiece of nutrition." It is so near perfection that scientists use it as a standard of measurement for protein value in other foods.

Aside from this, the egg has other remarkable properties. It is capable of playing almost any role assigned to it by the cook. When we make mayonnaise in our Fitness House Kitchen it is the emulsifier; it is the leavening in our cakes and soufflés; it often thickens our sauces, it may coat our croquettes or bind our meat loaves. And a delicious 80-calorie, five-cent omelet can be whipped up in 10 minutes.

In our cholesterol-conscious era, many health-oriented people avoid eggs. The truth is that cholesterol *intake* is not the core of the problem. Our bodies manufacture cholesterol; it is essential to life. What really counts is how our bodies handle it.

The egg is rich in lecithin (which works to prevent fatty deposits in the arteries) and the B vitamins along with its cholesterol. No food carries more built-in ammunition to deal with cholesterol. Since lecithin and the B vitamins are natural nutrients occurring in grains, nuts and seeds, it is clear that the foods to be avoided by the cholesterol-conscious person are refined flours, oils and hydrogenated fats, not the egg.


## Cheese

Cheese is one of the truly ancient foods. It takes 2,500 lbs. of milk to make 200 lbs. of some cheese, so that while milk is only 4 percent protein, cheese can be from 18-36 percent protein. It is also low in calories. A 2-ounce piece of cheese can supply up to 30 percent of your daily protein requirement while filling only 10 percent (200 calories) of the average woman's calorie allowance.

Unfortunately, the commercial manufacture of cheese today usually involves processing and the use of chemical additives. It is possible, however, to make cheese using raw milk and without adding imitation color and preservatives. Some of this cheese is available now in natural food centers and we hope that there will be a lot more in the future. This is of course the truly "natural" cheese. So-called natural cheese as opposed to "process" or processed cheese, is a far superior product.

Most natural cheeses are made from whole cow's milk though there are some which are made from skim milk, whey or mixtures of all three. In most cases the milk is coagulated with the help of rennet or some other suitable enzyme. The curd is then processed by heat, pressure, bacteria molds or other special treatment. Each natural cheese has its own characteristic flavor and texture, ranging from bland cottage cheese to sharp, Bleu, or Limburger, and from the smooth creaminess of cream cheese to the firm elasticity of Swiss.

These flavors and textures are closely related to ripening and aging. Some natural cheeses, such as cottage, cream, ricotta and factory-made mozzarella, are used unripened. The softer, ripened cheeses, which depend more on molds and bacterial growth for their flavor, include, Brie, Camembert, Muenster, Bleu, Roquefort, Bel Paese and Port du Salut. The firm, ripened cheeses are Cheddar, Colby, Edam, Gouda and Swiss.

Processed cheeses, or "process," as they are called in the industry, are basically one natural cheese or a mixture of several different natural cheeses, to which an emulsifying agent, a dye, a stabilizer, and a thickening agent have been added. Then there may be sugar, or a "smoked" flavor added as well. The end result is a poor excuse for cheese.

When you buy cheese, check the label carefully. Cheddar cheese labeled "mild" usually has been aged 2-3 months; "medium" or "mellow"—4-7 months and "aged" or "sharp"—8-12 months. Pasteurized process cheese labels will always include the name of the variety or varieties of cheese used—for example: "Pasteurized Process American Cheese" or "Pasteurized Process Swiss and American Cheese."

When we are lucky enough to get it, we serve natural cheese slices, with bread and crackers, along with a hearty soup for lunch. We have had some delicious goat milk cheeses.

In our kitchen, we use cheese in a number of dishes, sometimes as a major part of the main course—in a soufflé or fondue—often as one of the flavoring ingredients. We make our own cottage cheese from skim milk powder. It is quickly and easily made and very popular served with a fresh fruit salad or seasoned with chives and served atop a tomato. We also use cottage cheese in making cheesecake.

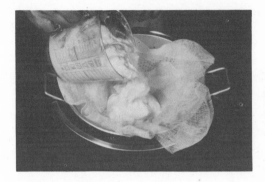

Put yogurt in cheese-cloth-lined strainer.

Semi-soft yogurt "cheese" is an excellent base for dips.

We have made yogurt "cheese" to be used in the place of cream cheese. It is easy to make. You simply put the yogurt in a cheese-cloth-lined strainer (don't squeeze it), and leave it to drip overnight in the refrigerator. Next morning you have a semi-soft curd-like "cheese" fine for use in salads, dips, or desserts.

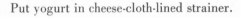

The Rodale Cookbook

# Soybeans

## Method for Cooking Soybeans

Wash soybeans, then remove any foreign particles. Cover soybeans with cold water. Refrigerate or freeze overnight. Freezing will lessen the amount of cooking time needed.

Next day put the soybeans and their soaking water on to cook, using a large enough pot and leaving the lid slightly to one side so that the soybeans will not boil over. Bring soybeans to a boil, then turn heat down and simmer until they are tender, 2-3 hours. (They will never be as soft as navy beans, for example, but they will get tender, when done.)

Soaking, or cooked soybeans ferment very quickly, so should never be left very long at room temperature. They will keep quite long in the freezer, but not more than a few days in the refrigerator.

1 cup dry soybeans will swell during soaking to 2½-3 cups. One pound of dry soybeans is about 2¼ cups.

## Baked Soybeans

Preheat oven to 350°F.
½ cup green pepper, chopped
¼ cup onions, chopped
3 tablespoons oil
1 lb. dry soybeans, soaked and cooked
    (see directions in this section)
water soybeans were cooked in
¾ cup catsup
1½ teaspoons salt
½ teaspoon kelp powder
2 tablespoons honey
1 tablespoon molasses

Sauté green pepper and onions in oil until tender.

Combine soybeans, cooking water, sautéed vegetables, catsup, salt, kelp powder, honey and molasses in casserole and bake in preheated oven for 1½ hours, stirring occasionally.

Yield: 8-10 servings.

see color photograph

## Barbecued Soybeans

Preheat oven to 350°F.
2¼ cups (1 lb.) large, dried soybeans,
    soaked and cooked (see directions
    in this section)
the water soybeans were cooked in
½ cup onion, chopped
1 clove garlic, minced
2 tablespoons oil
½ cup tomato juice
½ cup catsup
1 tablespoon molasses
½ cup green pepper, chopped
2 tablespoons honey
1½ teaspoons dry mustard
¼ cup parsley, freshly-chopped
⅛ teaspoon cayenne pepper
Bacon strips for garnish (optional)

Put cooked soybeans with their liquid into a lightly-oiled casserole.

Sauté chopped onion and minced garlic in 2 tablespoons oil until golden but not brown.

Remove from heat and add to cooked soybeans. Add the tomato juice, catsup, molasses, chopped green pepper, honey, dry mustard, chopped parsley and cayenne pepper. Mix together thoroughly.

**4!**

Lay strips of bacon on top of soybeans, if desired. Place in preheated oven and bake one and one-half hours or until soybeans are tender.

Yield: 6-8 servings.

# Soybean-Cheese Stuffed Peppers

Preheat oven to 350°F.
3 green peppers, cleaned, halved lengthwise
1 cup cooked soybeans (see directions in
        this section)
1 small onion, grated
1 cup cooked, brown rice
2 teaspoons nutritional yeast (optional)
$1\frac{1}{4}$ cups stock or water
$\frac{3}{4}$ cup sharp Cheddar cheese, grated
salt to taste
$\frac{1}{4}$ cup grated Parmesan cheese
$\frac{1}{4}$ cup wheat germ

Prepare peppers; set aside. Grind or chop soybeans coarsely and combine with onion and cooked rice.

Dissolve nutritional yeast in $\frac{1}{4}$ cup stock or water. Add with grated Cheddar cheese to rice-soybean mixture. Salt to taste.

Fill pepper halves and place them in casserole. Pour 1 cup stock or water into casserole or pan around (not over) peppers. Cover and bake in a preheated oven for 30 minutes.

Uncover peppers and top them with Parmesan cheese and wheat germ. Bake, uncovered, another 15 minutes or until peppers are tender.

Yield: 4-6 servings.

# Soybeans

## Soy Stuffed Peppers

Preheat oven to 350°F.
4 large green peppers
2 tablespoons oil
½ cup onion, minced
½ cup celery, finely-chopped
1 cup shredded carrots
2 cups cooked soybeans, puréed (see
  directions in this section)
⅔ cup tomatoes, peeled and chopped
½ teaspoon salt
½ teaspoon freshly-snipped thyme or ¼
  teaspoon dried thyme
½ teaspoon basil leaves, chopped, or ¼
  teaspoon dried basil
¼ teaspoon freshly-ground pepper
½ teaspoon kelp powder
4 tablespoons chopped parsley
1 cup tomato juice
3 tablespoons wheat germ
3 tablespoons grated Parmesan cheese

Wash and drain green peppers well. Cut green peppers in half lengthwise and carefully remove seeds and pith. Place pepper halves in a deep bowl and cover with boiling water; allow to stand for five minutes. Remove peppers from boiling water and drain.

**2**

In a large skillet heat two tablespoons oil over medium heat. Add chopped onion and celery and sauté until golden—about five minutes, stirring constantly. Add shredded carrots and cook, stirring until vegetables are tender—about 10 to 12 minutes.

**3**

Stir puréed soybeans into vegetable mixture. Add tomatoes, salt, thyme, basil, pepper and kelp powder, simmer for 15 minutes, stirring constantly.

**4!**

Remove skillet from heat and stir chopped parsley into cooked mixture. Allow to cool slightly before stuffing green peppers. Lightly season the inside half of each green pepper half with kelp powder. Stuff peppers with prepared mixture and place in a shallow baking pan or dish with cover. Pour tomato juice *around peppers*, not over.

Cover and place in a preheated oven and bake for 30 minutes. Baste occasionally.

Meanwhile combine wheat germ and grated Parmesan cheese. When stuffed peppers have baked for 30 minutes, remove from oven, uncover, and spoon wheat germ-cheese mixture over top of green peppers. Return to oven and continue to bake, uncovered, for 10 to 15 minutes longer or until peppers are tender.

**7**

Remove green peppers from oven and allow to stand for about 5 minutes before serving. Pour sauce into sauceboat and serve with green peppers.

Yield: 6-8 servings.

# Soybean Chili

$\frac{1}{3}$ cup onion, chopped
$\frac{1}{2}$ cup celery, chopped
$\frac{1}{2}$ cup green pepper, chopped
4 tablespoons oil
$\frac{1}{2}$ teaspoon cumin
$\frac{1}{2}$ teaspoon salt
$\frac{1}{4}$ teaspoon cayenne
$\frac{1}{2}$ teaspoon tamari soy sauce
2 cups fresh or canned tomatoes, chopped
$\frac{1}{2}$ cup tomato purée
2 cups cooked soybeans with liquid (see directions in this section)

In large skillet, sauté onion, celery and green pepper in oil. Add seasonings, tomatoes and tomato purée; bring to boil and simmer for 20 minutes.

Add soybeans and continue to simmer 30 minutes longer; correct seasoning to taste.

Yield: Approximately 5 servings.

# Soybeans

## Soybean Curry

Preheat oven to 350°F.
1 cup celery, diced
1 clove garlic, minced
1 onion, chopped fine
½ cup carrot, diced
¾ cup green pepper, diced
4 tablespoons oil
3 cups cooked soybeans (see directions this section)
1½ cups soybean cooking liquid
1½ teaspoons curry powder

In a large skillet, sauté celery, garlic, onion, carrot and green pepper in oil, until lightly brown and tender.

Add soybeans, soybean water and curry powder. Transfer to a casserole and bake in a preheated oven until liquid is absorbed—½ to 1 hour.

Yield: 6-8 servings.

## Soybean Loaf

Preheat oven to 350°F.
3 cups cooked soybeans, coarsely-chopped (see directions this section)
1 large carrot, grated (about 1 cup)
1 medium-sized onion, chopped
1 stalk celery and leaves, chopped
⅓ cup green pepper, chopped
2 tablespoons chopped parsley
1 tablespoon sesame seeds
1 tablespoon wheat germ
1 tablespoon oil
2 eggs, beaten

In large mixing bowl combine all ingredients.

Press into oiled 9 x 5 x 3-inch loaf pan and bake in preheated oven for 35 minutes.

Allow to cool in pan for 10 minutes, then remove carefully and slice in thick slices. Serve with tomato or mushroom sauce. (See recipe in meat-sauces section.)

Yield: 6 servings.

# Soybean-Rice Surprise Casserole

Preheat oven to 350°F.
½ cup soybeans, cooked (see directions
    this section)
2 cups whole corn, fresh or frozen
2 cups canned tomatoes (drained)
1 cup onion, chopped
1 clove garlic, crushed
½ teaspoon thyme
1 teaspoon salt
pinch of cayenne
¼ cup tomato paste
3 tablespoons nutritional yeast
½ cup stock (chicken or beef) (see recipe
    in soup section)
2½ cups cooked brown rice (see directions
    in grain section)
⅓ cup grated cheese
2 tablespoons wheat germ

Combine soybeans, corn, tomatoes, onion, garlic, thyme, salt and cayenne. Set aside.

Combine tomato paste, nutritional yeast, and stock. Set aside.

Place half the cooked rice on the bottom of an oiled 4-quart casserole. Cover the rice with the vegetable mixture. Spread the tomato paste over the vegetables and cover this layer with the rest of the rice.

**4!**

Sprinkle with grated cheese and then wheat germ. Bake uncovered for 30 minutes in preheated oven.

Yield: 6-8 servings.

## Soybean-Vegetable Casserole

Preheat oven to 350°F.
1 medium-sized onion, chopped
1 cup celery, diced
2 cups carrots, sliced
3 tablespoons oil
1 teaspoon salt
⅛ teaspoon cayenne
¼ teaspoon rosemary
2 teaspoons freshly-chopped parsley
2 cups tomato purée
2 cups bean liquid or water
3 cups cooked soybeans (see directions
            in this section)

In large skillet, sauté onion, celery and carrots in oil until tender but not brown (about 10 minutes).

Add seasonings and herbs to sautéed vegetables; slowly stir in the tomato purée and bean liquid or water. Simmer mixture for about 5 minutes.

Stir in cooked soybeans and simmer about 10 minutes longer. Turn mixture into a two-quart casserole and bake in a preheated oven for one hour or until beans are tender.

Remove from oven and serve immediately.

Yield: 8 servings.

# Soybean-Stuffed Eggplant

Preheat oven to 350°F.
1¼ lb. eggplant (2 medium-sized)
1 small onion, chopped
1 clove garlic, minced
3 tablespoons oil
2 cups cooked soybeans, chopped (see
      directions this section)
4 medium-sized fresh tomatoes, peeled
      and quartered, or 1 cup canned
      tomatoes
½ teaspoon salt
½ teaspoon basil (fresh or dried)
½ cup grated medium sharp Cheddar cheese
½ cup grated Parmesan cheese
¼ cup wheat germ

Halve eggplants lengthwise.

Scoop out pulp, leaving ½-inch border in shell.

3

Place shells in baking pan, add a little water, cover pan and bake 30 minutes in preheated oven.

Sauté onion and garlic in oil. Add chopped soybeans and diced eggplant pulp; continue to sauté.

5

Add tomatoes, salt and basil and cook on medium heat for 10 minutes, stirring several times.

6

Add grated Cheddar and mix in.

7

Pile filling into eggplant shells; top with grated Parmesan cheese and wheat germ.

8

Bake 25 minutes in preheated oven or until nicely browned on top.

Yield: 4 servings.

# Eggs

## Basic Omelette – with Spanish Sauce, Cheese or Mushroom Filling

8 eggs
1 cup water
1/4 cup oil
salt to taste
1 1/2 cups Spanish Sauce (see recipe in
      Meat-Sauce section)
         or
3/4 cup Cheddar cheese (grated)
         or
1 1/2 cups mushroom sauce (see recipe in
      Meat-Sauce section)
chopped parsley for garnish

Break eggs into a bowl. Beat lightly—just until yolks and whites are combined (overbeating toughens omelette). Add water and beat briefly.

Heat cast iron skillet to medium-high heat. Add enough oil to coat bottom of pan. Pour in just enough egg mixture to cover the bottom of the pan. It should sizzle and start to cook immediately. Salt to taste.

**3**

With a metal spatula, push cooked edges of omelette toward the center of the pan, tipping it so that the liquid can run to the outside rim and cook. When the omelette is almost all set, and the bottom of it is golden brown, spoon cheese, or filling onto one side and using spatula, lift up the other side, flipping it over the filling so that the omelette is a half-moon shape. Carefully turn out omelette onto plate. Garnish with chopped parsley and serve immediately. If making Spanish omelette, spoon hot sauce over omelette just before serving.

Yield: 6 servings.

# Egg Curry

16 eggs
2 teaspoons ground chilis or chili
        powder
1 teaspoon turmeric
1 pinch cumin
1 pinch coriander
1 pinch ginger
$\frac{1}{2}$ cup water or tomato juice
4 onions, sliced
2 cloves garlic, minced
$\frac{1}{4}$ cup oil
8 tomatoes, peeled and cut into eighths or
        4 cups canned tomatoes
salt to taste
1 cup yogurt

Hard boil eggs, peel, leave whole. With
tip of paring knife, slit egg white from end to
end around the whole egg, leaving $\frac{1}{4}$ inch
space between each slit to allow curry
flavor to penetrate egg, taking care to keep
the egg in one piece.

Combine chilis, turmeric, cumin, coriander,
ginger, and water or tomato juice.

Sauté onions and garlic in oil. Add spice
mixture and tomatoes, then simmer for one
hour. Salt to taste.

## 4!

Remove from heat and add one cup of yogurt
stirring until blended, and the eggs. Heat
together for about 30 minutes before
serving, to allow flavors to penetrate eggs;
but take care to keep the heat very low so
that eggs do not toughen.

Yield: 6-8 servings.

# Egg Puff Squares with Chicken Sauce

Preheat oven to 350°F.

**1.**
**Egg Puff:**
$2\frac{1}{2}$ tablespoons cornstarch
$\frac{1}{4}$ teaspoon salt
2 tablespoons oil
$\frac{1}{4}$ cup skim milk powder
1 cup water
$\frac{1}{8}$ teaspoon grated or ground nutmeg
4 egg yolks
4 egg whites

In medium-sized saucepan, combine cornstarch, salt and oil. Place over medium heat and stir until mixture bubbles; remove from heat. Combine skim milk powder and water with a wire whisk and add gradually, stirring constantly to prevent lumping. Return saucepan to heat, cook, stirring constantly, until mixture thickens. Remove from heat and stir in nutmeg.

**2**

In large bowl, beat egg yolks until thick and lemon-colored. Slowly add hot mixture to beaten yolks, blending with a wire whisk until all the sauce has been incorporated. Set aside while beating whites.

**3**

Beat egg whites until stiff peaks form when beater is slowly raised. Slowly add yolk mixture to beaten whites, folding in gently until thoroughly combined. Turn mixture into an oiled 9 x 9 x 2-inch baking dish or pan—do not oil sides of pan.

**4!**

Place on middle rack of preheated oven and bake for 30 minutes or until top is golden brown and puffed.

**5!**

Remove from oven; cut in squares. Serve at once with chicken sauce.

**2.**

**Chicken Sauce: (Prepare sauce while egg puff is baking)**
2 tablespoons oil
$\frac{1}{4}$ cup minced onion
$2\frac{1}{2}$ tablespoons cornstarch
$\frac{1}{4}$ teaspoon salt
$\frac{1}{2}$ cup skim milk powder
$1\frac{1}{4}$ cups water
$\frac{3}{4}$ cup shredded Cheddar cheese
$1\frac{1}{2}$ cups diced cooked chicken
2 tablespoons chopped pimiento
$\frac{1}{8}$ teaspoon paprika
Chopped parsley for garnish

**1**

Measure two tablespoons oil into medium-sized saucepan. Add one-fourth cup finely-chopped onion and sauté over medium heat until onion is tender—do not brown. Stir in cornstarch and salt and cook until mixture bubbles. Remove from heat.

**2**

Combine skim milk powder and water with a wire whisk. Add to saucepan, blending thoroughly with a wire whisk, to prevent lumping.

**3**

Return saucepan to heat and cook, stirring constantly, until mixture thickens and bubbles. Add cheese and stir until melted. Stir in chicken and pimiento. Add paprika and stir until chicken is thoroughly heated— do not bring to a boil.

**4!**

Remove from heat and turn into serving dish. Garnish with chopped parsley, if desired. Serve accompanied with Egg Puff Squares.

Note: Egg Puff is similar to a soufflé and should be served immediately upon removing from oven; however, it will not fall as quickly as a soufflé. If you should need to hold it over for a few minutes, turn oven off when puff is baked and leave in oven until ready to serve. Cut in squares just before serving.

Yield: 4-6 servings.

# Egg Foo Yung

5 eggs
1/2 cup water
1/4 cup chopped onions
1/2 cup sprouted mung beans
1/2 cup sliced mushrooms
salt and pepper to taste
1-2 teaspoons tamari soy sauce
1 tablespoon oil

Beat eggs and water with electric beater for
about 4 minutes. Add onions, mung bean
sprouts and mushrooms. Season to taste with
salt, pepper and tamari soy sauce

Heat oil in heavy-bottom skillet. Pour in the
batter and turn the heat down. Cook about
3 minutes, turn and cook the other side about
3 minutes.

Yield: 4 servings.

# Eggs Blackstone

2 cups mayonnaise (see recipe in salad
        dressing section)
6 slices whole grain bread, toasted or 3
        "pitas" (see recipe in bread section),
        split in half and toasted
6 fresh tomato slices (1 inch thick)
6 eggs
6 sprigs parsley for garnish

Set a bowl of mayonnaise in a larger bowl
of hot water in order to bring it to a warm
temperature. Stir it often and take care that
it does not separate.

Toast bread. Top each slice with a tomato
slice. Heat in a low oven (275-300°F.) while
poaching the eggs.

Place poached egg on top of tomato slice.

Spoon warm mayonnaise over the egg, letting
it run down over the tomato and bread.
Top with a sprig of parsley and serve
immediately.
Yield: 4-6 servings.

# Eggs Florentine

Preheat oven to 350°F.
2 lbs. fresh spinach (cooked, drained
      and chopped)
salt to taste
½ cup grated Parmesan cheese
6 eggs

Season spinach with salt to taste. Put into oiled, 2-quart casserole. Sprinkle with cheese.

With the back of a spoon, make 6 little wells, evenly spaced, about 1-inch deep, on the surface of the spinach. Break a raw egg into each well. Bake in preheated oven until the eggs are set (about 8 minutes).

Yield: 6 servings.

# Eggs Provencale

Preheat oven to 350°F.
1 tablespoon olive oil
4 medium-sized tomatoes (chopped), or
       4 cups canned tomatoes
1 clove garlic, minced
salt and pepper to taste
1 teaspoon chopped, fresh parsley
6 eggs
2 tablespoons Parmesan cheese, grated

Heat oil in medium-sized skillet; add tomatoes, garlic, salt, pepper and parsley. Cook slowly for 20 minutes.

Transfer to oiled medium-sized casserole. Break each egg separately into a saucer. Slip each egg carefully from the saucer into the tomato mixture, spacing uniformly and allowing egg to float on top of mixture. Cover eggs but not tomatoes with cheese, then put casserole into preheated oven for 8 minutes or until eggs are set and cheese is melted.

Yield: 6 servings.

# Eggs

## Mushroom Soufflé

Preheat oven to 350°F.
4 egg yolks
½ cup celery, diced
2 tablespoons oil
¾ lb. mushrooms, sliced
3 tablespoons oil
3 tablespoons cornstarch
3 tablespoons soy flour
½ teaspoon salt
¼ cup skim milk powder
1 cup water
¼ cup parsley, chopped
4 egg whites

Remove eggs from refrigerator and allow to remain at room temperature for at least one-half hour before using.

Separate eggs. Put whites in large bowl and yolks in medium-sized bowl. Beat egg yolks well; set aside.

Sauté celery in 2 tablespoons oil until tender. Lift celery out and set aside. Sauté mushrooms in same pan about 5 minutes. Lift out and chop coarsely.

Put 3 tablespoons oil in heavy, medium-sized saucepan. Stir in cornstarch, soy flour and salt. Combine skim milk powder and water with wire whisk and add slowly, stirring constantly to keep mixture smooth and free from lumps. Place saucepan over medium heat; cook, stirring constantly until the sauce thickens and bubbles. (It should be quite thick.) Reduce heat and add celery and mushrooms.

## 5

Remove from heat. Gradually pour into beaten egg yolks, stirring until well-blended. Stir in chopped parsley. Set aside to cool while beating egg whites.

## 6

Using electric mixer, set at high speed, beat egg whites until stiff peaks form when the beater is lifted out slowly. Gently fold mushroom mixture into beaten egg-whites, blending thoroughly until no trace of whites shows.

Turn mixture into ungreased, one and one-half quart soufflé dish or straight-sided baking dish.

Place soufflé on middle rack of a preheated oven and bake for 45 to 50 minutes; or until soufflé is puffed and golden and firm to the touch.

Remove from oven and serve immediately.

Note: Please keep in mind that a soufflé must be served immediately upon removing from the oven or it will fall. The egg whites in the soufflé make it rise and therefore, it is very delicate.

Yield: 5-6 servings.

## Stuffed Eggs

6 eggs
2 tablespoons mayonnaise
$\frac{1}{2}$ teaspoon mustard
$\frac{1}{2}$ teaspoon cider (or wine) vinegar
$\frac{1}{2}$ teaspoon salt
dash of pepper
4 green onions
2 tablespoons green pepper
1 teaspoon chopped chives
3 tablespoons sunflower seeds

Hard-cook eggs. Crack and drop immediately into cold water. Shell and cut in half lengthwise. Separate yolks from whites. Reserve egg whites.

Put egg yolks and rest of ingredients in blender. When completely combined and smooth, refill egg whites with the mixture.

Yield: 12 egg halves.

# Eggs

## Eggs Pierre

2½ lbs. ground pork or pork sausage
8 pita buns (see recipe in Bread section)
           or
8 rounds of whole grain bread, toasted
8 eggs, lightly poached
3½ cups Pierre sauce (see recipe in Meats,
       Poultry, Fish-Sauces section)
chopped parsley for garnish

Sauté ground pork or pork sausage, until it is thoroughly cooked. Drain off any remaining fat and discard.

Spread the pork ½ inch thick on pita buns or toast and place them on an ovenproof serving platter

**3!**

Top each bun with a lightly poached egg, cooked just enough to bear removal from the water. Place dish in a warm (not hot) oven until ready to serve.

**4!**

Just before serving, spoon Pierre sauce over each poached egg, allowing enough so that it drips down over the pork and bun. Top with chopped parsley.

Yield: 6-8 servings.

# Cheese

## Cheese Dreams
### (Open-Faced Sandwiches)

¼ cup skim milk powder
½ cup water
1 egg, beaten
¾ lb. Cheddar cheese, grated
¼ teaspoon mustard powder
¼ teaspoon salt
6 slices whole grain bread
6 slices tomato (optional)
6 strips bacon—partially cooked (optional)

In the top of a double boiler, combine skim milk powder with water using a wire whisk.

Add egg gradually to milk.

Combine grated cheese, mustard powder and salt. Add to milk mixture.

**4!**

Cook over hot water for 15 minutes, stirring occasionally.

**5**

Cool mixture. Refrigerate before using.

**6**

When ready to serve, spread cheese mixture on slices of bread and toast them in a 350 degree F. oven, or under the broiler, until they puff up and become golden brown.

**7**

Top the sandwiches with a slice of tomato and a strip of partially-cooked bacon before baking or broiling, if desired.

Yield: 4-6 servings.

# Cheese

## Cottage Cheese

2 cups skim milk powder
8 cups water

Combine skim milk powder with water using a wire whisk. Strain if necessary to remove any lumps.

**2**

Cover milk with a cloth. (Do not make it airtight.) Leave at room temperature for 1-2 days, until it sours.

**3**

Heat very slowly, watching carefully and testing the curds for cheese-like consistency by pressing between your thumb and forefinger. When you can keep the curds between your thumb and forefinger, without them slipping away, the cheese is ready.

**4!**

Put the cheese in a cheesecloth-lined strainer and drain off the whey, letting it drip until it is fairly dry. (Save whey to use in soups or beverages because it is full of nutrients.)

**5**

Refrigerate the cottage cheese for future use or season it as desired and use immediately.

Yield: Approximately 2 cups.

# Cheese Fondue

Preheat oven to 350°F.
$\frac{1}{3}$ cup soy powder
$\frac{1}{2}$ cup skim milk powder
3 cups water
2 tablespoons nutritional yeast (optional)
2 cups whole-grain bread cubes (1-inch)
6 eggs
3 cups sharp Cheddar cheese, grated
$\frac{1}{2}$ teaspoon basil
$\frac{1}{2}$ teaspoon marjoram
$\frac{1}{2}$ teaspoon dry mustard
$\frac{1}{2}$ teaspoon tamari soy sauce
$\frac{1}{4}$ teaspoon salt

Combine soy powder, skim milk powder and water by making a paste first and gradually adding the rest of the water. If you plan to use the nutritional yeast, blend it in at this time also.

**2**

Soak bread in milk mixture.

**3**

Beat eggs. Add eggs, cheese and seasonings to milk and bread mixture.

**4!**

Pour into oiled casserole. Bake in preheated oven until fondue has risen slightly, is brown, and set in the center. (An inserted knife will come out clean.)

Yield: 6-8 servings.

## Cheese Quiche in Brown Rice Shell

Preheat oven to 375°F.
1½ cups cooked brown rice
3 eggs
¼ cup skim milk powder
1 cup water
¼ teaspoon salt
dash of freshly-ground pepper
dash nutmeg
1 tablespoon potato flour or brown rice flour
1¼ cups, sharp, Cheddar cheese (or part natural Swiss and part Cheddar)

Press cooked rice into oiled, 9-inch pie plate. Bake in preheated oven just until dry (about 5 minutes); cool.

Using medium-sized bowl, beat eggs until light and fluffy. Combine skim milk powder and water with a wire whisk and add to eggs, along with salt, pepper and nutmeg.

**3**

Add potato or brown rice flour to shredded cheese; toss lightly but thoroughly. Put into cooled rice shell, spreading to edges of crust. Pour egg-milk mixture over all. Place in a preheated oven and bake 10 minutes. Reduce heat to 325°F. and continue to bake 25 to 30 minutes longer, or until filling puffs up and is golden brown.

**4!**

Remove from oven; allow to set for about 5 minutes; cut in wedges and serve.

Yield: 6 servings.

# Cheese Quiche with Bacon and Onion

Preheat oven to 350°F.
1 9-inch, unbaked pie shell (barley-oat or
      whole wheat crust—see recipes in
      desserts-pie section)
4-5 strips bacon (optional)
2 teaspoons rye flour
4 teaspoons soy powder
¼ cup skim milk powder
1¼ cups water
2 eggs
¼ teaspoon salt
tamari soy sauce, cayenne, dry mustard,
      paprika to taste
⅔ cup grated, sharp cheese
1 medium-sized onion, thinly-sliced

If using bacon in quiche, sauté 4-5 strips until crisp. Drain on paper towels; crumble into bits; set aside.

Make paste by mixing rye flour, soy powder and skim milk powder with ¼ cup water.

**3**

Beat the eggs and mix with remaining cup of water.

**4!**

Combine the two mixtures and add seasonings.

**5**

Put cheese into unbaked pie shell, spreading to edges of crust. Cover the cheese with thinly-sliced onion. Pour egg-milk mixture over all. If using bacon, sprinkle bacon bits over top and bake in a preheated oven for 40 minutes, or until set and nicely-browned.

**6**

Cool slightly (about 5 minutes); then cut pie into wedges.

Yield: 4-6 servings.

# Cheese

## Quiche with Spinach

Preheat oven to 350°F.
1 9-inch, unbaked pie shell (barley-oat or
      whole-wheat crust—see recipes in
      desserts-pie section)
3 eggs
1 tablespoon potato flour or brown rice flour
½ teaspoon salt
dash of freshly-ground pepper
¾ cup fresh spinach, cooked, drained and
      chopped
¼ cup grated, sharp cheese
¼ cup skim milk powder
1 cup water

Beat together eggs, flour, salt and pepper.

Combine spinach and cheese and place in
bottom of pie shell.

Mix skim milk powder and water with wire
whisk. Combine with egg mixture and pour
over spinach in shell.

Bake in preheated oven for about 35 minutes,
or until the custard is set and the top
nicely-browned. Serve warm.

Yield: 4-6 servings.

# Welsh Rarebit

2 tablespoons oil
1½ cups Cheddar cheese, diced
¼ teaspoon salt
¼ teaspoon dry mustard
dash of cayenne
1 teaspoon tamari soy sauce
¾ cup skim milk powder
2 cups water
2 egg yolks, beaten

Place oil in top of double boiler, over rapidly boiling water, stir in and melt Cheddar cheese.

Add salt, mustard, cayenne and soy sauce.

**3**

Combine (with wire whisk) skim milk powder and water. Add slowly to mixture, stirring constantly.

**4!**

When mixture is hot, remove from heat. Add a little of hot mixture to beaten egg yolks; mix well. Gradually pour yolk mixture into the hot sauce, blending well. Return to low heat for several minutes, stirring constantly. Remove from heat and serve immediately on whole-grain toast.

Yield: 6 servings.

# Cheese

## Cheese Soufflé

Preheat oven to 350°F.
4 egg yolks
½ lb. Cheddar cheese
3 tablespoons oil
3 tablespoons cornstarch
3 tablespoons soy flour
½ teaspoon salt
¼ teaspoon dry mustard
⅛ teaspoon cayenne
¼ cup skim milk powder
1 cup water
4 egg whites

Remove eggs from refrigerator and allow to remain at room temperature for at least one-half hour before using.

Separate eggs. Put whites in large bowl and yolks in medium-sized bowl. Beat egg yolks well; set aside.

Shred Cheddar cheese onto a piece of wax paper for easy handling and set aside

Put oil in heavy, medium-sized saucepan. Stir in cornstarch, soy flour, salt, mustard and cayenne. Combine skim milk powder and water with wire whisk and add slowly, stirring constantly to keep mixture smooth and free from lumps. Place saucepan over medium heat; cook, stirring constantly until the sauce thickens and bubbles. (It should be quite thick.) Reduce heat and add Cheddar cheese; continue to stir until cheese is melted.

**5**

Remove cheese sauce from heat. Gradually pour cheese mixture into beaten yolks, stirring until well blended. Set aside to cool while beating egg whites.

**6**

Using electric mixer, set at high speed, beat egg whites until stiff peaks form when the beater is lifted out slowly. Gently fold cheese mixture into beaten whites with rubber spatula; blending thoroughly until no trace of whites show.

Turn mixture into ungreased, one and one-half quart soufflé dish or straight-sided baking dish.

**8**

Place soufflé on middle rack of a preheated oven and bake for 45 to 50 minutes; or until soufflé is puffed and golden and firm to the touch.

Remove from oven and serve immediately.

Note: Keep in mind that a soufflé must be served immediately upon removing from the oven or it will fall. The egg whites in the soufflé make it rise, and therefore it is very delicate.

Yield: 5-6 servings.

# 6. vegetable

RICE RICE RICE

BEANS

BEANS

BEANS

peas

seas

leeks

celery

celery

rice

cabbage

vegetables

celery

6.

Asparagus

celery

vegetables

# Vegetables

Vegetable cookery is a sadly neglected culinary art. Considered mundane by some, vegetables may be overshadowed by a dramatic entrée or dessert. But a vegetable cooked so that it retains its maximum color, texture and flavor is the mark of a first rate cook.

The nutrients in vegetables are extremely fragile. The minerals, vitamins, natural oils and sugars can easily be lost—dissolved in water or destroyed by light or oxygen.

The preparation of fresh vegetables for cooking is essentially the same as for raw vegetable salads. They should be washed quickly in cold water, never soaked. Chopping or slicing should be done just before cooking. Most organically-grown vegetables do not need to be peeled. When they are, vitamins and minerals which are concentrated under the skin are thrown away.

General rules for cooking vegetables are to cook them quickly (using a fairly high heat and taking care not to overcook them); salt only before serving, if at all, not during the cooking; save any vegetable liquid which is left after cooking to use in gravy, sauces or soup.

Vegetables should never be boiled. They may be steamed, using as little water as possible. Greens, such as spinach, can be cooked using only the amount of water which clings to the leaves after they are washed. Start them off over high heat in a pot with a tight-fitting lid, then turn the heat low, watching them carefully to prevent overcooking. They will cook quickly in their own juices and have a delicious flavor.

Sautéing is another excellent method of cooking vegetables. The exposed surfaces are coated with the hot oil, sealing in the nutrients. Then the pan is covered so that the vegetables can steam in their own juices.

At Fitness House we try to obtain fresh, organic produce either from our own garden or from local suppliers, and to serve as wide a variety of vegetables as possible. But we prefer to eat fresh vegetables in season rather than frozen ones, so our choice is sometimes limited. If we happen to have an overabundance of any one kind, we may serve it in different forms for several days in a row. When fresh vegetables aren't available, we do serve frozen ones. They retain most of their nutrients when they are properly cooked.

Although we usually steam or sauté fresh vegetables, of course, we bake potatoes in their skins. And occasionally we broil some vegetables—zucchini or tomatoes, for example. When broiling it is important to brush the surface of the vegetable with oil, and to preheat the oven. After the vegetable is heated through, lower the oven temperature to 375 or 350 degrees F. and continue cooking until vegetable is tender.

There is such a variety of vegetable dishes! Stuffed eggplant, which combines the flavors of garlic, onion, tomato, and olive oil in such a marvelous way, and a curry dish which blends vegetables with turmeric, cumin and cardamom, are two of our more unusual recipes. Equally welcome at our buffet are garden beets and greens, braised cabbage or minted carrots. Any vegetable green such as turnip or beet tops, mustard greens, spinach, kale or Swiss chard, is so good coarsely-chopped and sautéed with a bit of onion. Greens of almost any kind disappear rapidly whenever we serve them.

Vegetable cookery takes undivided attention and painstaking care. It does not take *much* time, but the timing is crucial. Cook the vegetable last, just before serving time. It is worth the wait.

The Rodale Cookbook

# Sprouted Lentils, Bean and Rice Salad

for recipe see chapter on Salads and Salad Dressings

*Sweet-Sour Chicken*

for recipe see chapter on Meats, Poultry, Fish and Sauces

# Barbecued Soybeans

for recipe see chapter on Soybeans, Eggs and Cheese

# Curried Vegetables

for recipe see chapter on Vegetables

Coarse ends of Swiss chard should be
**dis**carded . . .

. . . then it can be coarsely-chopped . . .

. . . and sautéed with chopped onions for
**a** tasty treat.

# *Vegetables*

## Beets and Greens

2 lbs. young beets with fresh green tops
water to cover
1 medium-sized onion, diced
2 tablespoons oil
salt to taste

Cut tops off beets, leaving an inch of stem
on the beet to prevent the beet from
"bleeding" into the cooking water. Scrub
beets and cover them with cold water in a
medium size cooking pot. Cover pot with lid
and bring beets to a boil. Then turn heat
down and simmer until beets are tender
(about 45 minutes).

Drain cooked beets, reserving the cooking
water for Borscht. Slip skins from beets
while they are warm. Dice beets and keep
them warm in a low oven or in the top of a
double boiler.

**3**

Wash beet tops and slice them across in
one-inch lengths. Sauté diced onion in oil
until golden brown. Add beet greens and
sauté them briefly, just until they are tender
but have not lost their bright green color.
Salt to taste. Serve hot diced beets
surrounded with beet greens.

Yield: 6 servings.

# Skillet Fresh Asparagus

2-2½ lbs. asparagus
1½ teaspoons salt
¼ cup lemon juice or ½ cup mayonnaise
    (see recipe salad section)
lemon wedges for garnish

Break or cut off tough ends of asparagus
stalks. Wash asparagus tips thoroughly with
cold water; if necessary, use a brush to
remove grit.

In large skillet, put cold water 1½ inches
deep and bring to a boil. Add asparagus
spears, cover; simmer for about 10 to 12
minutes (depending on size and tenderness of
asparagus)— just until it is easily pierced
with a fork. Add salt.

Remove skillet from heat and remove
asparagus spears with slotted spoon to heated
serving dish. Sprinkle with lemon juice,
if desired, or warmed mayonnaise (used as a
mock Hollandaise sauce). Garnish with
lemon wedges.

Yield: 4-5 servings.

# Braised Cabbage

1 cup onions, chopped
1-3 tablespoons oil*
½ cup bacon, diced (optional)
1 3-lb. head green cabbage, cored and
    shredded
1 teaspoon caraway seeds
¼ cup cider vinegar
1 cup water
½ teaspoon salt
1 tablespoon honey
freshly-ground black pepper to taste

In saucepan, sauté chopped onions in oil
until golden in color. Add bacon (if using it)
and cook until it is lightly-browned. Add
cabbage, mixing it well with the onion and
bacon. Add caraway seeds. Cover pan and
steam over medium heat for 10 minutes.

Pour in vinegar and water, stirring and season
with salt, honey and pepper. Cover and
cook over medium heat about 10 minutes
longer. Serve immediately.

*Note: If not using bacon, add the extra oil
  to pan before sautéing cabbage.

Yield: 6 servings.

# Vegetables

## Curried Cabbage

1 large head green cabbage
1 onion, chopped
2 tablespoons mustard seed*
2 fresh chilis, chopped (optional)
1 teaspoon cumin, ground
1½ teaspoons chili powder
¼-½ cup oil
salt to taste

Cut cabbage head in quarters, remove core and slice as thin as possible with a sharp knife.

Sauté onions and spices in oil, starting with a small amount and adding more oil as you need it.

Add cabbage and toss lightly in skillet until tender. Salt to taste. Serve immediately.

*Cover pan with lid while mustard seeds cook, to keep them from "popping" out of the pan.

Yield: 6-8 servings.

## Red Cabbage

2 tablespoons oil
1 tablespoon onion, chopped
2 tart cooking apples, cored and thinly-sliced
2 tablespoons lemon juice or cider vinegar
½ cup water
2 tablespoons honey
1 head red cabbage (2 lbs.), cored and thinly-shredded
1 teaspoon salt
¼ teaspoon caraway seeds (optional)

Heat oil in a large skillet over medium heat. Sauté onion until golden.

Add sliced apple, lemon juice or cider vinegar, water, honey and cabbage. Stir thoroughly to combine. Season with salt. (Add caraway seeds, if desired.) Cover tightly and simmer over low heat for 15-20 minutes, stirring occasionally. Remove from heat and serve immediately.

Yield: 6 servings.

## Steamed Penny Carrots

⅓ cup water
2 cups sliced carrots
½ teaspoon lemon juice
¼ teaspoon salt
¼ teaspoon powdered kelp
freshly chopped mint or parsley for garnish

In a small, heavy saucepan, bring one-third cup water to boil over medium heat. Add sliced carrots and lemon juice. Cover tightly and simmer over low heat for 15 to 20 minutes or just until carrots are barely tender.

**2**

Remove from heat and stir in salt and powdered kelp. Turn into serving dish, garnish with chopped mint or parsley and serve.

Yield: 4-5 servings.

## Viennese Carrots

4 cups carrots, sliced
1 small onion, diced
2 tablespoons oil
salt to taste
1 tablespoon chopped parsley

Scrub carrots well. Peel, if desired and slice into thin rounds.

In a heavy bottom saucepan or a skillet, sauté onions in oil briefly. Add carrots, toss them until they are coated with the oil, cover the pot tightly and turn heat down as low as possible, letting them steam in their own juice. Watch closely and shake the pot from time to time so that carrots will not stick.

When carrots are tender (in about 8-10 minutes) season to taste. Stir in chopped parsley and serve immediately.

Yield: 4 to 6 servings.

# *Vegetables*

## Braised Celery

1 stalk or bunch celery
4 tablespoons oil
1 cup stock (chicken or beef)
salt to taste
chopped parsley for garnish

Wash and separate stalks of celery. Cut them crosswise, on the slant into 2 inch lengths.

**2**

In a large skillet or heavy-bottom saucepan, sauté celery in oil for about 2 minutes, stirring constantly.

**3**

Turn heat down, add stock, cover tightly and steam for 10 minutes or until celery is tender but still firm. Salt to taste. Garnish with chopped parsley.

Yield: 4-6 servings.

## Method of Cooking Garbanzo Beans (Chickpeas)

1 cup (6 ounces) dried garbanzo beans
      (chickpeas)
water to cover
salt to taste

Wash beans well. Discard water.

**2**

Soak washed beans in water to cover for 2-3 hours.

**3**

Freeze beans overnight in soaking water.

**4!**

Next morning, put frozen beans, salt and water into pot and bring to a boil. Turn heat down and simmer for 1-2 hours until tender. (Freezing lessens the amount of cooking time needed.)

Yield: Approximately 3 cups beans.

# Armenian Eggplant Soufflé

Preheat oven to 350°F.
1 large eggplant—2 to 2½ lbs.
⅓ cup olive oil
2 tablespoons lemon juice
1 clove garlic, minced fine (optional)
4 egg yolks
½ teaspoon salt
⅛ teaspoon cayenne pepper
½ teaspoon kelp, powdered
4 egg whites
2 tablespoons wheat germ
2 tablespoons sesame seeds
½ cup yogurt

Wash eggplant; peel and slice into one-half inch thick slices.

**2**

In a heavy 10-inch skillet, add two tablespoons olive oil. Place over medium heat. Sauté eggplant slices in hot oil, a few at a time, until soft and golden, adding more oil as needed.

**3**

Mash the cooked eggplant with a fork. Add lemon juice and minced garlic. Add egg yolks and beat mixture until well combined. Season with salt, cayenne pepper and kelp powder.

**4**

Beat egg whites until soft peaks form when beater is raised. Fold beaten whites into eggplant mixture.

**5**

Pour mixture into a one and one-half quart casserole which has been lightly oiled and sprinkled with wheat germ. Place casserole in a preheated oven and bake for 30 to 35 minutes. (During last ten minutes of baking, sprinkle sesame seeds over top of casserole.)

**6**

Remove from oven and serve accompanied with yogurt.
Yield: 5-6 servings.

# Vegetables

## Garbanzos (Chickpeas) and Rice

Preheat oven to 350°F.
2 cups water
1 teaspoon salt
½ cup uncooked brown rice
1½ cups cooked garbanzo beans (chickpeas)
        (see method of cooking garbanzo
        beans in vegetable section)
2 tablespoons honey
reserve garbanzo cooking liquid
chopped parsley for garnish

**1**

In saucepan, bring two cups of water to a boil; add one teaspoon salt and slowly stir in rice. Cover saucepan and cook over low heat for 20 to 25 minutes, stirring occasionally. Remove from heat and turn the undrained rice into an oiled, one and one-half quart casserole. Add the chickpeas and honey; mix together.

**2**

Bake in a preheated oven, stirring occasionally, for 35 to 40 minutes or until rice is tender. If liquid becomes absorbed while baking, add chickpea liquid to casserole.

**3**

Remove from oven, garnish with chopped parsley and serve immediately.

Yield: 4-6 servings.

## Herbed Green Beans with Sunflower Seeds

1 lb. fresh green beans
2 cups water
½ teaspoon basil
½ teaspoon marjoram
½ teaspoon chervil
1 tablespoon freshly-snipped parsley
2 teaspoons freshly-chopped chives (or 1
       teaspoon dried chives)
⅛ teaspoon savory
⅛ teaspoon thyme
1 small onion, chopped
1 clove garlic, minced
2 tablespoons oil
½ cup sunflower seeds
1 teaspoon salt
¼ teaspoon freshly-ground pepper

Wash fresh young green beans; drain. Cut off ends. Cook them, tightly covered, in 2 cups boiling water for 10-15 minutes, until tender, but still crisp.

Meanwhile, combine herbs in a small bowl. Then sauté chopped onion and garlic in oil, adding the herbs toward the end, and lastly the sunflower seeds.

**3**

Add cooked beans to herb mixture, season to taste, toss lightly and serve immediately.

Yield: 4-6 servings.

# *Vegetables*

## Mung Beans and Rice

1 cup dried mung beans
water to cover
1 cup uncooked brown rice
2½ cups water
½ cup onion, chopped or thinly-sliced
½ cup green pepper, chopped
3 tablespoons oil
2½ cups fresh tomatoes (chopped), or
       canned
2 teaspoons tamari soy sauce
⅛ teaspoon cayenne pepper
¼ teaspoon crushed basil
salt to taste

Wash mung beans and cover with water; soak overnight in refrigerator or for 5 to 6 hours at room temperature.

Pour beans and liquid used for soaking into a medium-size saucepan and bring to a boil. Simmer until tender (about 40 minutes). Drain beans, reserve liquid.

While mung beans are cooking, prepare brown rice. In medium-size saucepan, bring 2½ cups of water to boil; add rice. Cover and simmer until rice is tender (about 40 minutes), stirring occasionally to prevent sticking.

**3**

Remove rice from burner and drain any remaining liquid; set aside.

**4!**

In large skillet, sauté onion and green pepper in oil until tender, but not brown. Add drained mung beans and rice to sautéed vegetables. Add tomatoes and seasonings along with ½ cup reserved liquid from beans and rice.

**5**

Cover and continue to simmer mixture adding more liquid, if necessary, until flavors have blended (about 15 minutes).

Yield: 8-10 servings.

# Creamed Leeks

1 lb. leeks
¼ cup olive oil (or safflower)
¼ cup potato flour (or brown rice flour)
¼ cup olive oil
1 cup water
salt to taste
pepper to taste

Trim and slice leeks crosswise, then wash them well.

In a heavy bottom pot or skillet, (not cast-iron), sauté leeks in ¼ cup olive oil for about five minutes. Turn heat down, cover with a tight-fitting lid and allow to steam for 10 minutes or so.

Put ¼ cup olive oil in saucepan. Dissolve potato flour, (or brown rice flour), in oil and heat until mixture bubbles. Stir in water and continue to cook a minute or two. Add to leeks and stir until well combined. Cook for about 10 minutes longer. Add salt and pepper to taste.
Yield: 6-8 servings.

# Caraway Potatoes

Preheat oven to 400°F.
8 large potatoes (about 3 lbs.)
6-8 tablespoons oil
salt, pepper to taste
caraway seeds

Scrub but do not peel potatoes. Slice them crosswise about one-inch thick. Lay them in an oiled casserole.

Brush potatoes with oil. Sprinkle them with salt, pepper and caraway seeds. Bake in preheated oven for 45 minutes to an hour, until nicely browned.

Yield: 6 servings.

# *Vegetables*

## Avocado-Stuffed Baked Potatoes

Preheat oven to 400°F.
3 baking potatoes
1 tablespoon oil
1/2 cup avocado, diced
2/3 cup yogurt
2 teaspoons salt
freshly ground pepper to taste
2 tablespoons wheat germ

Scrub potatoes thoroughly. Pat dry with
paper towels. Rub potatoes lightly with some
oil. Place them in a shallow pan and bake
in a hot oven for 45 minutes to one hour, or
until potatoes are soft to the touch.

Prepare avocado by peeling, removing seed
and dicing.

Remove baked potatoes from oven and cool
for 10 minutes until easily handled. Halve
the potatoes lengthwise and scoop out the
insides with care, reserving shells.
Mash pulp well with a fork or place in a

large mixing bowl and beat on low speed until
potatoes are blended. Add yogurt gradually
along with diced avocado and continue to
beat until potatoes are light and fluffy.
Season with salt and freshly-ground pepper
to taste. Meanwhile, preheat oven to 375°F.

Fill the reserved potato shells, sprinkle wheat
germ over top. Place in a preheated oven
for about 10 minutes until lightly browned.

Remove from oven and serve immediately.

Yield: 6 stuffed potato halves.

# Stuffed, Baked Potatoes

Preheat oven to 400°F.
4 large Idaho potatoes for baking
1 cup yogurt
2 teaspoons salt
3 tablespoons freshly-snipped chives
1/8 teaspoon cayenne pepper
grated Parmesan cheese
paprika

Scrub potatoes thoroughly. Pat dry with paper towels.

Place potatoes in preheated oven and bake, on middle rack, until potatoes are crisp on the outside and soft inside—about 45 minutes to one hour.

Remove baked potatoes from oven and allow to cool for 10 to 15 minutes.

## 4!

Halve the potatoes lengthwise and scoop out the insides with care; reserving shells. Mash well with a fork; or place in a large mixing bowl and beat with the electric beater, set at medium speed, until mixed. Add yogurt gradually and continue to beat until well-blended and potatoes are light and fluffy. Season with salt, freshly-snipped chives and cayenne pepper. Meanwhile preheat oven to 350°F.

## 5

Spoon mixture into reserved shells; sprinkle with Parmesan cheese and paprika. Place in a shallow baking dish and bake in a preheated oven for 15 to 20 minutes, or until heated thoroughly.

## 6

Remove from oven and serve immediately.

Yield: 6-8 servings.

# Vegetables

## Scalloped Potatoes Supreme

Preheat oven to 400°F.
6-8 medium-sized potatoes, scrubbed and
sliced thin (unpeeled)
2 onions, sliced very thin
2 tablespoons chopped parsley (reserve half
for garnish)
½ teaspoon salt
3 tablespoons oil
1 cup hot stock (preferably chicken—
see recipe in soup section), or 1
cup boiling water

Combine potatoes, onions, parsley and salt.

Spread mixture about two inches deep in a
shallow baking dish.

**3**

Pour oil evenly over top of potatoes; add
hot stock or water.

**4!**

Bake in preheated oven for about one hour
or until they are brown and crusty on top and
the liquid is absorbed.
Garnish with fresh parsley before serving.

Yield: 6 servings.

# Grated Sweet Potato Casserole

Preheat oven to 325°F.
2 lbs. sweet potatoes (about 5 large potatoes)
grated rind from 1 lemon
grated rind from 1 orange
4 eggs
½ cup honey
½ cup oil
1 cup soy milk
½ teaspoon salt
½ teaspoon cinnamon
½ teaspoon allspice (optional)

Scrub sweet potatoes well. Do not peel.
Scrape with knife, if desired, and remove eyes.
Grate coarsely.

Grate lemon and orange rind.

In a bowl, beat eggs and add honey, oil,
lemon and orange rind, and remaining
ingredients. Stir in grated sweet potatoes.

Bake in a well-oiled casserole dish, uncovered,
for one hour in a preheated oven, until
the mixture is set (no longer liquid).

Yield: 6-8 servings.

# Vegetables

## Sweet Potato-Apple Casserole

$1\frac{1}{4}$ lbs. sweet potatoes
$\frac{1}{2}$ cup water
1 lb. apples
1 cup apple juice
2 tablespoons cornstarch
3 tablespoons water
$\frac{1}{2}$ cup honey
$\frac{1}{3}$ cup wheat germ

Steam sweet potatoes in a pot with a tight-fitting lid, using $\frac{1}{2}$ cup water, for 15-20 minutes, until tender. Peel, slice lengthwise, $\frac{1}{2}$ inch thick, and layer them in a casserole.

Peel and core apples, slicing them $\frac{1}{2}$ inch thick. Lay apple slices on top of sweet potatoes.

**3**

Heat apple juice to the boiling point. Combine cornstarch and water and add to juice, cooking until sauce is clear and thickened. Add honey.

**4!**

Spoon sauce over apples, then top with wheat germ.

**5**

Bake in preheated oven for 45 minutes to an hour or until apples are tender.

Yield: 6 servings.

# Potato Pancakes (Latkes)

3 medium-sized potatoes
1 small onion
2 tablespoons potato flour
½ teaspoon salt  *1 egg*
⅛ teaspoon pepper  *PINCH BAKING POWER*
¼ cup oil

Grate potatoes and onion. Drain in a fine sieve, pressing out all liquid. Put in medium-sized bowl.

Add dry ingredients. Mix well.

*lot*
Fry in skillet, ~~using as little oil as possible~~ and adding more as it is necessary.

Yield: About 12 pancakes.

# Method of Cooking Pumpkin

Preheat oven to 350°F.
1 pumpkin (any variety)

Cut pumpkin into pieces, whatever size is most convenient.

Place, skin side up, on rack in baking pan and bake in a preheated oven for about 40 minutes, or until the pumpkin is tender when pierced with a fork.

Remove from oven. Scoop pumpkin pulp out with a spoon. Purée pulp. Cool and if not using immediately, refrigerate or freeze.

# *Vegetables*

## Swiss Chard – Almond Loaf

Preheat oven to 350°F.
½ lb. Swiss chard (kale, spinach, or beet
       tops can also be used)
1 medium-sized onion, chopped
1 clove garlic, minced
¼ cup oil
2 cups ground almonds (walnuts can also
       be used)
1 cup dry whole grain bread crumbs
½ cup wheat germ
1 egg, beaten
2 tablespoons chopped parsley
1 teaspoon oregano
½ teaspoon cumin
½ cup catsup
1 tablespoon tamari soy sauce

Wash, chop and steam greens for 5 minutes,
using only the amount of water which
clings to them after being washed.

Sauté onion and garlic in oil.

**3**

Grind almonds in blender.

**4!**

Combine almonds, crumbs, wheat germ,
egg, greens, sautéed onions and garlic. Add
remaining ingredients. Mix well.

**5**

Pack into well-oiled 9 x 5 x 3-inch loaf pan.
Bake in preheated oven for 30 minutes.
Serve either hot or cold.

Yield: 1 loaf.

## Swiss Chard with Onions

3 lbs. young Swiss chard
1 bunch (about 6) green onions, sliced
       thin or 2 medium-sized ordinary
       onions, diced
2-4 tablespoons oil*
½ cup bacon, diced (optional)
salt to taste

Wash and slice, crosswise into 1 inch
lengths young stalks of Swiss chard, using
stem and leaf.

Sauté thinly-sliced green onions or ordinary
onions in oil until golden in color. If using
bacon, add it to the onions and sauté until
it is lightly-browned.

Add Swiss chard and sauté briefly just until
it is tender but has not lost its green color.
Salt to taste. Serve immediately.

*Note: If not using bacon, add the extra oil
  to the pan before sautéing the Swiss chard.

Yield: 4-6 servings.

## Baked Acorn Squash

Preheat oven to 375°F.
3 acorn squash
3 tablespoons oil
¾ teaspoon salt
¾ teaspoon kelp powder
6 teaspoons honey (optional)

Cut acorn squash into halves, remove seeds,
and put squash, cut side down, in a baking
pan with half inch of water. Bake in
preheated oven for a half hour or so, until
almost tender when pierced with a fork.

Turn halves cut side up, brush with oil,
sprinkle each half with ⅛ teaspoon salt and
kelp powder. Drizzle 1 teaspoon honey into
center of each half, if desired.

Bake another 20 minutes or so until brown.

Yield: 6 servings.

# Vegetables

## Yellow Summer Squash with Yogurt

2 lbs. summer squash (about 3 small squash)
2 tablespoons oil
1/2 cup onion, finely-chopped
1/2 teaspoon salt
1/2 teaspoon paprika
2 tablespoons freshly-chopped dill or 1
      teaspoon dried dill weed
3 teaspoons lemon juice
2/3 cup yogurt
2 tablespoons freshly-chopped parsley

Wash squash. Cut, unpeeled, into quarters, lengthwise. Cut squash into long, thin strips— three inch by one-half inch.

In a ten-inch skillet, heat two tablespoons oil over medium heat. Add onion and sauté until golden and tender—about 5 minutes.

**3**

Add strips of squash, salt, paprika, dill and lemon juice. Cover and simmer over low heat for 10 to 15 minutes, stirring occasionally. Remove cover and continue to cook over medium heat, stirring occasionally, until squash is tender.

**4!**

Remove from heat. Stir in yogurt (do not reheat or yogurt will curdle). Pour into serving dish and garnish with two tablespoons of chopped parsley.

Yield: 6 servings.

# Ratatouille

2 medium-sized onions, peeled and sliced
1 clove garlic, minced
5 tablespoons olive oil
2 small zucchini squash (one-pound size),
    washed and thinly-sliced
2 small eggplants (about one pound each),
    peeled and cubed
2 medium-sized green peppers, washed;
    stem and seeds removed, cut into
    one-inch strips
5 medium-sized tomatoes, peeled and
    quartered, or two cups canned
    tomatoes, coarsely-chopped
2 tablespoons freshly-snipped basil or $\frac{1}{2}$ to 1
    teaspoon dried basil leaves
2 tablespoons freshly-snipped parsley
1 teaspoon salt
1 teaspoon kelp powder
$\frac{1}{4}$ teaspoon freshly-ground pepper

Using a large, heavy skillet, sauté onions and garlic in 2 tablespoons olive oil for 5 minutes.

Add zucchini squash, eggplant and green pepper to skillet, adding more oil as needed. Stir gently, but thoroughly. Sauté mixture for 10 minutes. Stir in the fresh or canned tomatoes, basil, parsley, salt, kelp and pepper. Reduce heat, cover skillet tightly and continue to simmer for 15 minutes longer. Serve immediately.

Yield: 8-10 servings.

see color photograph

## Curried Vegetables

1 medium-sized onion, chopped
2 tablespoons oil
1 small head cauliflower, broken into
　　flowerets
1 medium-sized eggplant, peeled and cut
　　into 1-inch cubes
2 green peppers, cut into $\frac{1}{4}$-inch strips
4 medium-sized carrots, sliced into $\frac{1}{4}$-inch
　　rings
$\frac{1}{2}$ lb. green string beans, broken in half
1 teaspoon chili powder
1 teaspoon cumin (ground)
$\frac{3}{4}$ teaspoon turmeric
$\frac{1}{2}$ teaspoon cardamom (ground)
1 bay leaf
$\frac{1}{2}$ cup boiling water
$\frac{1}{2}$ cup tomato juice

Sauté onion in oil until yellow.

Add vegetables, spices and bay leaf, cook about 5 minutes. Add boiling water and simmer 10 minutes. Add tomato juice and cook until vegetables are tender.

Remove bay leaf. Correct seasoning.
Yield: 6-8 servings.

# Corn Pudding

Preheat oven to 350°F.
2 cups frozen corn (approximately ⅔
     package)
1 cup boiling water (approximately)
2 tablespoons butter
2 tablespoons rye flour
1 cup water
¼ cup skim milk powder
¼ cup green pepper, chopped (optional)
2 egg yolks
½ teaspoon salt
¼ teaspoon paprika
2 egg whites

Cook corn in boiling water until tender. Blend corn and liquid together briefly to mash it, but not long enough to purée it.

In large saucepan, melt butter and stir in flour gradually, until blended. Combine water and skim milk powder with a wire whisk, and add gradually, cooking over low heat until sauce is thickened.

Add corn mixture to sauce and then the chopped green pepper.

### 4

In a small bowl, beat egg yolks and pour a small amount of the corn mixture over them, stirring constantly, and then return it to the corn mixture. Stir and cook over low heat for several minutes to allow egg yolks to thicken slightly. Add salt and paprika.

### 5

Beat egg whites until stiff but not dry and fold them lightly into the corn mixture.

### 6

Bake in a preheated oven for 30 minutes.

Yield: 4-6 servings.

SESAME RICE

7.

KASHA

PILAF

RICE

RICE

7.

fritters

fried rice

CORNBEAN

rice

fritters

grains

Grains

RICE PIE

RICE

RICE

KASHA

KASHA

KASHA

RICE

PILAF

fried rice

7.

SESAME

# *Grains*

Working with whole grains has been one of the most exciting and creative aspects of our experience at Fitness House Kitchen. A whole new world of possibilities has opened up. When served with meat, Bulgur pilaf, Millet soufflé, Polenta or Kasha provide an exciting alternative to potatoes.

Bulgur, a precooked, cracked wheat, has been developed recently by the U.S. government for export to needy countries. Closely resembling brown rice, it can be used in any way that rice is used. Pleasant, nutty-tasting bulgur requires very little cooking. We use it not only in pilaf, we make salads with it and add it to our turkey soup. It is true that some of the B vitamins are lost in the processing of bulgur but this is somewhat balanced by the increased availability of its protein.

With millet meal or millet flour, we make delicious muffins, casseroles and even desserts.

Polenta is a gourmet version of corn meal mush and is especially good with Italian meat sauce, Beef Stroganoff or stew. Besides corn meal, we derive two other products from corn—corn oil and cornstarch—very useful staples in our Fitness House Kitchen.

Buckwheat's greatest claim to fame is that it "stays with you." It has been said that six buckwheat pancakes will fill you for six hours. In the 1860's, the U.S. used ten times as much buckwheat as it does today. This grain, presently enjoying a comeback in America, as kasha, or cooked buckwheat groats—has long been a favorite in Russia and Eastern Europe where buckwheat is also used in making bread, for puddings, in cakes and beer. The groats can be cooked in water, then served as breakfast cereal with dates or raisins added—a good way to begin a cold day.

The traditional way to cook kasha is to stir a whole egg into the dry groats over low heat, until the egg is absorbed, then to add stock, seasonings and cover tightly—steaming the groats until tender and fluffy. For those who find groats a bit too unusual, try combining about ⅓ kasha with ⅔ bulgur.

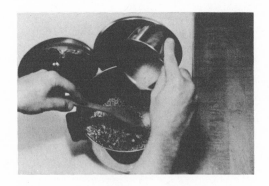

To make Kasha, add an egg to groats and cook over low heat until egg is absorbed.

Add stock and seasoning to groats and egg.

Buckwheat flour, low in calories and cost, contains important protein, plus valuable minerals, vitamins and enzymes.

Rice is the principle food for over half the human race. But for flavor and food value, we recommend using the "brown" version. Once you have started serving and eating brown rice, you will probably look upon white rice as a "mere shadow of the real thing." In comparison, the polished product seems pale, anemic and tasteless.

There are two basic ways to cook brown rice: in a measured amount of water, until the rice is tender and the liquid absorbed; or lightly sautéed in a little oil and then cooked in stock, just enough so that when the liquid is absorbed, the rice will be done. The timing depends on whether or not the rice has been soaked, the intensity of the heat, and the speed of the cooking. When the rice is almost cooked, a tight-fitting lid should be put on the pot so that the rice can steam and get fluffy and somewhat dry before serving.

Rice pilafs, made by combining rice with meat, fowl or fish, are delicious. There must be a different variation of this dish for every Asian, or Middle-Eastern country. We've tried many of them at Fitness House. Rice and bean salads, and rice-nut-and-seed combinations make unusual, imaginative luncheon fare. A special favorite in our dining room is Quiche Lorraine baked in a brown rice shell.

Brown rice flour is one of our staples. We use it as a thickening agent, along with soy flour, and in cookies, bread and cakes.

Oats are as Scottish as bagpipes and kilts. To most Americans, oats mean hot cereal, (the kind that sticks to the ribs on cold winter mornings) and those good old-fashioned oatmeal-raisin cookies.

Oatmeal, used in combination with whole-wheat flour to make bread, produces a moist, tasty loaf. Oat flour blends particularly well with soy flour. This mixture makes an excellent coating for oven-baked chicken. Oat flour also blends nicely with barley, rice or rye flour. Two of our pie crust recipes are made with combinations of these.

We use barley mostly in its flour form, as a good thickener, or in combination with other flours in breads, cookies or pie crusts.

Wheat germ is not only a healthful food, but a delicious one. It works well as a substitute for bread-crumbs in breading, in meat loaves or as a dessert topping. It serves as a replacement for some of the flour in cookies, breads or cakes, and it can be added to cereals, or sprinkled over fruit salads and vegetables.

Rye, like wheat, contains some gluten. It is the only other grain that does. Commercial rye bread usually contains whole wheat flour or white flour, so we are especially proud of our Fitness House rye bread because it is an all-rye-flour loaf. The all-rye loaf is, of course, fairly solid, but remarkably good. It is similar to our pumpernickel, and our Swedish Limpa bread which we make partly with whole wheat flour. Rye flour combines well with oat and rice flours, also with corn and buckwheat. An excellent breading for liver or kidneys before sautéing them, this versatile flour is also a tasty thickener for meat gravies.

Whole grains keep best in a cool dry place, in air-tight containers. However, grains should be bought as fresh as possible and milled close to the time they are to be used.

Grains provide almost half the protein in the world's diet. They are inexpensive, readily available, and they represent infinite possibilities for the talents of an imaginative cook.

# Grains

## Kasha (Buckwheat Groats)

1½ cups buckwheat groats
1 egg, beaten
2½ cups boiling water or stock (see recipe
    in soup section)
1 teaspoon salt

Put groats in heavy skillet. Stir in beaten
egg and place over medium heat, stirring
until grains separate.

Gradually add the boiling water or stock,
stirring constantly. Add salt; cover, and cook
over low heat for about 15 minutes. All the
liquid should be absorbed; if not, drain
thoroughly after removing from burner.

Serve immediately as an accompaniment to
any meat dish.

Yield: 6 servings.

## Bulgur Pilaf

2 tablespoons oil
1 tablespoon onion, chopped
1 cup bulgur
2 cups water or chicken stock (see recipe in
    soup section)
½ teaspoon salt
dash of pepper
chopped parsley for garnish

Put oil in skillet; add onion and sauté until
almost tender (about 8 minutes). Add bulgur
and cook until golden.

Add stock or water and seasonings. Cover
and bring to a boil; reduce heat and simmer
15 minutes. Garnish with chopped parsley
and serve.

Yield: 4 servings.

# Grains

## Spanish Bulgur

2 tablespoons oil
1¼ cups bulgur
½ cup onion, chopped
1 clove garlic, minced
½ cup green pepper, diced
2 cups tomatoes, fresh or canned
¼ cup dried beans, cooked
1 teaspoon salt
⅛ teaspoon pepper
1 teaspoon paprika

Heat oil in heavy-bottom saucepan. Add bulgur and sauté until golden.

Add remaining ingredients; cover and bring to a boil. Reduce heat and simmer for about 15 minutes.

Yield: 4-6 servings.

## Cornbean Pie

Preheat oven to 350°F.
*CRUST:*
2 cups yellow corn meal
½ teaspoon salt
2 tablespoons nutritional yeast
3 tablespoons oil
½ cup hot stock (see recipe in soup section)
    —enough to make stiff batter

Mix all ingredients and pat into a well-oiled, 9-inch pie plate.

*FILLING:*
1 onion, chopped
½ cup carrots, chopped
½ cup celery, chopped
1 clove garlic, minced
½ cup green pepper, chopped
2 tablespoons oil
1 cup dry kidney beans, cooked
pinch cayenne
1 tablespoon cumin, ground
½ cup tomatoes, fresh or canned
3 tablespoons tamari soy sauce
⅓ cup grated sharp cheese

Sauté onion, carrot, celery, garlic and green pepper in oil for about 5 minutes.

**2**

Add beans and spices and put into corn meal crust.

**3**

Combine tomatoes with soy sauce and pour over the beans. Bake in preheated oven about 25 minutes. Remove from oven, sprinkle with cheese and bake 5 minutes longer.

Yield: 6 servings.

## Cashew-Millet Casserole

Preheat oven to 325°F.
2 cups water
1 teaspoon salt
½ cup millet meal (whole millet which has been ground in blender)
3 tablespoons oil
1 medium-sized onion, chopped
1 cup unsalted raw cashew nuts (ground)
3 eggs, slightly-beaten
⅔ cup wheat germ
½ cup skim milk powder
¼ cup parsley, chopped
¼ cup pimiento, chopped
½ cup water
⅛ teaspoon of the following herbs: ground mace, sage, rosemary, ground marjoram

Prepare millet meal: In top of double boiler bring two cups of water to a boil; add salt and millet meal to rapidly-boiling water very slowly, stirring constantly with wire whisk to avoid lumping. Place over hot water and continue to cook 15 to 20 minutes, or until millet has absorbed all water. Remove from heat and cool slightly.

Heat oil in skillet and saute onion.

please turn page

# Grains

**3**

Combine cooked millet and ground cashew nuts in mixing bowl. Add slightly-beaten eggs, wheat germ, skim milk powder, sautéed onion, chopped parsley, and pimiento. Add ½ cup water, blending together thoroughly. Stir in herbs. Adjust seasoning according to taste.

**4!**

Turn mixture into an oiled 1½ quart casserole and bake in preheated oven, uncovered, for 45 minutes or until tested to firmness and lightly browned. Serve immediately.

Yield: 6-8 servings.

## Millet Soufflé

Preheat oven to 350°F.
4 cups boiling water
½ teaspoon salt
2 tablespoons oil
1 cup millet meal (whole millet which has been ground in blender)
4 egg yolks
¼ cup skim milk powder
1 cup water
½ teaspoon crushed dill seeds (optional)
3 tablespoons minced chives or grated onion
1 cup sharp cheese, grated or shredded
4 egg whites

In saucepan, bring 4 cups water to a boil, add salt and oil. Gradually add millet meal to boiling water, stirring constantly with a wire whisk until all of it has been incorporated. Place in top of double boiler and cook for about 20 to 30 minutes, or until all water has been absorbed. Stir mixture occasionally. Remove from heat and cool slightly.

**2**

In large mixing bowl, beat egg yolks until thick. Combine skim milk powder with water, using a wire whisk, and beat gradually into yolk mixture.

With beater set at medium speed, blend cooked millet into yolk mixture until thoroughly combined. Stir in dill seeds, chives or grated onion. Add grated cheese.

**4!**

Beat egg whites until soft peaks form; gently fold into millet mixture.

**5**

Pour mixture into an oven-proof casserole (2-quart size) and bake in a preheated oven for 35 to 45 minutes. Remove from oven and serve immediately.

Yield: 6 servings.

# Polenta Cheese Squares

5 cups cold water
1 teaspoon salt
$1\frac{1}{2}$ cups white or yellow corn meal
1-2 tablespoons oil
1 cup grated, sharp Cheddar cheese
$\frac{1}{3}$ cup grated Parmesan cheese

In a large, heavy saucepan, bring 5 cups cold water and 1 teaspoon salt to a boil. Add corn meal very slowly, stirring constantly with wire whisk or long wooden spoon until mixture is thick and free from lumps.

**2**

Transfer corn meal mixture to top of double boiler. Place over boiling water and cook, covered, for thirty minutes, stirring occasionally. Corn meal is finished when it leaves sides of pan.

Remove from heat and turn corn meal mixture into a lightly oiled 9 x 9 x 2-inch baking pan; cool, refrigerate until stiff enough to cut (three to four hours or overnight).

please turn page

# Grains

**4!**

Preheat oven to 400°F. Cut polenta into 16 squares. Arrange in an oiled baking dish. Sprinkle with Cheddar and Parmesan cheese*, place in preheated oven, and bake for 15 minutes or until cheese is melted and nicely-browned. Serve immediately.

Note: Serve with beef stew or Italian Meatballs.

*Polenta may also be prepared by adding Cheddar cheese to corn meal mixture just before removing from heat. Proceed as above. Sprinkle with Parmesan cheese before placing in oven.

Yield: 6-8 servings.

## Brown Rice

1 cup uncooked brown rice
2½ cups water
¼ teaspoon salt

Put all ingredients into saucepan which has a tight-fitting lid. Bring to a boil, then turn down to a low simmer and continue to cook for about 35-40 minutes, or until all water is absorbed, rice is tender and the grains are separate. Do not stir, once rice is boiling.

Yield: 4-6 servings.

# Brown Rice – Chinese Style

1½ cups uncooked brown rice
3 cups water

Soak rice in water for an hour, in a saucepan.

**2**

Bring rice to boil in soaking water over high heat, without a lid.

**3**

Once it is boiling hard, reduce heat to medium and simmer rice until the water has disappeared from view and there are "holes" in the rice surface (20-30 minutes).

**4!**

Cover with a tight-fitting lid, and turn fire as low as possible, watching it closely, until the rice is quite dry, yet tender (about 15 minutes). Do not stir at any time during this process, as that tends to make the rice sticky.

Yield: 6 servings.

# Rice-Bulgur-Soy Pilaf

3 tablespoons oil
1 cup uncooked brown rice
¾ cup bulgur
⅔ cup soy grits
4 cups chicken or beef stock (see recipe in soup section) or water

Heat oil in heavy-bottom pot. Add grains and sauté for about 10 minutes, stirring often.

**2**

In separate saucepan, bring stock to a boil; add to sautéed grains. Cover and simmer for about 30 minutes or until all liquid is absorbed and grains are tender.

Yield: 6 servings.

# Grains

## Fruity Rice

Preheat oven to 350°F.
2 tablespoons oil
⅓ cup peanuts, chopped
⅓ cup sunflower seeds
⅓ cup sesame seeds
1 cup mixed, dried fruits, chopped
½ teaspoon ground cloves
½ teaspoon salt
1 cup brown rice, cooked

Heat oil in heavy-bottom skillet; add peanuts, sunflower seeds and sesame seeds. Cook and stir until slightly browned.

Stir in the mixed fruit, cloves and salt. Then add cooked rice.

Place in a 2-quart, oiled casserole; bake in preheated oven for 15-20 minutes.

Yield: 4-6 servings.

## Fried Rice

¼ cup onions, diced
¼ cup green pepper, diced
¼ cup celery, diced
2-3 tablespoons oil
3 cups cooked long-grain, brown rice
        (about 1 cup uncooked) (cooked
        1 day ahead)
½ cup cooked green peas (fresh or frozen)
½ cup cooked chicken, diced
3 eggs, beaten slightly
¼ cup bean sprouts (fresh or canned)
tamari soy sauce (optional)

Sauté onions, green pepper, celery in 2 tablespoons oil until just tender. Remove from pan.

Add more oil to pan, if necessary, and sauté rice. Add sautéed vegetables, peas, chicken and slightly-beaten eggs.

Stir for 2 or 3 minutes or until eggs are set but not dry or brown. Add bean sprouts. Season with soy sauce to taste. Serve at once.

Yield: 6-8 servings.

# Sesame Rice

½ cup celery, chopped
½ cup onions, chopped
½ cup green pepper, chopped
½ cup carrots, chopped
1 clove garlic, minced
3 tablespoons oil
¼ teaspoon each of paprika, sage, marjoram
    and rosemary
1 cup uncooked brown rice
2 cups chicken or beef stock (see recipes
    in soup section)
½ teaspoon salt
2 tablespoons nutritional yeast
2 tablespoons sesame seeds toasted (in a
    200°F. oven for 20 minutes)

Sauté all the vegetables in the oil until the onions are golden and the celery is tender (about 10 minutes). Stir in the herbs and uncooked rice.

Heat the stock, add to vegetable-rice mixture and bring to a boil. Stir in the salt, nutritional yeast and toasted sesame seeds.

Lower heat, cover and simmer until all the liquid is absorbed and rice is tender (about 40 minutes).

Yield: 4 servings.

# *Grains*

## Pungent Rice

1 medium-sized onion, finely-chopped
3 tablespoons oil
1 cup uncooked brown rice
3 cups chicken stock (see recipe in soup
      section)
salt to taste
1 tablespoon freshly-snipped basil or ½
      teaspoon dried
1 tablespoon freshly-snipped marjoram or
      1 teaspoon dried
2 teaspoons fresh thyme, chopped or ¼
      teaspoon dried
¼ teaspoon curry powder
fresh parsley for garnish

In medium-sized saucepan or skillet, sauté chopped onion in oil. Add rice and continue to sauté for 5 minutes longer.

Add chicken stock, stirring constantly. Salt to taste and stir in remaining ingredients (except parsley). Heat to boiling. Lower temperature, cover, and cook slowly for 25 to 30 minutes without stirring, until rice is tender and liquid is absorbed. Garnish with chopped parsley.

Yield: 5-6 servings.

## Sesame-Rice Fritters

¼ cup sesame seeds
2 tablespoons skim milk powder
¼ cup water
2 egg yolks
2 tablespoons whole wheat flour
⅛ teaspoon pepper
dash of salt
⅔ cup brown rice, cooked
2 egg whites
oil for frying

Toast sesame seeds until golden (about 20 minutes in a 200°F. oven).

Mix skim milk powder and water with wire whisk. Add egg yolks, flour, pepper and salt.

Combine milk mixture, sesame seeds and rice; mix well. Fold in stiffly beaten egg whites.

Drop by tablespoonfuls onto hot, oiled griddle and fry until brown. Drain on paper towel.
Yield: 16 fritters.

see color photograph

## Spinach and Rice Casserole

Preheat oven to 350°F.
2 cups cooked brown rice
1 cup grated Cheddar cheese
4 eggs, beaten
4 tablespoons parsley, chopped
1 teaspoon salt
2 lbs. fresh spinach, washed, drained and
      chopped
1 tablespoon oil
4 tablespoons wheat germ

Combine the cooked rice and cheese.

**2**

Add eggs, parsley and salt.

**3**

Stir in the raw spinach and pour into an oiled casserole.

**4**

Top with wheat germ which has been mixed with the oil.

**5**

Bake in preheated oven for 35 minutes.

Yield: 6-8 servings.

# Grains

## Spaetzle (Fresh Noodles)

1½ cups barley flour
1 cup soy flour
1 teaspoon salt
3 eggs
¾ cup water
2-3 tablespoons oil
2 tablespoons onion, minced (optional)
freshly minced parsley for garnish

In medium-sized bowl, sift barley and soy flours with salt. Make a well in the center of the flour mixture and break the eggs into it. Pour about ½ cup water into mixture and beat until smooth; gradually adding the remaining ¼ cup water (use wooden spoon for beating). Beat mixture until well-blended and smooth.

In a four-quart container, bring three quarts water to a boil.

**3**

Add about two or three tablespoons of batter or dough to a spaetzle (or noodle) press, which has been rinsed in cold water. (Rinse press each time before refilling with batter.) Slowly press batter into gently boiling water, holding the press 4 to 5 inches above boiling water for long noodles or 2 to 3 inches for short noodles.

**4**

As soon as noodles rise to the surface of the gently boiling water, remove with slotted spoon and place in a container of cold water (to prevent noodles from sticking together).

## 5

Rinse spaetzle press and continue to use as directed above until all batter has been used. Drain noodles into colander or strainer, rinse them with additional cold water and allow to drain for several minutes. Place in an oiled casserole and cover. Place in 300°F. oven until ready to use.

## 6

To reheat noodles; put 2 to 3 tablespoons oil in heavy skillet, add noodles and heat over medium burner, turning noodles gently with turner to prevent them from breaking apart. Serve immediately—garnished with freshly-minced parsley. Two tablespoons of minced onion may be sautéed first in the oil for added flavor.

Note: Serve with beef stew, Stroganoff or Italian meat balls: (see recipes in meat section).

# Breads

Making bread is definitely one of "my favorite things." Working with yeast is fascinating. Every woman I've ever asked agrees, and as for children, they adore it. Kneading dough is a great way to work off those blue-Monday morning depressions too.

One such morning, when I was pounding and kneading and feeling better with each punch, the milkman appeared at the back door. As we chatted he wistfully remarked that his mother had baked all the bread for the family when he was growing up. I gathered that he didn't come across many women thus occupied on his morning rounds.

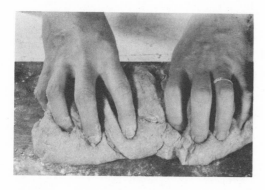

Knead bread dough first with your fingers . . .

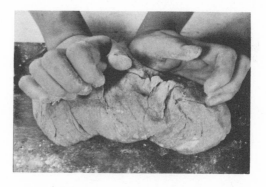

. . . then with the heels of your hands.

I remember my mother baking bread and the wonderful aroma that pervaded the house. To me it is reminiscent of a happy, secure childhood. Today, happily, this experience is being revived in many new young families, and it bodes well for the future.

If the idea of fresh-baked bread appeals to you, and you want to introduce your family to the true "staff of life," get your children to make a loaf of white bread, but add some wheat germ and soy flour to the recipe. Try substituting 2 tablespoons of soy flour and 2 tablespoons of toasted wheat germ for 4 tablespoons ($1/4$ cup) of white flour, in the next loaf of bread you make. As they get used to the taste, increase the amounts. This can be done easily without changing the appearance of the bread very much. If your children are like some others I know, you must be subtle and change things gradually and quietly.

When you do use soy flour, be sure to sift it as it tends to be lumpy. Also, lower the baking temperature of the oven by 25 degrees; soy flour browns at a lower temperature than other flours. Soy flour is among the best sources of protein, so if you add even 2 tablespoons of it to your dough, the bread will be decidedly richer in protein. If you include the bonus of wheat germ, your loaf will be substantially enriched with the B vitamins, iron and vitamin E.

This kind of "enriching" makes a lot more sense than the commercial practice of stripping 12 or more nutritional substances from the flour, then adding four and calling the final product "enriched."

Not only is most commercially made bread practically devoid of nutrients, it is also a "Trojan Horse" that holds an astounding assortment of chemicals. To begin with, the grain these bakeries use is harvested from fields that have been doused with chemical fertilizers, and herbicides. Then it is subjected to milling and refining processes which remove the bran and the germ. The flour that remains is bleached with toxic chemicals then disinfected and conditioned with other chemicals. A softening agent is even added to enhance its "squeezability!"

How did this ever come about? It probably goes back a long way, to the time when only the aristocratic elite had access to white bread and the peasants had to be content with the dark heavier variety. The concept of white bread as the most desirable has persisted, even though the aristocracy has all but disappeared from the world. It's time we got back to eating the nutritious and tasty whole grain breads.

Stone-ground, freshly-milled whole grain flours are becoming more easily available, either through mail order wholesalers, or from local cooperatives. Some of the organic food centers have acquired their own mills and will grind flours to order. Once you purchase the flour it must be either refrigerated or kept in a cool, dry place. It may also be stored in the freezer.

At Fitness House we have developed a number of bread recipes using grains other than wheat, and using only yeast and eggs as leavening, because baking powder and baking soda contain chemicals which destroy nutrients. Here are some tips we offer:

The amount of yeast, its freshness, the temperatures of the ingredients used with the yeast, the temperature and humidity of the room in which the dough is left to rise, and the gluten content of the flours used, are all very important in determining how high a loaf of bread will rise. Yeast is a living organism. There are billions of tiny plants in just one ounce of yeast. They feed on sugars and release carbon dioxide which is held in the bread dough and makes it rise.

There is a common, mistaken assumption that 1 package of dry yeast is equivalent to 1 tablespoon. It actually measures only 2 teaspoons. Be sure to check the expiration date on the yeast package; if it is too old, it won't work the way it should. Many pre-measured packaged yeasts contain chemical preservatives. We use 8-ounce packages of dry yeast obtained from natural food stores. They must, of course, be refrigerated.

All ingredients for baking bread should be at room temperature when they are used. If your flour has been refrigerated or frozen, warm it in a low oven, stirring it, until it reaches room temperature.

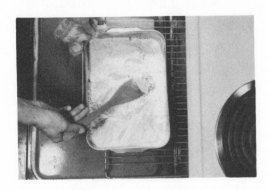

If flour has been refrigerated, warm it in a low oven before using it in bread.

The liquid in which the yeast is dissolved should be lukewarm. Yeast stops growing when it is chilled and overheating kills it. If your recipe calls for molasses or honey, add it to dissolving yeast; this will hasten the action, as yeast feeds on sugars.

For the rising process put the dough in a draught-free, warm, humid room. If you don't have access to such a room, warm your oven briefly and put the dough, covered with a damp cloth, in the oven, and place a pan of water on a lower oven shelf, for humidity. It is gluten, a protein substance found in wheat, that will make your bread rise best.

Unfortunately, a significant number of people are allergic to wheat gluten. For this reason we have considered it important to develop bread recipes using other grains. Rye flour contains a gluten-like substance which helps dough rise and many of those who are sensitive to wheat gluten are able to enjoy rye bread with no allergic reaction. Only wheat and rye flours contain enough gluten to make yeast bread rise.

Most recently we have been experimenting with sourdough breads. The recipes which have proven most successful are those which require both yeast and a sourdough starter. The result is a delicious, somewhat tangy, soft-textured loaf.

Basically the starter is made by mixing flour and water together and allowing it to ferment with yeast. It can be used in muffins, biscuits, corn bread and pancakes as well. Once you have a crock or jar of sourdough starter, it can be used and replenished indefinitely. In the old West, starter was made by combining equal parts of flour and milk. The basic recipe used most often today combines equal parts of flour and water, although potato water, milk and buttermilk can all be used for variation.

The surest way to start the first batch is with yeast although it is possible to make it from the "wild yeast" present in the air. The yeast-flour-water mixture is put into a covered jar or crock and left at room temperature for three days, until it reaches the sourness desired. Then it is refrigerated. To start from scratch without yeast or a bit of left-over starter, mix equal amounts of flour and water and leave to ferment for 3-5 days at room temperature, uncovered, until it is thick and bubbly. Equal parts of flour and water must always be added to replace the amount of starter taken out to use in baking. And the fresh batch of starter must be left at room temperature until it is "working" again. Then it should be covered and refrigerated. Remember to let the starter called for in your recipe, come to room temperature before you use it.

In our recipes for corn bread, some muffins and pancakes, we use a combination of yeast with separated eggs. The eggwhites when beaten stiff contain air. During baking, the trapped air becomes steam and expands, causing the batter to rise. Potatoes, used in some of our bread recipes, seem to add to the moisture and tenderness of the bread.

Sometimes bread has a "yeasty" taste. This happens if the dough is allowed to rise too much before being stirred down, or if it is not kept warm enough while it is rising. It is *not* a result of using too much yeast. Either stir the dough as soon as it has doubled in bulk and keep it near 85 degrees F. or else refrigerate it to stop the yeast from growing temporarily. The smaller the amount of yeast the slower the dough rises, the more yeast, the faster it rises.

Your breadmaking can be quite flexible, once you understand the basic principles involved. You can make the dough, let it rise once, stir it down, put it into the pan, let it rise briefly and bake it all within a total time of only 3 hours. Or you can make a "sponge" (using only half of the flour with the yeast and liquid) letting it grow (even overnight), stirring it down or chilling it and adding the rest of the flour at a later date. Remember, once dough has been refrigerated, it must be allowed to come to room temperature again so that the yeast can become active.

Bread should be baked on the center rack in the oven. When the loaf is done, it will pull away slightly from the sides of the pan and be firm when tapped. To be sure, stick a toothpick into the center of the loaf. If it comes out clean, the bread is baked. Remove the loaf from the pan carefully, loosening the sides with a knife. Be sure the sides are a bit crusty. If they are not, let the loaf dry out in the oven for an additional 10 minutes or so. Cool loaf on a rack completely before cutting and serving or storing it. To keep bread for longer than a few days it should be refrigerated or frozen. One further tip—whole grain breads are apt to stick to the bread pan more than ordinary breads, so oil your pan generously.

We are still testing and experimenting, trying numerous combinations. We encourage you to be adventurous and try some bread recipe ideas of your own.

The Rodale Cookbook

# Breads

## Banana-Nut Bread

Preheat oven to 350°F.
1 tablespoon dry yeast
3 tablespoons lukewarm water
½ cup oil
⅓ cup honey
2 eggs
4 bananas* (very ripe, mashed) about
       1¾ cups
½ cup potato starch
½ cup oat flour
½ cup soy flour
½ teaspoon salt
½ cup wheat germ
⅛ teaspoon nutmeg, grated (optional)
½ teaspoon pure vanilla extract
⅔ cup chopped walnuts

Dissolve dry yeast in lukewarm water; stir and set aside.

In mixing bowl, combine oil, honey and eggs. Beat together until well-blended. Gradually add mashed bananas and beat until thoroughly-combined.

Sift together potato starch, oat and soy flour, and salt. Stir into banana mixture and blend together. Add wheat germ, grated nutmeg (if desired), vanilla extract, and chopped nuts. Slowly blend in the yeast mixture.

**4!**

Pour batter into a well-oiled 9 x 5 x 3-inch loaf pan and allow to rest in a warm place for 20 minutes. Bake in a preheated oven for one hour and 15 minutes.

**5**

Remove from oven and allow to cool for about 10 minutes; invert pan and turn bread out onto wire rack. Cool thoroughly before cutting.
*Note: Frozen bananas may be used. Use 3 instead of 4, mashed thoroughly with the accumulated juice.
Yield: one loaf.

# Breads

## Bran Bread

Preheat oven to 375°F.
1 tablespoon dry yeast
1 cup lukewarm water
3 egg yolks
1½ tablespoons oil
3 tablespoons honey
6 tablespoons brown rice flour
6 tablespoons soy flour, sifted
6 tablespoons skim milk powder
½ teaspoon salt
¾ cup bran
6 tablespoons wheat germ
½ cup raisins (optional)
3 egg whites

**1** Oil a 9 x 9-inch square pan.

**2** Sprinkle yeast over lukewarm water. Let soak for 5 minutes.

**3** Beat egg yolks. Add oil and honey. Combine with dissolved yeast.

**4** In a bowl, combine brown rice flour, sifted soy flour, skim milk powder, salt, bran and wheat germ. Add raisins at this time if using them. Stir wet ingredients into dry ones.

**5** Beat egg whites until stiff but not dry. Gently fold them into batter. Turn into prepared pan and leave in a warm place for 30 minutes.

**6** Bake bread in preheated oven for 20 minutes.

Yield: 6-8 servings.

# Carrot Bread

Preheat oven to 350°F.
2 cups raw carrots
2 teaspoons dry yeast
⅓ cup lukewarm water
1 cup oat flour
½ cup potato starch
⅓ cup soy flour
3 tablespoons skim milk powder
½ teaspoon salt
1½ teaspoons cinnamon
¼ teaspoon nutmeg
2 eggs
½ cup honey
⅔ cup oil
½ cup date sweetener
¾ cup coarsely-chopped walnuts

Oil a 9 x 3 x 5-inch loaf pan.

Prepare carrots by scrubbing them well and shredding them.

**3**

Dissolve dry yeast in ⅓ cup warm water, set aside.

**4**

Sift dry ingredients (except date sweetener) together in medium-sized bowl.

**5**

In mixing bowl, beat eggs lightly; gradually add honey. Stir in oil and date sweetener.

**6**

Gradually stir in sifted, dry ingredients and blend until well combined. Stir in shredded raw carrots and nuts. Slowly blend in the yeast mixture.

**7**

Pour batter into loaf pan and allow to rest in warm place for 20 minutes. Bake in a preheated oven for one hour and 15 minutes.

**8**

Remove from oven and allow to cool for about 10 minutes. Invert on wire rack and allow to cool thoroughly. Remove carefully from pan.
Yield: one loaf.

# Breads

## Corn Bread

Preheat oven to 350°F.
4 teaspoons dry yeast
1 cup lukewarm water
1 cup corn meal (white or yellow)
½ cup oat flour
¼ cup soy flour
½ cup skim milk powder
¾ teaspoon salt
2 tablespoons nutritional yeast (optional)
2 tablespoons honey
3 tablespoons oil
2 eggs, beaten

**1**

Dissolve dry yeast in lukewarm water and allow to stand for ten minutes.

**2**

Combine in a mixing bowl: corn meal, oat and soy flours, skim milk powder, salt and nutritional yeast, if desired.

**3**

Combine honey, oil and beaten eggs and add to dry ingredients, mixing well.

**4**

Gradually add dissolved yeast mixture, blending well into other ingredients.

**5**

Pour batter into a well-oiled (9 x 9-inch) square pan. Place pan in warm area and allow corn bread to rise thirty to forty minutes.

**6**

Bake in a preheated oven for 30-35 minutes.

Yield: 6-8 servings.

# Millet Bread

Preheat oven to 350°F.
⅔ cup millet flour
⅓ cup barley flour
1 cup grated raw carrots
1 tablespoon honey
1 teaspoon salt
2 tablespoons oil
¾ cup boiling water
3 egg yolks
3 egg whites

Combine millet flour, barley flour, grated carrots, honey, salt and oil in a bowl; mix well. Gradually add the boiling water, mixing thoroughly.

**2**

Beat egg yolks until light and lemon-colored. Stir into the flour and carrot mixture.

**3**

Beat egg whites until they peak, but are not dry. Fold carefully into batter.

**4!**

Oil 8 x 8-inch pan or 9 x 5 x 3-inch loaf pan. Line bottom with brown paper and oil again. Spoon mixture into prepared pan and bake for 30 to 40 minutes in preheated oven or until done.

**5**

Remove from oven; set pan on wire rack and allow to cool for about 5 to 10 minutes. Remove from pan. Serve warm.

Yield: 5-6 servings.

# Breads

## Spoon Bread

Preheat oven to 375°F.
½ cup skim milk powder
1 cup cold water
1 cup corn meal
1½ cups boiling water
1½ teaspoons salt
4 egg yolks
1 tablespoon honey
3 tablespoons soy flour
2 teaspoons nutritional yeast (optional)
2 tablespoons oil
4 egg whites

Oil a two-quart casserole.

Dissolve skim milk powder in water with a wire whisk.

In medium-sized saucepan, combine corn meal and milk mixture. Gradually add boiling water, blending thoroughly. Add salt. Cook over medium heat, stirring constantly, until consistency of thick mush. Remove from heat. Let cool slightly.

**4!**

Beat egg yolks until thick. Add honey. Combine soy flour, nutritional yeast and oil; add to egg mixture; mix well. Combine egg and corn meal mixture.

**5**

Beat egg whites until stiff peaks form when beater is raised. Fold gently into batter and pour into prepared casserole.

**6**

Bake in preheated oven for 35-45 minutes or until golden brown and puffy. Remove from oven and serve immediately.

Yield: 8 to 10 servings.

# Steamed Brown Bread

2 tablespoons dry yeast
$\frac{1}{4}$ cup water
$\frac{1}{2}$ cup whole wheat flour
$\frac{1}{2}$ cup yellow corn meal
$\frac{1}{3}$ cup skim milk powder
$\frac{1}{2}$ teaspoon salt
1 cup raisins or chopped dates
$\frac{3}{4}$ cup yogurt
$\frac{1}{2}$ cup molasses
$\frac{1}{2}$ cup wheat germ

Soak yeast in water and set aside.

**2**

Combine dry ingredients thoroughly. Add raisins or dates and stir until each piece is coated.

**3**

Add yogurt and molasses to soaked yeast, combine with dry ingredients and add wheat germ.

**4!**

Pour into 2 well-oiled pint cans; let rise until almost double in bulk. Then cover with heavy paper tied with string.

**5**

Place a rack in a large kettle. Set the filled cans on the rack. Add boiling water to kettle until it comes halfway up the sides of the cans. Cover kettle tightly—adjust the heat to keep the water boiling slowly for $1\frac{1}{2}$ to 2 hours.

Yield: about 6 servings.

# Breads

## Chappatis

1 cup whole wheat flour
1 cup corn flour
⅛ teaspoon salt
1 cup cold water (approximately)

Mix whole wheat flour, corn flour and salt together.

Add water gradually, adding just enough to keep dough from sticking to hands (about 1 cup).

Divide into 8 portions and roll out each portion as thin as possible, with a rolling pin.

Toast over medium-high heat in a dry cast-iron skillet about 30 seconds on each side, or until lightly toasted and cooked through.

Yield: 8 chappatis—about 5 inches in diameter.

## Barley Pancakes

4 teaspoons dried yeast
½ cup lukewarm water
1-2 tablespoons honey
2 eggs
⅓ cup soy milk powder
¼ cup skim milk powder
1 cup water
1 cup barley flour
2 tablespoons oil
1 cup wheat germ

Sprinkle the yeast over the surface of ½ cup warm water in a mixing bowl. Stir in honey and allow mixture to "work" in a warm place for about 25 minutes.

Gradually blend in eggs. Combine soy milk powder and skim milk powder with water, using wire whisk, add to mixture; then add barley flour, oil and wheat germ.

Bake (¼ cup batter for each pancake) on lightly-greased griddle, over medium heat. When bubbles form on surface, turn pancake and cook about 2 minutes longer, or until nicely-browned on underside.
Yield: about 5 servings.

# Buckwheat Blini (Pancakes)

¼ cup skim milk powder or soy milk powder
1 cup water
2 teaspoons dry yeast
4 egg yolks
1 teaspoon honey
4 tablespoons oil
1½ cups sifted buckwheat flour
4 egg whites

Combine skim milk powder or soy milk powder with water, using wire whisk. Heat over medium heat until bubbles form on sides of saucepan. Remove from heat and cool to lukewarm. Add yeast and stir until softened.

In mixing bowl, beat egg yolks until thick. Blend the yeast mixture into beaten yolks. Stir in honey and oil.

Sift buckwheat flour and gradually blend it into batter, mixing thoroughly.

**4**

Set bowl over a pan of warm water, cover and let rise until double in bulk—about 1¼ hours.

**5**

Beat egg whites until soft peaks form when beater is raised. Fold gently but thoroughly into batter.

**6**

Preheat a lightly-oiled griddle, on medium heat, until it is hot. Using one tablespoon of batter for small pancakes and two tablespoons batter for larger pancakes, bake on griddle until bubbles form on edges and pancake is golden brown; turn pancake and bake two minutes longer. If pancakes begin to stick to the griddle, oil it lightly again.

Yield: 8-12 pancakes.

# Breads

## Mexican Pan-Bread

Preheat oven to 350°F.
1 onion, chopped
1 clove garlic, minced
1 tablespoon oil
½ cup dried kidney beans, cooked
¾ cup bean liquid (reserved from cooking
     the beans)
1 egg, beaten
1 cup corn meal
1 tablespoon chili powder
½ teaspoon cumin, ground
½ teaspoon salt
⅓ cup grated cheese

In a heavy-bottom skillet, saute onion and
garlic in oil.

In a medium-sized mixing bowl, mix
together all the remaining ingredients except
the cheese. Pour this mixture into the
skillet and stir to mix well.

Sprinkle grated cheese on top and bake in
preheated oven for about 10 minutes.

Yield: 4 servings.

## Pizza

*Dough*
2 tablespoons dry yeast
1¼ cups lukewarm water
1 teaspoon honey
1 cup soy flour
1 tablespoon nutritional yeast
2 cups rye flour
¾ teaspoon salt
¼ cup oil
corn meal to dust pans

Sprinkle dry yeast over surface of lukewarm
water. Add 1 teaspoon honey. Let soak
for five minutes.

Combine sifted soy flour and nutritional
yeast, rye flour and salt. Add along with oil
to dissolved yeast mixture and knead until
dough is smooth and elastic. Place in
oiled bowl, cover with a damp cloth and let
rise 1-2 hours in a warm place until
doubled. Stir down and knead once more,
briefly.

Divide into 4 balls and roll each one out ⅛-inch thick on a cookie sheet or pizza pan which has been dusted with corn meal. Make a rim around the pizza by pinching the crust into an edge. It can be either round and cut into wedges or oblong, cut into squares. Preheat oven to 450°F.

*Tomato Sauce*
1 cup onions, chopped
3 cloves garlic, minced
2 green peppers, diced
2 tablespoons olive oil
2 tablespoons oil (sesame or safflower)
4 cups tomatoes (canned)
1 small can tomato paste
1 tablespoon oregano
1 tablespoon basil
2 teaspoons honey
2 teaspoons salt
2 cups grated Mozzarella cheese
        (approximately 1 lb.)
½ cup grated Parmesan cheese

In a heavy-bottom pot, sauté onions, garlic, green pepper in mixed oils until tender. Add tomatoes, tomato paste, herbs and

seasonings and simmer over low heat for ½ hour or so until flavors are well blended.

Top each pizza with about 1 cup tomato sauce, then ½ cup grated Mozzarella cheese and 2 tablespoons grated Parmesan cheese.

Bake in a preheated 450°F. oven for 15 minutes.

Yield: four 10-inch pizzas.

# Breads

## Millet Muffins

2 tablespoons soy powder
1 cup warm water
¾ cup millet flour
2 tablespoons rye flour
¼ cup wheat germ
2 teaspoons dry yeast
¼ cup lukewarm water
1 egg, beaten
1 tablespoon honey
1 tablespoon oil
½ teaspoon salt
¾ cup brown rice flour
½ teaspoon caraway seeds (optional)

Oil muffin tins lightly and place one paper baking cup (cup-cake size) which has also been well-oiled, in each muffin cup.

**2**

Combine soy powder and warm water, using a wire whisk and blend with millet flour, rye flour, and wheat germ.

**3**

Dissolve yeast in warm water and add to flour mixture. Let rise about 30 minutes. Meanwhile, preheat oven to 400°F.

**4!**

Add egg, honey, oil, salt, rice flour and caraway seeds. Mix the batter well and pour into prepared paper cups.

**5**

Bake in preheated oven for about 20 minutes.

Yield: one dozen.

# Orange Muffins

⅔ cup oat flour
½ cup brown rice flour
⅓ cup soy flour
½ teaspoon salt
3 tablespoons wheat germ
2 teaspoons dry yeast
2 egg yolks
3 tablespoons honey
2 tablespoons oil
¼ cup skim milk powder
1 cup water
¼ teaspoon ground mace
1 tablespoon grated orange rind
¼ cup seedless raisins
2 egg whites

Prepare a 12-cup muffin pan by brushing with oil. (2 ½-inch size cups)

Sift together flours and salt into a medium-sized bowl. Add wheat germ and dry yeast; mix together.

In a mixing bowl, beat egg yolks until thick. Add honey and oil. Combine skim milk powder and water with a wire whisk, and add to egg mixture. Stir in flour mixture. Add mace, orange rind and raisins.

Beat egg whites until soft peaks form. Gently fold beaten egg whites into batter until well-combined.

Spoon batter into prepared muffin-pan cups, filling two-thirds full. Place in a warm area or over a shallow pan of hot water, cover, and allow to rise for 30 minutes. Meanwhile, preheat oven to 375°F.

**6**

Place raised muffins on middle of rack in preheated oven and bake 30 minutes or until nicely-browned.

**7**

Remove from oven and loosen edge of each muffin with a spatula; remove and serve immediately.
Yield: 12 medium-size muffins.

# Breads

## Popovers or Yorkshire Pudding

Preheat oven to 450°F.
3 tablespoons oil for oiling pans
½ cup rye flour
¼ cup soy flour
¼ cup cornstarch
½ teaspoon salt
¼ cup skim milk powder
1 cup water
3 eggs, beaten
1 teaspoon oil

Prepare muffin tin or 9 x 9-inch pan by coating the surface with oil, tilting to distribute evenly. Place pan in preheated oven while preparing batter.

Sift flours, cornstarch, and salt into medium-sized bowl. Combine skim milk powder and water with a wire whisk. Add beaten eggs, milk and 1 teaspoon oil; beat with rotary beater or wire whisk until batter is smooth.

Pour batter into heated, prepared pan and place immediately in preheated oven. Bake 20 to 25 minutes or until popovers have "popped" and are deep golden-brown. Serve immediately.

Yield: one dozen.

# Pita

**(An Ancient Arabian Bread Surprisingly Like Hamburger Buns)**

8 teaspoons dry yeast
1 cup lukewarm water
1 teaspoon honey
10 cups whole-wheat flour
$1\frac{1}{2}$ cups brown rice flour
$\frac{1}{2}$ cup wheat germ
6 tablespoons oil
4 cups lukewarm water
4 teaspoons salt
1 egg, beaten
$\frac{1}{4}$ teaspoon water
$\frac{1}{4}$ cup sesame seeds (toasted in 200°F. oven for 20 minutes)

**1**

Combine yeast with 1 cup lukewarm water and 1 teaspoon honey and set aside.

**2**

Sift flours together and add wheat germ.

**3**

Mix oil with 4 cups lukewarm water. Add salt. Make a well in the center of the mixed flours and gradually add oil and water mixture. Stir in yeast mixture.

**4!**

Knead dough for 12-15 minutes. Place in an oiled bowl, cover with a cloth and leave in a warm spot to rise for an hour and a half.

**5**

Stir down dough. On a floured board, using a rolling pin, roll out dough $\frac{1}{2}$ inch thick. Cut buns in circles about 4 inches in diameter, using a lid or regular cutter.

**6**

Place buns on oiled cookie sheet. For shiny tops, brush tops with beaten egg to which $\frac{1}{4}$ teaspoon water has been added. Then sprinkle with sesame seeds. Let rise for an hour. Meanwhile preheat oven to 500°F.

**7**

Bake for 10 minutes in preheated oven, until golden in color.

Yield: approximately 3 dozen buns.

# Breads

## Buckwheat Bread
### (Wheatless)

1 large potato
2 cups water
1 cup brown rice flour
½ cup oat flour
1 cup rye flour (plus ¼ cup to knead with)
1 cup buckwheat flour
¾ teaspoon salt
2 tablespoons dry yeast
2 tablespoons oil
2-4 tablespoons molasses

Cook potato in 2 cups water until tender.

**2**

Combine and sift brown rice, oat, rye and buckwheat flours and salt.

**3**

While potato is hot, push it through ordinary strainer, or ricer. Save potato water and add more lukewarm water if remaining liquid is less than 1½ cup. Measure 1 cup riced potatoes into a bowl.

**4**

Sprinkle 2 tablespoons dry yeast over surface of 1½ cups lukewarm potato water and leave to soak for a few minutes.

**5**

Add oil and molasses to riced potatoes and mix well.

**6**

Combine dissolved yeast mixture and potato mixture. Add dry ingredients and mix well.

**7**

Sift some rye flour onto board, and turn out dough onto it. Knead briefly, adding flour until the dough is stiff enough to handle.

**8**

Form dough into a ball. Place in oiled bowl, turn dough over so it is oiled on top, and cover bowl with a damp towel. Put it in a warm place to rise for about ½ hour.

**9**

When dough has doubled itself, place it in an oiled bread pan, 9 x 5 x 3-inch, cover it again and put it in a warm place to rise to top of pan. Meanwhile preheat oven to 350°F.

**10**

Bake in preheated oven for 45-50 minutes. Test bread with toothpick to be sure it is done. Loosen sides with knife, turn out onto rack and cool completely before cutting. Store in refrigerator.

Yield: one loaf.

## Buckwheat – Sesame Bread

1/4 cup molasses
1 cup lukewarm water
2 teaspoons dry yeast
2 cups buckwheat flour
2 cups rye flour
2 cups whole wheat flour
1 teaspoon salt
1 cup sesame seeds
1/4 cup oil
1 cup water

Mix 1/4 cup molasses and 1 cup lukewarm water. Add yeast. Let soak a few minutes.

Combine the flour, salt and sesame seeds in a bowl.

Add 1/4 cup oil and 1 cup water, blending well.

Add molasses-yeast mixture and work it into dough with hands. It will be sticky.

please turn page

# Breads

Form dough into a ball. Place in oiled bowl, then turn dough over, so top is coated with oil. Cover bowl with damp cloth and let rise in warm place for 3 hours until double in bulk.

**6**

Knead dough and form into 2 round loaves on cookie sheets. Let rise an additional 45-60 minutes. Meanwhile, preheat oven to 350°F.

**7**

Bake in preheated oven for 40 minutes or until done.

Yield: 2 round loaves.

## 4-Grain Bread
### (Using Whole Wheat or Rye Flour)

1 large potato
2 cups water
¼ cup soy flour
½ cup oat flour
⅔ cup brown rice flour
1 teaspoon salt
2 tablespoons dry yeast
2 tablespoons oil
1 tablespoon honey
1 tablespoon molasses
2 cups whole wheat flour or rye flour

Cook potato in 2 cups water until tender.

**2**

While potato is cooking, measure out and sift soy, oat and brown rice flours and salt.

Push cooked potato, while still hot, through ordinary strainer or ricer. Save potato water, adding more water if less than 1½ cups remain. Measure 1 cup riced potato into a bowl.

**4**

Sprinkle 2 tablespoons dry yeast over the surface of 1½ cups lukewarm potato water and leave to soak for a few minutes.

**5**

Add oil, honey, molasses to the riced potato.

**6**

Combine dissolved yeast and potato mixture and add 1 cup wheat or rye flour and stir until mixed well. This is the "sponge." Cover "sponge" with a damp towel and leave in a warm spot to double in bulk—about ½ hour.

**7**

When "sponge" is doubled, stir soy, oat, rice flours and salt into it and add ⅔ cup wheat or rye flour.

**8**

Using the remaining ⅓ cup wheat or rye flour, knead dough on a board until you can form a ball with it. Oil the bottom of the bowl, lay the dough in upside down and then turn it over, thus oiling the top of the dough. This prevents a dry crust forming. Cover the bowl with a damp cloth and put it in a warm spot once again to double itself (about 45 minutes).

**9**

Stir the dough down and turn it into a well-oiled bread pan (9 x 5 x 3), patting it smooth. Let it rise to the top of the bread pan (about 10-20 minutes). Meanwhile, preheat oven to 325°F.

**10**

Then bake it in a preheated oven for 1 hour or until loaf is firm to the touch and has drawn away slightly from the sides of the pan. Remove from pan by loosening sides with a knife and turn out onto a rack. Cool completely before cutting. Store in refrigerator.
Yield: 1 loaf.

# Breads

## Fitness House Rye Bread
### (Wheatless)

3 tablespoons yeast
½ cup lukewarm water
1 pint lukewarm water
1½ tablespoons caraway seeds
2 teaspoons salt
4 cups rye flour
¼ cup oil
2 cups rye flour (more if needed for
    kneading)

Soak yeast in ½ cup lukewarm water and leave for 5 minutes. Make "sponge."

**2**

Stir in 1 pint of lukewarm water, caraway seeds, salt and 4 cups of rye flour. Leave in a warm spot for 1½ hours, covered.

**3**

Stir in oil and 2 more cups rye flour. Knead until smooth. Place in oiled bowl and let rise in a warm spot, covered, for about 2¼ hours, until double in bulk.

**4!**

Knead dough down, shape into round, high loaves (making 1 large or 2 smaller loaves), place on an oiled cookie sheet, cover and let rise in a warm spot for about 4 hours. Meanwhile preheat oven to 350°F.

**5**

Bake in preheated oven for about one hour or until done. Place a pan of hot water in the bottom of the oven to provide moisture during baking. Brush loaf with oil when loaf is removed from oven. Cool.

Yield: 1 large or 2 small round loaves.

# Fitness House Rye-Oat-Rice Bread

## (Wheatless)

1 cup mashed potatoes (about 1 large potato)
1 tablespoon dry yeast
$\frac{1}{4}$ cup lukewarm potato water
1 teaspoon honey
1 cup oat flour
1 cup brown rice flour
2 teaspoons salt
$1\frac{1}{2}$ cups potato water
4 tablespoons oil
5 cups rye flour
1 tablespoon caraway seed
$\frac{1}{4}$ cup corn meal

Boil potato in approximately 2 cups water until tender. Force potato, while hot, through ordinary strainer or ricer. Reserve potato water.

Dissolve yeast in $\frac{1}{4}$ cup lukewarm potato water. Add 1 teaspoon honey to yeast mixture.

Add oat flour, brown rice flour and salt to mashed potato. Measure out $1\frac{1}{2}$ cups potato water and add it along with the yeast mixture, the oil, the rye flour and caraway seed. Mix well.

Knead dough well on board, adding more flour if necessary. Oil bowl, place dough in bowl and cover with a damp cloth setting it in a warm place to rise until double. (approx. 2 hours.)

Stir dough down and shape it into a round loaf. Shake corn meal over cookie sheet and place loaf on it. Prick loaf all over with a fork. Allow to rise for another hour. Meanwhile preheat oven to 400°F.

**6**

Brush loaf with cold water. Bake in preheated oven for about 45 minutes. After removing from oven, brush once more with cold water. Cool completely on a rack before slicing. Yield: 1 round loaf.

# Breads

## Herbed Batter Bread

**(An All-Rye, No-Knead, Casserole Bread)**

¼ cup skim milk powder
1 cup lukewarm water
1 tablespoon honey
1½ teaspoons salt
1 cup lukewarm water
4 teaspoons dry yeast
3 tablespoons chopped parsley
2 tablespoons chopped fresh basil or 1
    teaspoon dried crushed basil
1 tablespoon freshly-snipped chives
1 teaspoon dried, crushed oregano
½ teaspoon fresh chopped thyme or ¼
    teaspoon dried thyme leaves
½ teaspoon freshly-snipped marjoram or
    ¼ teaspoon dried marjoram leaves
4½ cups rye flour
2 tablespoons oil

Combine skim milk powder and warm water in a small bowl, using a wire whisk. Add honey and salt.

In a larger mixing bowl, place the lukewarm water and sprinkle the yeast over the top, stirring until dissolved.

Add the milk mixture to the dissolved yeast. Stir in the fresh and dried herbs. Add two cups of rye flour. Beat for two minutes on medium speed of electric mixer, scraping sides of bowl frequently; or beat vigorously with a wooden spoon, about 200 strokes, until batter looks satiny. Using a wooden spoon, blend in the additional two and one-half cups rye flour.

## 4!

Scrape batter from sides of bowl. Cover with a clean towel and set in a warm place (85°F.), away from drafts, to rise until light and doubled in size—about 45 to 50 minutes. (Do not allow batter to over-rise.)

## 5

Stir the batter down. Turn into a well-oiled one and one-half quart casserole or soufflé dish. (Batter will be sticky. Smooth out top of loaf by flouring hand and patting into shape.) Again, allow to rise in a warm place, covered, for 20 minutes. Preheat oven to 375°F.

Place in preheated oven and bake for 45 to 50 minutes or until bread is golden brown.

Remove from oven and brush top of bread lightly with oil. Cool for ten minutes. Turn bread out onto wire rack to cool.

Yield: one round loaf.

# Peanut-Rye-No-Knead Bread
## (Wheatless)

2 cups lukewarm water
4 teaspoons dry yeast
1 tablespoon molasses
3½ cups rye flour
½ cup soy flour
½ cup peanut flour (raw peanuts finely-ground either in electric blender or nut grinder)
½ cup rye flour
2 tablespoons oil
2 teaspoons salt

Put lukewarm water into electric mixer bowl. Sprinkle yeast over surface of water. Add molasses. Let soak a few minutes.

When yeast is dissolved, stir in 3½ cups rye flour.

Beat in electric mixer for 10 minutes on low speed.

please turn page

# Breads

**4!**

Sift soy flour and add it along with the peanut flour and remaining $\frac{1}{2}$ cup rye flour, oil, and salt to dough. Stir just until combined. Cover bowl with damp cloth and set in warm place. Let rise until double in bulk (about 45 minutes).

**5**

Stir dough down and turn out into very-well-oiled 9 x 5 x 3-inch bread pan. Shape into loaf with wet spatula.

**6**

Let rise again for about 30 minutes until almost to top of pan. Meanwhile, preheat oven to 350°F.

**7**

Bake for 45-50 minutes, or until toothpick comes out clean. Remove from pan and cool completely before cutting. Store in refrigerator.

Yield: one loaf.

## Pumpernickel Bread

2 large potatoes
water to cover
2 teaspoons dry yeast
$\frac{1}{2}$ cup potato water
1 teaspoon honey
3 cups cold water
$\frac{3}{4}$ cup corn meal
$\frac{1}{2}$ cup molasses
1 tablespoon caraway seeds
2 tablespoons oil
4 teaspoons salt
5 cups rye flour
$6\frac{1}{2}$ cups wheat flour
1 egg, slightly-beaten
$\frac{1}{2}$ teaspoon water

Cook potatoes in water to cover. Drain, save $\frac{1}{2}$ cup potato water. Push potatoes, while still hot, through ordinary strainer or ricer. Measure 2 cups potatoes into bowl and leave to cool slightly.

Soften yeast in lukewarm potato water. Add honey and let soak a few minutes.

**3**

Combine cold water and corn meal and boil, stirring constantly until thick—about 3 minutes.

**4!**

Add molasses, caraway seeds, oil and salt to corn meal mixture. Let mixture cool to lukewarm.

**5**

Add 2 cups riced potatoes and all of yeast mixture to lukewarm corn meal mixture and blend well.

**6**

Add rye flour gradually, then wheat flour, reserving enough to knead with. Knead thoroughly, 10-15 minutes. Place in large oiled bowl to rise. Cover with a damp cloth. Allow $2\frac{1}{2}$ hours for rising in warm, draft-free place.

**7**

Stir down and shape into four round loaves. For a glistening crust, mix together one slightly beaten egg and $\frac{1}{2}$ teaspoon water and brush surface of loaves. Prick tops with fork design. Allow to rise for one hour in warm place. Meanwhile, preheat oven to 375°F.

**8**

Bake in preheated oven for 45 minutes.

Yield: 4 loaves.

see color photograph

# Traditional Irish Oatmeal Bread

8 teaspoons dry yeast
1 cup lukewarm water
1 tablespoon honey
1/4 cup skim milk powder
1 cup water
1/2 cup oil
1 1/2 teaspoons salt
4 tablespoons honey
2 eggs (well-beaten)
2 cups oatmeal
6 1/2 cups whole-wheat flour
1 cup currants
1 egg (slightly-beaten)
1/2 teaspoon water

Dissolve yeast in 1 cup lukewarm water. Add 1 tablespoon honey.

Combine skim milk powder and 1 cup water with wire whisk, and heat almost to scalding point. Add oil, salt and honey. Cool to lukewarm.

In large mixing bowl, combine milk mixture, 2 well-beaten eggs, and yeast mixture. Mix in oatmeal and 6 cups of the whole-wheat flour, 3 cups at a time, reserving 1/2 cup for the second kneading.

Knead until smooth and elastic, for about 10 minutes.

Put into an oiled bowl. Cover with damp cloth and let rise in a warm place until double in bulk—1 1/2 hours (approximately).

Stir dough down and knead with remaining 1/2 cup whole-wheat flour, gradually working in currants. Shape into 3 round loaves. Brush with beaten egg to which 1/2 teaspoon water has been added. Put loaves on oiled cookie sheets to rise. Let rise 1 hour in draft-free spot. Meanwhile preheat oven to 375°F.

Bake in preheated oven for 25 minutes until golden brown. Remove from pan and cool before slicing.
Yield: 3 round loaves.

# Swedish Limpa Rye Bread

4 teaspoons dry yeast
1/2 cup lukewarm water
1/3 cup honey
2 teaspoons salt
1 tablespoon orange rind, grated
1 teaspoon anise seed
1 teaspoon caraway seed
1/3 cup molasses
2 tablespoons oil
1 1/4 cups hot water
4 cups rye flour
2 1/2 cups wheat flour
1 egg, lightly-beaten
1/2 teaspoon water

Sprinkle dry yeast over lukewarm water. Add 1 teaspoon honey and let stand 5-10 minutes.

Meanwhile put remaining honey, salt, orange rind, anise seed, caraway seed, molasses and oil into a large bowl.

Pour hot water into this mixture and stir well. Cool to lukewarm. Blend in 1 cup rye flour, beating until smooth.

**4!**

Stir softened yeast into mixture, beating well. Add remaining 3 cups rye flour, mixing until smooth. Beat in 2 1/2 cups wheat flour with a spoon, turning dough out onto board, to knead in the rest of the flour if necessary. Let rest for 10 minutes.

**5**

Knead dough until smooth and no longer sticky. Put it into an oiled bowl, cover it with a damp cloth and set it in a warm place to double itself in bulk (about 2 hours).

**6**

Stir dough down. Cover and let rise again until nearly double in bulk (about 1 1/2 hours).

please turn page

# Breads

Shape into two loaves and place either in (9 x 5 x 3-inch) bread pans which have been oiled or on a cookie sheet. Brush with beaten egg to which ½ teaspoon water has been added. Let rise an hour or so more. Meanwhile preheat oven to 350°F.

**8**

Bake in a preheated oven for 45-50 minutes or until a deep golden brown. Remove from pan, cool on a rack. Store in refrigerator.

Yield: 2 loaves.

## Whole Wheat Bread

4 teaspoons dry yeast
1 cup lukewarm water
1 teaspoon honey
⅓ cup oil
¼ cup molasses
2 cups lukewarm water
1 tablespoon salt
2 cups wheat germ
7 cups whole-wheat flour
1 egg, beaten
¼ teaspoon water
sesame seeds

Sprinkle yeast over the top of 1 cup lukewarm water, adding honey. Leave to soak 5-10 minutes.

Mix oil and molasses with 2 cups lukewarm water. Add salt and wheat germ.

Add yeast mixture to oil-molasses-water mixture, stirring to combine.

**4**

Stir in 3½ cups whole-wheat flour, then stir in 3 more cups, mixing the flour in as well as possible.

**5**

Turn dough out onto board and using the remaining ½ cup flour, knead dough until it is smooth and "springy"—about 12 minutes.

**6**

Put dough into oiled bowl, turning it in order to coat the surface with oil. Cover with a damp towel. Let rise for 1½ hours or until doubled in bulk.

Punch down dough. Let it rest about 20 minutes. Knead about 5 minutes. Divide dough into two loaves. Place in well-oiled (9 x 5 x 3-inch) bread-pans. Brush tops with beaten egg to which ¼ teaspoon water

has been added. Sprinkle with toasted sesame seeds. Let rise until loaves are well-rounded and are high in the pans—about an hour. Meanwhile preheat oven to 350°F.

**8**

Bake in preheated oven for 1 hour or until loaf tests done. (Sides of loaf will pull away from the pan and an inserted toothpick in the center of the loaf will come out clean.) Remove from pans, and cool on rack before serving.

Yield: 2 loaves.

# Breads

## No-Knead Raisin Whole-Grain Bread
### (Wheatless)

2 teaspoons dry yeast
1/3 cup lukewarm water
2-3 tablespoons honey
1¾ cups boiling water
2 teaspoons salt
2 tablespoons oil
1 cup brown rice flour
1 cup oat flour
1½ cups rye flour
1 teaspoon clove or mace (optional)*
1/3 cup raisins (optional)*

**1**

Dissolve dry yeast in 1/3 cup lukewarm water to which honey has been added.

**2**

Combine boiling water, salt and oil in electric mixer bowl.

**3**

Combine brown rice, oat and rye flours with spice and raisins (if using them) and add to boiling water mixture. Cool to lukewarm.

**4**

Add yeast mixture and beat for 2-3 minutes.

**5**

Cover bowl with damp cloth and set in larger bowl of hot water to rise for two hours.

**6**

Beat dough again for 2-3 minutes.

**7**

Turn dough into oiled 9 x 5 x 3-inch loaf pan and set in unheated oven to rise for 40-45 minutes or until it has just reached the top of the pan.

**8**

Set oven at 400°F. and leave it at that temperature for 10 minutes. Then turn heat down to 325°F. and bake bread for 40-45 minutes longer. Turn loaf out of pan and cool on a rack before slicing.

*Note: Spice and raisins can be omitted for a plainer, but still delicious loaf. For this, use 2 tablespoons of honey.

Yield: 1 loaf.

# Whole-Wheat – Oatmeal Bread

3 cups oatmeal
4 cups boiling water
⅓ cup oil
¼ cup molasses
2 tablespoons honey
2 teaspoons salt
4 teaspoons dry yeast
½ cup lukewarm water
1 teaspoon honey
9 cups (approximately) whole-wheat flour

In large mixing bowl, soak 3 cups oatmeal in 4 cups boiling water.

**2**

Add oil, molasses, honey, salt.

**3**

Sprinkle dry yeast over surface of lukewarm water. Add 1 teaspoon honey.

**4**

Stir 4 cups whole-wheat flour into oatmeal mixture to help cool it down.

**5**

When oatmeal mixture is lukewarm, add dissolved yeast. Stir in 4 more cups of whole-wheat flour.

**6**

Turn out onto floured board and knead (using approximately 1 cup more of whole-wheat flour) until a workable dough is formed.

**7**

Place in oiled bowl, cover with a damp cloth and let rise in a warm place until double in bulk (about 1 hour).

**8**

Stir dough down and let rise again (about ½ hour). Form into 2 loaves. Place in oiled bread pans, 9 x 5 x 3-inch, and let rise to top of pan (about ½ hour). Meanwhile, preheat oven to 325°F.

**9**

Bake in preheated oven for an hour. Turn out of pans. If sides of loaf are not crusty, set in oven on rack without pan for another 10 minutes, to dry out a little. Cool before slicing. Store in refrigerator.
Yield: 2 loaves.

# Breads

## Wheat – Soy – Sesame Bread

1 tablespoon dry yeast
2 cups lukewarm water
¼ cup honey
4-5 cups whole-wheat flour
¾ cup sesame seeds
½ cup soy flour, sifted
2 tablespoons soy grits
1 teaspoon salt
¼ cup oil

**1**

Dissolve yeast in lukewarm water.

**2**

Add honey to yeast mixture.

**3**

Stir 2 cups whole-wheat flour into yeast mixture. Cover with a damp cloth, put in warm place and allow "sponge" to rise for about ½ hour.

**4!**

Meanwhile, combine sesame seeds, soy flour, soy grits, salt and remaining whole wheat flour.

**5**

When "sponge" has risen, stir in oil and rest of ingredients. If dough isn't firm, add more whole-wheat flour. Knead until dough is elastic. Let rise in a covered bowl in a warm place for about an hour more, until dough is doubled.

**6**

Stir dough down, knead briefly to shape into one loaf. Place in oiled 9 x 5 x 3-inch pan. Let rise again until nearly doubled. Meanwhile, preheat oven to 350°F.

**7**

Bake for 30 minutes, until golden brown in color.

Yield: one loaf.

# Whole-Wheat Crescent Rolls

4 teaspoons dry yeast
1 cup lukewarm water
1 teaspoon honey
1 cup oil
3 tablespoons honey
2 teaspoons salt
1 cup boiling water
2 eggs, beaten
6 cups whole-wheat flour (more, if necessary,
    for rolling out crescents)
1 egg, beaten
1/2 teaspoon water
4 tablespoons sesame seeds (toasted for
    about 20 minutes in a 200°F. oven)

Dissolve yeast in lukewarm water. Add 1
teaspoon honey.

**2**

In large bowl, mix oil, 3 tablespoons
honey, salt and boiling water. When
lukewarm, add 2 beaten eggs, then dissolved
yeast. Gradually stir in whole-wheat flour,
mixing well, but do not knead. Put in
refrigerator to chill until firm.

**3**

Divide dough into 3 parts and roll each one
out on floured board into a large circle,
as thin as possible. Brush with beaten egg
to which 1/2 teaspoon water has been added.
Sprinkle sesame seeds over the surface.
Cut each circle into wedges about two
inches wide at the outside edge. Roll each
wedge toward the center, lift off board,
dip top in egg mixture and then in sesame
seeds. Place on oiled cookie sheet, leaving
enough room for each crescent to rise. Let rise
in draft-free place for 11/2 hours. Meanwhile,
preheat oven to 425°F.

**4!**

Bake for 25 minutes until golden brown.
Serve warm.

Yield: 4 dozen rolls.

# Breads

## No-Knead Whole-Wheat Bread

**from County Cork, Ireland**

7½ cups whole-wheat flour
6 teaspoons dry yeast
1 cup water (lukewarm)
1 tablespoon honey
4 tablespoons molasses
1 cup warm water
2 tablespoons salt
2 cups warm water (approximately)

Place whole-wheat flour in large bowl and set it in a very low oven for about 20 minutes, to warm flour and bowl. If it is a gas oven, the pilot light will give sufficient heat; if electric, set at lowest temperature.

Dissolve yeast in 1 cup lukewarm water and add honey.

**3**

Mix molasses with 1 cup warm water.

**4!**

Combine yeast mixture with molasses mixture and add with salt to warmed flour. Add enough water to make a sticky dough (about 2 cups).

**5**

Oil 2 large loaf pans, at least 9 x 5 x 3-inches or larger, or 3 small loaf pans and put entire mixture directly into pans. No kneading is involved. Let rise 1 hour. Meanwhile, preheat oven to 400° F.

**6**

Bake for 30 to 40 minutes or until crust is brown. Remove pans from oven and leave to cool on racks for 10 minutes. Remove loaves from pans and continue to cool on racks before slicing.

Yield: 2 large or 3 small loaves.

# Basic Sourdough Starter

2 teaspoons dry yeast (or 1 cup starter)
1 cup lukewarm water
1 cup whole grain flour (rye or wheat)
1 cup lukewarm water (added at a later date)
1 cup whole grain flour (rye or wheat)
         (added at a later date)

Sprinkle yeast over 1 cup lukewarm water and leave to dissolve—about five minutes.

**2**

Stir dissolved yeast into 1 cup flour, making a paste first and gradually adding the liquid.

Put starter into a glass jar. Cover it and leave it at room temperature for three days, or until it has developed the sourness desired and is bubbly and thick.

If planning to bake the next day, stir in the other cup lukewarm water and flour and leave at room temperature overnight. Next morning take out the amount of starter needed for baking and refrigerate the remaining starter.

If not planning to bake the next day, refrigerate the starter as soon as it is ready and take it out the night before you plan to use it, let it come to room temperature, add the other cup of water and flour and leave it at room temperature overnight. Next morning take out the amount needed and refrigerate the remainder.

Note: If the starter is kept for longer than 2 weeks or if it becomes too sour, shake it up, throw half of it away and add extra water and flour to make up for what you have discarded. Always keep 1 cup of starter for the next batch. If your recipe calls for 1 cup of starter and you wish to double the recipe, do not double the starter. Use only 1 cup.

# Breads

## Danish Sour Bread

2 teaspoons dry yeast
1 cup starter (lukewarm)*
2½ cups whole-wheat flour
¾ cup rye flour
1 tablespoon salt
1 tablespoon powdered caraway seed
      (ground in electric blender or nut
      grinder)
¼ cup oil
1⅓ cups warm water
caraway seeds

Dissolve dry yeast in lukewarm starter.

Mix flours, salt and powdered caraway seeds in a large bowl.

Make a well in the center, and add the starter-yeast mixture and oil. Stir in the warm water, a little at a time, and mix the dough thoroughly, kneading it for 6-8 minutes.

**4!**

Set the bowl in a pan of warm water, cover with a towel and let dough rise in a warm place for an hour or until it is doubled in bulk.

**5**

Stir dough down, knead it into a round loaf. Roll it in the whole caraway seeds (or sprinkle them over the top). Place loaf on an oiled cookie sheet. Let rise in a warm place for an hour. Meanwhile preheat oven to 425°F. Put pan of water on oven floor for an extra crusty loaf.

**6**

Bake bread in preheated oven for 15 minutes. Then turn oven to 300°F. and remove pan of water from oven. Bake bread 45 minutes longer.
Yield: 1 large round loaf.
*Note: If you want to double this recipe, double all ingredients except starter. Use only 1 cup starter. If starter is cold, it can be quickly brought to room temperature by placing the cup in a bowl of hot water and stirring it.

# Old Country Sourdough Rye Bread
## (Made with Onion Starter)

2 teaspoons dry yeast
$\frac{1}{3}$ cup lukewarm water
1 teaspoon honey
1 cup lukewarm water
3 tablespoons molasses
1 tablespoon oil
$\frac{1}{2}$ cup mashed potatoes
1 cup onion starter*
1 tablespoon caraway seeds
1 tablespoon salt
$2\frac{1}{2}$ cups whole-wheat flour
$\frac{1}{2}$ cup wheat germ
$1\frac{1}{2}$ cups rye flour
2 tablespoons corn meal
1 egg, beaten
1 teaspoon caraway seeds

Sprinkle yeast over $\frac{1}{3}$ cup lukewarm water. Add 1 teaspoon honey. Let dissolve for five minutes.

In a large mixing bowl, combine 1 cup lukewarm water, molasses, oil, mashed potatoes and mix until smooth.

Add yeast mixture, onion starter, caraway seeds and salt. Mix until well-blended.

## 4!

Add whole-wheat flour, (reserving $\frac{1}{2}$ cup for kneading), and wheat germ, mix well for about five minutes. Let dough rest for 10 minutes.

please turn page

# Breads

**5**

Add rye flour. Knead on a board for about 10 minutes, using 1/2 cup whole-wheat flour, until dough is elastic and "springy."

**6**

Place dough in an oiled bowl, turning it over to coat surface with oil. Cover, set bowl in hot water and leave to rise in a warm place for 1 1/2 hours until doubled in bulk.

**7**

Stir down dough. Allow to rise for one hour. (This second rising can be omitted if time is of the essence.)

**8**

Stir down and divide dough into two loaves. These can be shaped in rounds and placed on an oiled cookie sheet which has been sprinkled with corn meal, or they can be place in oiled loaf pans (9 x 5 x 3-inch). Glaze tops with beaten egg and sprinkle with caraway seeds.

**9**

Set to rise in an unheated oven for approximately one hour. Turn oven to 400°F. for 20 minutes, then turn it down to 375°F. and bake for 30 minutes longer or until bread tests done. (For a crustier loaf, put a pan of hot water on oven floor during the first 20 minutes when oven is at 400°F.) Cool on rack before serving.

*To make onion starter, add 1 small, peeled, onion—loosely wrapped in cheesecloth, to fresh batch of basic sourdough starter mixture and leave to sour at room temperature for at least three days. Before making OLD COUNTRY SOURDOUGH RYE BREAD, add a second cup of water and a second cup of flour to the onion starter, leaving it at room temperature overnight.

Yield: 2 loaves.

# Sourdough English Muffins

1 cup skim milk powder
3 cups water
1 cup starter (see sourdough starter method
    in this section)
10 cups whole-wheat flour
3 teaspoons dry yeast
1 tablespoon honey
4 tablespoons oil
3 teaspoons salt
¼ cup cornmeal
¼ lb. butter (for skillet)

Combine skim milk powder and water with a
wire whisk and heat to boiling point. Cool
to lukewarm.

**2**

When milk is lukewarm, add sourdough
starter and gradually stir in 4 cups of the
whole-wheat flour until it is thoroughly mixed.
Leave in a warm place overnight.

**3**

In the morning, stir down the mixture and
add yeast, honey, oil, salt and remaining 6
cups of flour. Turn out onto light-floured
board and knead for 10-12 minutes.

**4!**

Sprinkle floured board with cornmeal and
roll out dough to thickness of English muffins
(about ⅜ inch). Cut with large round cutter
and place on cookie sheet to rise for an
hour in a warm place.

**5**

Heat iron skillet to medium low heat, lightly
grease it with butter and bake muffins
approximately 12 minutes on each side. Be
very careful not to burn them. If the heat is
too high, they may not bake evenly inside
before browning too much on the outside.
Serve muffins hot, or cool and store them,
splitting and toasting them before serving.

Yield: 24 muffins.

AMBROSIA

SHERBET

raisin

9.

Desserts

PIE

compote

pund
puffs

cream

Chees

9.

Cak

Desserts

apricot

tart

CUSTARD

OATMEAL

PUMPKIN 9.

# Desserts

To most people, a meal isn't complete without dessert. The diners at Fitness House are no exception. But their requirements are exceptional. They present us with the challenge of providing tempting desserts that are totally free from refined sugar, chocolate, white flour and similarly undesirable ingredients, most of which seem to be synonymous with dessert.

The discoveries we've made in meeting this challenge have broadened our ideas of what a dessert can be. The limitations imposed on us led to the creation of some delectable sweets that have become favorites at Fitness House and will surely score the same success with your family. For example, we found that "sweet" doesn't have to mean white sugar; it can mean something much more interesting, much more flavorful and distinctive.

Refined sugar is dangerous to health because it's so concentrated and makes unnatural demands on the body much as a drug does. It can disturb the calcium-phosphorus balance of the body, and it is now thought to be a cause of dangerously high cholesterol levels.

The so-called "raw" sugar which is sold in many health stores, is commonly thought of as unrefined. This is apparently a misconception, for according to Fred Rohe, spokesman for the Organic Merchants Association on the West coast, it is against the law to sell unrefined sugar.

We found that raw, unstrained honey is the best sweetener to use because it contains natural vitamins and minerals. Clover honey has the mildest flavor and is the best choice for a wide variety of dishes. When you buy honey, remember that the darker and cloudier the honey, the more minerals and vitamins it contains. Avoid the light, clarified honeys sold in most stores.

Generally speaking, in a recipe which requires sugar, honey in half that amount may be substituted. However, the fact that honey is a liquid must be taken into consideration; often more flour must be added to the recipe to give the final product the right consistency.

Honey sometimes needs to be thinned if it is to be added successfully to beaten egg-whites for a meringue or a cake frosting. We do this by setting the container of honey in a large pan of hot water and leaving it at room temperature briefly, stirring occasionally, until it is thin enough. Never put honey over direct heat, as this will destroy some of the vitamins. If it becomes grainy or crystallized, warming it in this way will soften it. Honey will keep indefinitely. It has even been discovered, perfectly preserved, after centuries of storage in some of the Egyptian tombs.

We use date sugar (ground dried dates) in some our our dessert recipes. A natural sweetener, this is a good addition to many fruit-crisp toppings, cookies and date desserts. But because it doesn't dissolve, its use is limited.

We have never used chocolate at Fitness House. It is true that cocoa and chocolate are rich in calcium but they are also high in oxalic acid which interferes with the absorption of calcium in the body to such an extent that whatever calcium value there is is nullified. So we use carob—a food that tastes remarkably like chocolate and is just as beneficial as chocolate is detrimental. Carob is composed largely of carbohydrates. It contains natural sugars and a generous supply of B vitamins and minerals, especially calcium. Compared to cocoa, carob has approximately half the calories, one-hundredth the amount of fat and $2\frac{1}{2}$ times the amount of calcium.

Carob looks and acts much like cocoa. It should be dissolved in oil before being mixed with water. Like cocoa, it has a somewhat raw taste and should be heated slightly, either by being mixed with a hot liquid or heated briefly in a double-boiler on the stove.

Carob should be dissolved in oil before it is mixed with water.

Try using soy flour, peanut flour, nuts, seeds, or eggs to add tasty protein to a dessert. Often, when a meal at Fitness House consists of a hearty soup and salad, we serve a more substantial dessert, such as a nut torte, baked custard, rice pudding or apple crisp. Brazil nuts, sunflower seeds, almonds and soy grits are some of the flour substitutes we use in our cakes. Since we use no chemical leaveners, separated eggs, well beaten give our cakes lightness. The combinations of ground nuts or seeds, honey and eggs make delicious tortes, which can be served plain, frosted or with a fruit glaze. Nut and seed butters, such as peanut, sesame, sunflower, almond can all be made using a blender. (See recipes in Snack section.) We combine these with coconut, carob, honey, soy flour, chopped nuts, seeds, or dried fruit to make a variety of unusual, tempting confections.

Yogurt is so easily made it is never necessary to buy it commercially. (See recipe in Salad Dressing section.) It has become one of our staples at Fitness House. We make it from skim milk powder and use it as a basic ingredient in many of our desserts. Cheesecake becomes a low-calorie, high-protein food when you make it with cottage cheese and yogurt, instead of cream cheese and sour cream. Yogurt adds smoothness and a richer quality to our pineapple chiffon pie. Combined with fresh or dried fruits, nuts and oatmeal or coconut, yogurt becomes a filling dessert after a meal of soup and salad.

It is quite possible, we have found, to make smooth, creamy sherbets and ice creams using gelatin, egg whites and honey with skim milk powder, or even without milk of any kind. The secret seems to be in beating it at least twice—once after the initial freezing and again just before serving it.

At Fitness House, we do not use hydrogenated fats. We use vegetable oil when a recipe calls for shortening. Our experience is that safflower oil (unrefined), because of its mild flavor, is the best one to use in desserts. Of course, allowance must be made for the fact that the oil is a liquid; it does not take as much oil as it would shortening or butter to make pie-crust, crumb topping, or cookies for example.

Pie-crust made from barley and oat flour, safflower oil and ice-water is tender and tasty. We press the dough into the pie-plate making it as thin as possible and building up a nice edge all around it. The dough can also be rolled between two sheets of waxed paper. It is equally good baked before being filled (as for a chiffon pie) or filled and then baked (as for a dried fruit custard pie). Other combinations may also be used for crusts. An especially good one for a pineapple chiffon pie is the coconut-wheat germ mixture pressed into a pie-plate—just as you would a graham-cracker crust. The toasted coconut adds a delectable flavor to the pineapple and provides an elegant setting for it.

Press pie dough into pie plate.

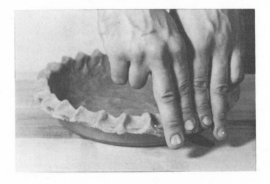

Make pie-crust as thin as possible and build up a nice edge around it.

Fresh fruit in season, especially when it is grown locally and organically, is the best dessert you can get. If fresh fruit is not available, unsulphured, dried fruits such as apricots, peaches, pears and even prunes offer year-round possibilities. We use them in whips, pies, and compotes. Dates, figs and raisins are tasty additions to cookies, cakes and puddings. In fall and winter our Fitness House dessert is often a big bowl of apples and a prettily arranged plate of dried fruits with nuts and seeds. Russet pears and persimmons sometimes grace our fall buffet. We serve beautiful fruit cups all year round, using citrus fruits, unsweetened pineapple (canned), and bananas in winter, and melons, berries and peaches in summer.

To our delight we've found that desserts can be a nutritious, as well as a pleasant, way to end a meal.

# *Fruit Desserts*

## Ambrosia

8 medium-sized oranges (Valencia or Navel)
2-4 tablespoons honey
⅓-½ cup coconut

Peel oranges and slice them crosswise in rounds about ¼ inch thick.

Layer orange slices in dessert serving dish, drizzling honey between each layer and over the top layer. Sprinkle coconut liberally over the top layer. Chill for 1 hour before serving to allow flavors to blend together.

Note: The amount of honey and coconut will vary according to taste.

Yield: 4-6 servings.

## Apple Delight

4 apples, washed, unpeeled
1 tablespoon lemon juice
1 tablespoon honey
½ cup dates, pitted and chopped
1 cup yogurt
chopped nuts for garnish

Core apples and shred into a large bowl.

Blend in lemon juice, honey and dates. Fold in yogurt.

Serve, topped with chopped nuts, as a dessert or salad.

Yield: approximately 4 servings.

# Apple Betty

Preheat oven to 325°F.
2½ lbs. baking apples (6-8 apples)
⅓ cup honey
2½ tablespoons lemon juice
1 teaspoon grated lemon rind
½ cup raisins
¼ teaspoon cinnamon
½-¾ cup cider or apple juice (use larger
        amount if apples are dry)
3 cups whole grain bread cubes
¼ cup oil
⅓ cup honey
½ cup wheat germ
½ teaspoon cinnamon

Wash apples. Peel and remove core. Cut into ½ inch-thick slices and put in a large bowl.

**2**

Mix together honey, lemon juice, lemon rind. Add to apples and toss together lightly. Add raisins, cinnamon, and cider or apple juice. Toss to combine. Turn into shallow baking dish.

**3**

Lightly sauté whole grain bread cubes in oil for a few minutes. Remove from heat. Add honey and toss to combine; then add wheat germ and cinnamon.

**4!**

Cover apples with topping. Bake in a preheated oven on the middle rack, for 45 minutes to an hour or until apples are tender.

**5**

Remove from oven and cool to room temperature before serving.

Yield: 6-8 servings.

# Fruit Desserts

## Honey-Baked Apples

Preheat oven to 350°F.
6 large baking apples
3 tablespoons walnuts, chopped
3 tablespoons raisins
1 cup water
⅓ cup honey
1 cinnamon stick, about two-inch length
1 tablespoon lemon juice

Wash and core apples.

Mix chopped walnuts and raisins together. Fill apple cavities with the mixture and place in a shallow baking dish.

**3**

In a small saucepan, combine water, honey, and cinnamon stick. Place over medium heat and bring to a boil. Simmer for five minutes.

**4!**

Remove from heat and stir in the lemon juice. Remove cinnamon stick and pour syrup over apples in baking dish. Place in a preheated oven and bake, uncovered, for 45 minutes or until the apples are tender, basting occasionally. Remove from oven and cool to room temperature before serving.

Yield: 6 servings.

Spinach and Rice Casserole

for recipe see chapter on Grains

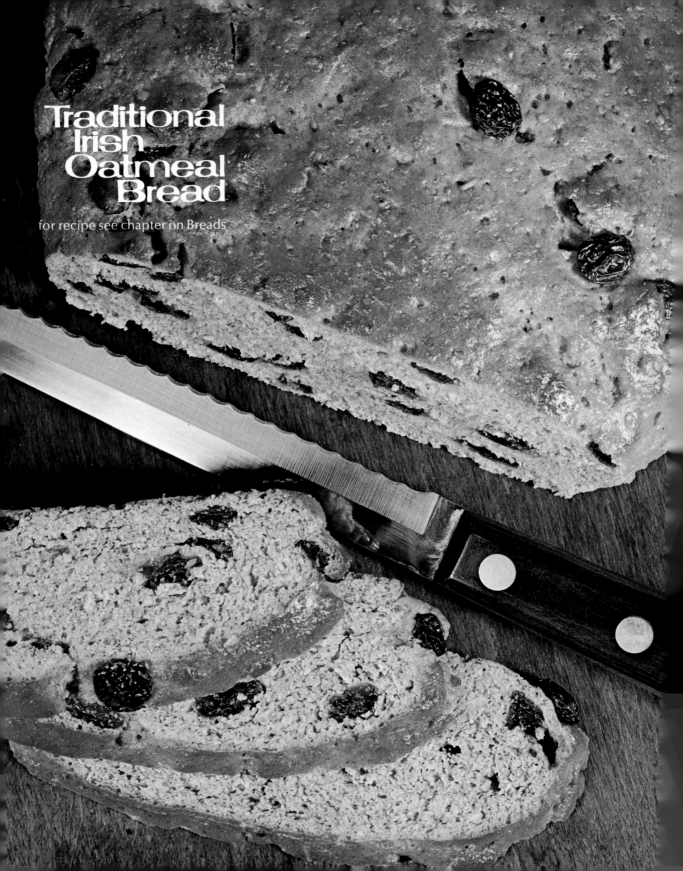

# Traditional Irish Oatmeal Bread

for recipe see chapter on Breads

Strawberry Cheesecake

Pineapple Sherbert

Brazil Nut Torte

Tutti-Frutti

recipes see
apter on Desserts

Peanut Butter-Sesame Balls

Fudgies

for recipe see chapter on Desserts

*Pineapple Chiffon Pie*

# Apple Crisp

Preheat oven to 325°F.
2½ lbs. baking apples (6-8 apples)
⅓ cup honey
2½ tablespoons lemon juice
1 teaspoon grated lemon rind
¼ teaspoon cinnamon
¼ cup raisins (optional)
½ cup old-fashioned, rolled oats
⅓ cup wheat germ
½ cup raw peanut flour (raw peanuts ground
      fine, either in blender or electric
      nut grinder)
¼ cup brown rice flour
½ cup date sweetener (ground dried dates)
½ teaspoon ground cinnamon
¼ cup oil

Wash apples; peel and cut into quarters,
remove core and seeds. Cut into ½-inch thick
slices and put in a large bowl. Mix
together honey, lemon juice, lemon rind,
and cinnamon. Add to sliced apples and toss
together thoroughly. Stir in raisins. Place
mixture in a baking dish. (If baking in
large quantities, bake apples without topping
until the apples are almost tender, then
put topping on and bake until topping
is light and brown.)

Prepare topping: In a medium-sized bowl,
combine rolled oats, wheat germ, raw peanut
flour, brown rice flour, date sweetener and
cinnamon. Mix ingredients together
thoroughly. Add oil gradually, mixing
ingredients with a fork until mixture is
crumbly. Sprinkle over apples, covering them
completely.

Place in a preheated oven, on middle rack,
and bake for 45 minutes-1 hour, or until
apples are tender.

**4!**

Remove from oven and cool to room
temperature before serving.

Yield: 6-8 servings.

# *Fruit Desserts*

## Avocado Dessert

2 ripe avocados, peeled and pits removed
1 cup green, seedless grapes
2 bananas
1 cup yogurt
2 tablespoons honey
3 tablespoons orange juice
1 teaspoon grated orange rind
1/8 teaspoon salt
1 tablespoon lemon juice
2 teaspoons grated lemon rind
fresh mint sprigs and orange slices for
      garnish

Cut avocados into bite-size pieces and put into
a medium-sized bowl. Wash grapes and
add to avocado pieces. Slice bananas and
add to avocado and grape mixture.

Place yogurt in small bowl and beat, with
wire whisk, until smooth. Stir in the honey,
orange juice and rind, salt, lemon juice
and lemon rind. Blend together and pour
over fruit mixture. Toss gently to combine.

Garnish with fresh mint sprigs and orange
slices before serving.

Yield: 4-5 servings.

## Broiled Grapefruit

2 grapefruit
6 teaspoons honey

Wash grapefruit. Cut them in half. Remove
seeds and cut around sections.

Spread 1½ teaspoons honey evenly over the
cut surface of each grapefruit half.

Broil grapefruit, about 3 inches below the
broiler unit, for 5-10 minutes until golden
brown. Cool for 5 minutes before serving.

Yield: 4 servings.

# Banana Ice Cream

2 teaspoons gelatin
1/4 cup cold water
6 tablespoons honey
2 egg yolks, beaten
1 1/2 cups soy milk
3/4 cup concentrated frozen orange juice
1 cup banana pulp
2 egg whites
1/8 teaspoon salt

Sprinkle gelatin over 1/4 cup cold water and let soak about 5 minutes.

Put gelatin mixture into the top of a double-boiler and heat over boiling water, stirring until gelatin is dissolved. Remove from heat. Add honey.

3

In a bowl, combine egg yolks, soy milk, concentrated frozen orange juice and banana pulp. Add gelatin-honey mixture, stirring to blend well. Pour into ice-cube tray and freeze.

4

Put unbeaten egg whites and salt into a mixing bowl. Spoon frozen mixture into egg whites. Beat at medium speed for 5-10 minutes until ice cream is fluffy and of desired consistency. Serve at once.

Note: It is best to beat homemade ice cream each time it is removed from the freezer before serving it.

Yield: 6-8 servings.

# *Fruit Desserts*

## Heavenly Dessert or Salad

1 cup orange sections
1½ cups canned pineapple cubes,
      unsweetened
1 cup seedless green grapes, halved if desired
½ cup fresh blueberries
1 cup coarsely-shredded coconut,
      unsweetened
2 teaspoons lemon juice
1 teaspoon grated orange rind
2 tablespoons honey
1 cup yogurt, stirred with a wire whisk to
      remove any lumps
½ cup fresh strawberries, halved
2 bananas, sliced
iceberg, romaine lettuce or fresh mint for
      garnish

Drain orange sections and pineapple cubes well. Reserve for another time.

**2**

In large bowl, combine orange sections, pineapple cubes, grapes, blueberries and coconut. Add lemon juice, orange rind, honey and yogurt. Toss together lightly. Cover bowl and place in refrigerator for at least one hour before serving.

Remove fruit mixture from refrigerator and add strawberry halves and sliced bananas. Mix lightly.

**4!**

Serve as a salad on serving dish lined with iceberg or romaine lettuce leaves; or as a dessert in a large serving dish or individual dishes, garnished with fresh mint.

Yield: 6-8 servings.

# Orange Whip

1 tablespoon gelatin, unflavored
1/4 cup cold water
3/4 cup boiling water
1/4 cup honey
1/3 cup concentrated, frozen orange juice
3 tablespoons lemon juice
1/4 cup cold water
3 egg whites
dash of salt

**1**

In a medium-sized bowl, soak gelatin in 1/4 cup cold water for 5 minutes. Dissolve this mixture in 3/4 cup boiling water.

**2**

Add honey and stir until it is dissolved; then add concentrated orange juice, lemon juice, and remaining 1/4 cup cold water.

**3**

Cool in refrigerator, or by setting bowl of gelatin in a larger bowl of ice cubes and water, until gelatin is thick but not set completely.

**4**

Beat egg whites and salt together until stiff (but not dry) peaks form.

**5**

Whisk gelatin briefly and fold it carefully into beaten egg whites. Refrigerate several hours or overnight. Serve garnished with orange slices or segments.

Yield: 6 servings.

## Fruit Desserts

### Dried Fruit Compote

1 cup dried figs
1 cup dried prunes
2 cups dried apricots
¾ cup raisins
2 cups water
2 cups apple juice
1 piece cinnamon stick, about 2-inch length
1 large apple, peeled and chopped coarsely
¼ cup lemon juice
2 tablespoons honey
¼ teaspoon salt

In saucepan, combine figs, prunes, apricots, raisins, water and apple juice. Add cinnamon stick and bring slowly to a boil. Turn heat low and simmer 15 minutes or so.

Add chopped apple, lemon juice, honey, salt and cook for 5 to 10 minutes longer, until apple is tender. Cool and serve cold.

Yield: 6-8 servings.

### Pineapple-Orange Gelatin

1 envelope unflavored gelatin
1 cup cold water
3 tablespoons honey
1¼ cups pineapple juice (unsweetened)
2 tablespoons concentrated orange juice (frozen)
1 cup unsweetened, canned pineapple chunks, drained
2 medium-sized oranges, peeled and separated into segments
1 banana, sliced

Soften gelatin in cold water.

In small saucepan, warm gelatin mixture and honey, just enough to dissolve gelatin and soften honey.

Add pineapple juice and frozen *undiluted* orange juice; cool until almost set.

Add pineapple chunks, orange segments and sliced bananas; chill until set.
Yield: 4-6 servings.

# Fresh Peach Crisp

Preheat oven to 350°F.
2½ lbs. fresh ripe peaches (about 7-8)
2 teaspoons lemon juice
¼ cup honey
1½ tablespoons tapioca granules
¼ teaspoon grated or ground nutmeg
⅓ cup brown rice flour
½ cup date sweetener
4 tablespoons wheat germ
4 tablespoons sunflower-seed meal
¼ cup unsweetened coconut meal
¼ cup oil

Wash peaches and peel. Cut in halves; remove pits. Slice peaches into a mixing bowl. Add lemon juice, honey, tapioca granules and grated or ground nutmeg. Toss together lightly. Turn peach mixture into an oiled 8 x 8 x 2-inch baking dish.

Prepare topping: In a separate bowl, combine brown rice flour, date sweetener, wheat germ, sunflower-seed meal and coconut meal. Mix ingredients together lightly. Add oil gradually, stirring with a fork, until mixture is crumbly. Sprinkle topping evenly over peach mixture.

Place in a preheated oven, on middle rack, and bake for 40 to 45 minutes, or until peaches are tender. Remove peach crisp from oven and cool to room temperature before serving.

Yield: 6-8 servings.

*Fruit Desserts*

## Peach-Apricot Whip

¾ cup dried apricots
¾ cup dried peaches
1 tablespoon lemon juice
1 teaspoon grated lemon rind
3 egg whites
pinch of salt
1½ tablespoons honey*

Cover dried fruit with water, bring to a boil
and simmer ten minutes. Drain and reserve
liquid for use another time.

Purée fruit. (Use blender or purée utensil.)
Add lemon juice and rind.

Beat egg whites with salt until stiff. Pour
honey into egg white mixture gradually while
continuing to beat. Then fold egg white
mixture into puréed fruit mixture carefully,
using an over and under motion with a
wire whisk or rubber spatula.

Serve with custard sauce (see recipe this
section).

*Note: Honey must be very liquid in order
to pour it into beaten egg whites. If it is too
stiff, soften it by setting in a container
of hot water briefly.

Yield: 6-8 servings.

# Party Peaches

Serve this light, refreshing dessert to company or to your family after a heavy meal.

4 cups thinly-sliced peaches, washed and peeled
4 teaspoons lemon juice
¼ cup honey
1 cup yogurt
2 teaspoons grated orange rind
2-3 drops almond extract
fresh mint leaves for garnish

In a large bowl, combine sliced peaches with lemon juice and honey. Toss together lightly.

**2**

Combine yogurt, orange rind and almond extract (be careful with the almond extract—it is powerful), mix together and pour over sliced peach mixture. Mix gently, but thoroughly.

**3**

Cover and place in refrigerator for one hour to blend flavors.

**4!**

To serve, turn peach mixture into a glass serving dish or large brandy snifter; garnish with fresh mint leaves.

Yield: 6 servings.

*Fruit Desserts*

## Persimmon Whip

½ cup persimmon pulp
2 envelopes unflavored gelatin
1½ tablespoons honey
2 teaspoons lemon juice
1½ cups persimmon pulp
⅛ teaspoon salt
2 egg-whites, beaten stiff

Put ½ cup persimmon pulp into the top of a double boiler. Sprinkle gelatin over it and let it soak for 5 minutes.

Heat over boiling water, stirring until gelatin is dissolved.

Remove from heat. Add honey, lemon juice, remaining persimmon pulp and salt.

**4!**

Pour into a bowl and cool. Refrigerate until almost set.

**5**

Fold in stiffly beaten egg-whites. Pour into serving dish and refrigerate several hours until it is set.

Yield: 6 servings.

# Pineapple Sherbet

2 cups unsweetened pineapple juice
⅓ cup honey
2 tablespoons lemon juice
1 tablespoon unflavored gelatin
1 cup unsweetened, crushed pineapple,
     drained
2 egg whites
⅛ teaspoon salt

In saucepan, combine pineapple juice, honey and lemon juice. Sprinkle gelatin over juice and blend together. Place over medium heat and stir until gelatin dissolves.

**2**

Remove from heat and cool mixture. Stir in drained, crushed pineapple. Pour mixture into freezing tray and freeze until almost firm but still mushy.

Remove sherbet from freezer and spoon into large mixing bowl; add unbeaten egg whites and salt; beat until mixture is fluffy but still thick.

**4!**

Return mixture to freezer for several hours or until firm. To retain a light and fluffy consistency, spoon sherbet into a cold mixing bowl, about one hour before serving, and beat until smooth. Return to freezer.

Yield: 6 servings.

# *Fruit Desserts*

## Lemon Sherbet

¾ cup skim milk powder
2 cups water
1 envelope unflavored gelatin
½ cup honey
⅓ cup lemon juice
1½ tablespoons grated lemon rind
2 egg whites

In medium-sized saucepan, combine skim milk powder and water, using wire whisk. Add gelatin, then honey. Place over medium heat and bring mixture just to boiling point; remove from heat and cool slightly.

Stir in lemon juice and rind. Pour mixture into freezing tray and freeze until almost firm but still mushy.

Spoon mixture into cold mixing bowl and add unbeaten egg whites. Beat until fluffy but still thick. Return to freezing tray and freeze several hours or until firm. Before serving, beat once more until sherbet is fluffy.

Note: Sherbet will keep for several weeks in freezer if placed in a covered container.

Yield: 6 servings.

# Vanilla Ice Cream

2 cups skim milk powder
4 cups water
1 2-inch piece vanilla bean or 1 teaspoon
      vanilla extract
7 tablespoons honey
1 envelope unflavored gelatin
1/4 cup water
3 egg yolks
3 egg whites

Combine skim milk powder and 4 cups water
in top of double boiler. Add 2-inch piece
vanilla bean. (If using vanilla extract do
not add at this time.) Put double boiler on
to heat. Stir in honey.

Sprinkle gelatin over 1/4 cup cold water
and leave to soak for a few minutes. Then
add to hot milk mixture, stirring to dissolve.

**3**

Beat egg yolks and add a little of the milk
mixture to them, then add this to milk
mixture, blending well. Cook until mixture
coats spoon, stirring constantly.

**4**

Remove from heat. Remove vanilla bean
or add vanilla extract, if using it. Pour into
refrigerator trays. Cool completely before
freezing.

**5**

10 minutes before serving, remove from
freezer and let soften at room temperature.
Scoop into mixing bowl, add unbeaten
egg whites and beat until fluffy. Serve
immediately. Ice cream can be refrozen.
Before serving second time beat once again.

Yield: 8-10 servings.

# Puddings

## Applesauce Pudding

4 cups crumbs (cookie, cracker, or dried
     breadcrumbs)
3-4 tablespoons honey
$1\frac{1}{2}$ teaspoons cinnamon
1-2 tablespoons oil (optional)
wheat germ, sesame seeds, ground almonds
     (optional)
4 cups seasoned applesauce

Blend all but last ingredient into crumbs
well, using fingers. If using cracker or cookie
crumbs, it is not necessary to add the oil,
but if using bread crumbs, it may improve
the flavor. Wheat germ, sesame seeds or
ground almonds may also be added if
using plain breadcrumbs. There should be 4
cups of crumbs in all, including any
additions.

**2**

In a glass serving bowl, make a layer using
$\frac{1}{3}$ of crumb mixture. Then make a layer
of applesauce, using half the amount.
Next make another layer of crumbs, using $\frac{1}{3}$
of the mixture. Spread the remaining
applesauce over the layer of crumbs and
top the bowl with the remaining crumbs,
covering the surface evenly. In all there
should be three layers of crumbs and two
layers of applesauce. Chill and serve.

Yield: 6-8 servings.

# Carob Pudding

⅓ cup carob powder, sifted
½ cup boiling water
3 tablespoons cornstarch
1 cup skim milk powder
¼ teaspoon salt
2½ cups cold water
⅓ cup honey
3 egg yolks
1 teaspoon pure vanilla extract
chopped pecans for garnish (optional)

In small bowl, combine carob powder and boiling water, stirring until mixture is smooth. Set to one side.

In top of double boiler, combine cornstarch, skim milk powder and salt. Using a wire whisk, gradually add 2½ cups cold water, blending thoroughly. Blend in the honey and carob-water mixture until well-combined.

Place double boiler over hot water. (Water in lower part of double boiler should not touch upper section.) Cook, stirring constantly until pudding thickens. Cover and continue to cook 10 to 15 minutes longer. (Do not undercook or carob will have a powdery taste.)

Beat egg yolks; spoon about one-half cup hot pudding into beaten yolks, blend together. Turn mixture into hot pudding, stirring constantly. Cook 3 minutes longer; do not boil.

Remove double boiler from heat. Stir in vanilla extract. Pour pudding into serving dish or bowl to cool. Cover pudding to prevent film from forming on surface.

Place pudding in refrigerator, covered, to chill.

Serve plain or with low-calorie whipped cream (see recipe in this section) and garnish with chopped pecans.
Yield: approximately 6 servings.

# *Puddings*

## Carob Spanish Cream

1 tablespoon unflavored gelatin
¼ teaspoon salt
1 tablespoon honey
3 egg yolks, slightly-beaten
⅔ cup skim milk powder
1½ cups water
4 tablespoons carob powder, sifted
1 teaspoon pure vanilla extract
3 egg whites
3 tablespoons honey, softened by placing
      container in bowl of hot water

**1**

Mix gelatin, salt and one tablespoon honey.
Add egg yolks.

**2**

Mix skim milk powder and water with wire
whisk. This will make 2 cups of milk
mixture. Add 1 cup milk mixture and carob
powder to gelatin. Cook over low heat
until gelatin is thoroughly dissolved (about
8 minutes).

**3**

Remove from heat; add the other 1 cup
milk mixture and vanilla. Chill until slightly
firm.

**4!**

Beat egg whites until stiff peaks form,
gradually adding the honey as you beat. Fold
by small amounts into the pudding.

**5**

Pour into large mold or individual molds
and chill for several hours or overnight. As
the cream cools, it divides into a foamy top
over a layer of smooth custard.


Yield: 6 servings.

# Carob Tapioca

2 eggs, slightly-beaten
6 tablespoons tapioca granules
4 tablespoons honey
¼ teaspoon salt
1 cup skim milk powder
3 cups water
4 tablespoons carob powder, sifted
4 tablespoons boiling water
1 teaspoon pure vanilla extract

In a saucepan, beat eggs with fork, just
enough to blend the yolks and whites. Add
tapioca, honey, salt. Combine skim milk
powder with 3 cups water (using wire whisk)
and add to egg mixture.

Dissolve carob powder in 4 tablespoons
boiling water. Add to mixture and cook,
stirring constantly, over moderate heat until
the pudding boils. Let stand 15 minutes.
Stir in vanilla.

Pour into large dish and chill before serving.

Yield: 6 servings.

# Cashew – Carob Pudding

¾ cup (6 ounces) cashew nuts
3 cups water
3 tablespoons oil
3 tablespoons carob powder, sifted
6 tablespoons honey
6 tablespoons cornstarch
6 tablespoons soy powder
¼ teaspoon salt
5 whole eggs, or egg yolks

Make cashew milk by putting cashew nuts
and water into the container of an electric
blender and blending on high speed for
2 minutes.

Combine oil and carob powder in a saucepan.
Add honey and mix with a whisk until
smooth.

Sift cornstarch and soy powder into a
medium-sized bowl. Add cashew milk and
stir with whisk until mixture is smooth.
Stir into carob mixture. Add salt.

please turn page

# *Puddings*

Cook over medium heat, stirring constantly until mixture has boiled for approx. 2 minutes. (If you prefer, you may cook it in a double boiler.)

**5**

Beat eggs or egg yolks and add a little of the pudding mixture to them, then add egg mixture to pudding. Remove from heat. Pour into serving dish. Cool completely before serving.

Yield: 6-8 servings.

## Coconut Bread Pudding

1 cup skim milk powder
4 cups water
½ cup whole grain bread crumbs
2 eggs, beaten
1½ tablespoons oil
5 tablespoons honey
⅛ teaspoon salt
½ cup coconut

Combine skim milk powder and water using a wire whisk. Strain if necessary.

Pour milk over whole grain bread crumbs and let soak for one hour.

Preheat oven to 350°F. Combine eggs, oil, honey and salt, blending well and add to soaked crumbs.

**4**

Stir in coconut. Turn into casserole. Bake in preheated oven for about 1 hour until custard is firm.

Yield: 4-6 servings.

# Date Pudding

1 lb. dates, pitted and diced
2 cups hot water
½ cup date sugar
⅛ teaspoon salt
1 2-inch piece cinnamon stick
⅓ cup cornstarch
¼ cup cold water
½ cup walnuts, chopped
1 tablespoon lemon juice
2 egg whites

**1**

Combine in a saucepan: dates, hot water, date sugar, salt and cinnamon stick.

**2**

Dissolve cornstarch in cold water and stir into date mixture. Cook over medium heat until it thickens. Remove from heat, discard cinnamon stick.

**3**

Add walnuts and lemon juice.

**4**

Beat egg whites until stiff but not dry. Gently fold them into pudding and chill.

Note: Serve with custard sauce if desired (see recipe in this section).

Yield: 6-8 servings.

# *Puddings*

## Hasty Pudding

Preheat oven to 250°F.
1 cup skim milk powder
3 cups water
½ cup corn meal
3 tablespoons oil
½ cup molasses
1 teaspoon salt
½ teaspoon nutmeg
1 cooking apple, pared and diced

Oil a two-quart baking dish, with cover.
Combine skim milk powder and water with a
wire whisk.

In a medium-sized saucepan, bring one
and one-third cups of the milk and water
mixture to a boil; gradually add the
corn meal, stirring constantly.

Remove saucepan from the heat and add the
oil, molasses, salt and nutmeg. Stir in
the diced apple. Mix well and add the
remaining milk.

**4!**

Pour the mixture into prepared baking dish
and cover. Bake in a slow oven for three
and one-quarter hours.

**5**

Remove from oven and cool slightly
before serving. Serve plain or with yogurt or
whipped topping (see recipes in this section).

Yield: 6 servings.

# Indian Pudding

Preheat oven to 325°F.
¼ cup soy grits
½ cup water
1½ cups skim milk powder
3¾ cups water
1 cup corn meal
¼ cup oil
¼ cup honey
⅔ cup molasses
¾ teaspoon salt
½ teaspoon cinnamon
¼ teaspoon cloves
¼ teaspoon ginger
⅛ teaspoon allspice
2 eggs
yogurt, served separately

Soak soy grits in ½ cup water.

**2**

Combine skim milk powder with 3¾ cups water using wire whisk.

**3**

Scald milk, add corn meal and soaked soy grits gradually.

**4**

Lower heat and beat with wire whisk to make a smooth mixture. When mixture begins to thicken, remove from heat.

**5**

Add remaining ingredients, except eggs, and allow mixture to cool.

**6**

Beat eggs and add to cooled mixture; blend thoroughly.

**7**

Pour into oiled dish, and bake 45 to 60 minutes in a preheated oven, or until pudding is firm.

**8**

Pudding can be served hot or cold. Yogurt can be used as a topping for the pudding.

Yield: 4-6 servings.

# Puddings

## Lemon Meringue Pudding

Preheat oven to 325°F.
4 egg yolks
¾ cup honey
2 tablespoons oil
6 tablespoons lemon juice
2 teaspoons grated lemon rind
2 tablespoons cornstarch
½ cup skim milk powder
1¼ cups water
4 egg whites
⅛ teaspoon salt

Prepare a two-quart ovenproof casserole by brushing bottom lightly with oil; set aside.

In small bowl, beat egg yolks until light and lemon-colored. Slowly add the honey and oil, beating until well-combined. Add lemon juice and rind; blend thoroughly.

In a medium-sized bowl, mix cornstarch and skim milk powder. Slowly add water and blend well with wire whisk. Add yolk mixture and combine thoroughly.

**4!**

Beat egg whites with salt and fold gently into yolk mixture. Pour into prepared casserole and bake in preheated oven for 35 to 45 minutes, or until custard is set.

**5!**

Remove pudding from oven and allow to cool at room temperature. Chill before serving.

Note: Pudding will separate into two layers—custard on the bottom and meringue on top.

Yield: 6 servings.

# Old-Fashioned Rice Pudding

½ cup uncooked brown rice
1 cup skim milk powder
3½ cups water
⅓ cup honey
½ teaspoon salt
¼ teaspoon ground (or grated) nutmeg
⅓ cup seedless raisins

Wash rice and remove any foreign particles.

**2**

In top of double boiler, combine skim milk powder, water, honey, rice, salt and nutmeg.

**3**

Cook covered, over hot water 2½ hours, or until rice is tender. Stir mixture occasionally.

**4!**

During the last half hour of cooking, stir in raisins. Serve warm or cold.
Yield: 5-6 servings.

# Baked Rice Pudding

Preheat oven to 275°F.
½ cup skim milk powder
2 cups water
⅓ cup honey
½ teaspoon salt
2 cups cooked, brown rice (see directions in grain section)
1 teaspoon pure vanilla

In medium-sized bowl, combine skim milk powder, water, honey and salt. Mix thoroughly, then add rice and vanilla.

Turn mixture into oiled, 1½-quart casserole and bake in preheated oven for 2 hours. Stir mixture occasionally. Serve warm or cold.

Yield: 5-6 servings.

# Puddings

## Soy Milk Custard

Preheat oven to 350°F.
2 eggs
1/4 cup skim milk powder
2 tablespoons soy powder or soy flour
1/8 teaspoon salt
2 cups warm water
2 tablespoons honey
1 teaspoon pure vanilla extract

Beat eggs until frothy.

**2**

Mix skim milk powder, soy powder or flour, and salt. Make a paste of them by adding some of the water gradually.

**3**

Dissolve honey in rest of warm water. Add this to dry paste gradually, stirring until it is smooth.

**4!**

Stir in beaten eggs. Mix thoroughly. Add vanilla.

**5**

Pour into ungreased casserole. Set casserole into a pan with warm water and place in oven. (This is to insure slow cooking so that the custard won't overcook and separate.) Bake for 30-45 minutes or until knife inserted in custard comes out clean.

BLENDER METHOD
Instead of steps 1, 2, 3, and 4, simply put all ingredients into blender and blend until thoroughly mixed. Then continue with step 5.

Yield: 4 servings.

# Wheat–Soy Dessert

Preheat oven to 450°F.
¾ cup skim milk powder
½ cup whole wheat flour
2 cups water
dash of salt
¼ cup raisins
2 tablespoons soy flour, sifted
1 tablespoon honey
1 egg yolk
1 egg white
2 tablespoons honey
1 tablespoon sesame seeds

Combine skim milk powder, whole wheat flour and water with a wire whisk. Put in saucepan; bring to boil; add salt. Cook over low heat, stirring constantly until mixture is thickened.

Remove from heat and stir in combined raisins and soy flour. Cook for 10 more minutes. Add 1 tablespoon honey.

**3**

Beat egg yolk; add some of the hot mixture to it; then return it to the saucepan. Beat the egg white until stiff and fold it into the hot mixture.

**4!**

Turn hot mixture into an 8-inch round casserole; drizzle 2 more tablespoons of honey over the top of the pudding, sprinkle with sesame seeds, and bake for about 25 minutes in preheated oven.

Yield: 4 servings.

*Pies*

## Pie Crust

Preheat oven to 400°F.
1 cup barley flour
½ cup oat flour
½ teaspoon salt
⅓ cup oil
4 tablespoons ice water

Prepare one 9-inch pie pan by brushing bottom and sides lightly with oil.

Sift dry ingredients into bowl.

Mix oil and ice water.

Add liquid to dry ingredients using fork. Stir until a ball is formed.

**5**

Press into prepared pie pan, or roll out between wax paper and place in pie pan, making a high edge around the outside. Prick with fork, and bake in preheated oven for 10-12 minutes.

Note: This crust can be made with whole wheat flour: simply use 1½ cups whole wheat instead of the combination of barley and oat.

Yield: one 9-inch pie shell.

# Coconut Pie Shell

Preheat oven to 325°F.
1 cup coconut shreds, unsweetened
½ cup wheat germ
2 tablespoons oil
2 tablespoons honey

Prepare one 9-inch pie pan by brushing
bottom and sides lightly with oil.

Combine ingredients and mix together. Press
into prepared pie pan, building up a
high edge around the outside, and bake
on middle shelf of preheated oven, 5 to 8
minutes or until lightly browned.

Remove from oven and cool. Fill with your
favorite filling for a crumb crust.

Yield: one 9-inch pie shell.

# Sunflower-Seed Meal – Coconut Pie Crust

Preheat oven to 325°F.
1 cup coconut shreds (unsweetened)
½ cup sunflower-seed meal
2 tablespoons wheat germ
⅓ teaspoon salt
¼ teaspoon cinnamon
⅓ cup oil
1 tablespoon honey

Mix first five ingredients thoroughly.

Add oil and honey; mix well.

Oil 9-inch pie pan lightly, press crumbs into
pan building up a high edge around outside.
Bake in preheated oven for 12 minutes
or until lightly browned.

Yield: one 9-inch pie shell.

# Carrot Chiffon Pie

1 9-inch, baked pie shell (see recipes in
        this section)
3 teaspoons unflavored gelatin
⅓ cup cold water
½ cup skim milk powder
½ cup cold water
1¼ cups cooked carrots, puréed or strained
¼ cup honey
½ teaspoon ginger
½ teaspoon nutmeg
½ teaspoon cinnamon
¼ teaspoon mace
3 egg yolks, slightly-beaten
½ teaspoon pure vanilla extract
3 egg whites
½ teaspoon salt.

Dissolve gelatin in cold water. Set aside.

Combine skim milk powder with water, using
a wire whisk. In top of double boiler,
combine carrots, honey, milk mixture,
spices and slightly-beaten egg yolks. Place
over hot water and cook until mixture
thickens, stirring occasionally. Add softened
gelatin to the hot mixture and stir until
dissolved.

Remove from heat and add vanilla extract;
cool.

![4!]

In medium-sized mixing bowl, combine egg
whites and salt and beat until stiff peaks
form when beater is raised.

![5]

When mixture begins to thicken, fold in
stiffly-beaten egg whites. Turn into baked pie
shell and chill.

Yield: one 9-inch pie.

# Cinnamon Apple Tart

Preheat oven to 400°F.
1 9-inch, unbaked pie shell (barley-oat or
        whole-wheat crust—see recipes in
        this section)
7 large cooking apples
2 tablespoons cornstarch
¼ cup honey
½ teaspoon cinnamon

Pare, halve and core apples; slice 6 halves
into prepared shell, making an even layer.

**2**

Mix cornstarch, honey and cinnamon, drizzle
half over sliced apples; arrange remaining
apple halves cut side down, in single layer
on top of sliced apples; drizzle remaining
honey mixture over top.

**3**

Bake in preheated oven for 10 minutes.
Reduce heat to 375°F., bake another 35
minutes or until apples are tender but
still hold their shape. (Syrupy juices will
thicken as pie cools.)

**4!**

Remove from oven. With a fork, press apple
halves down into juices. Serve warm or
cold.

Yield: one 9-inch pie.

## Cherry Tart

1 9-inch baked pie shell (barley-oat or
   whole wheat crust—see recipes in
   this section)
3 cups pitted sour cherries, drained
$\frac{1}{3}$ cup cherry juice
$\frac{3}{4}$ cup honey
3 tablespoons cornstarch
$\frac{1}{2}$ teaspoon cinnamon
2 teaspoons tapioca granules

Combine cherries, cherry juice, honey,
cornstarch, cinnamon and tapioca in
heavy-bottom saucepan. Bring to a boil,
stirring constantly.

**2**

Simmer slowly for about 5 minutes until
tapioca is clear and mixture has thickened.

**3**

Cool and spoon into baked pie shell. Serve
chilled or at room temperature.

Yield: one 9-inch pie.

## Coconut Custard Pie

Preheat oven to 450°F.
1 9-inch, unbaked pie shell (barley-oat or
   whole wheat crust—see recipes in
   this section)
$\frac{1}{2}$ cup skim milk powder
1 cup water
2 eggs, lightly-beaten
2 tablespoons honey
$\frac{1}{4}$ teaspoon salt
$\frac{1}{4}$ teaspoon pure vanilla extract
$1\frac{1}{2}$ cups unsweetened coconut

With wire whisk combine skim milk powder
and water. Add eggs, honey, salt and
vanilla.

Combine custard mixture with coconut. Pour
into pie shell.

Bake 10 minutes in preheated oven, then
reduce heat to 300°F. and bake until firm
when tested with a silver knife (about 30
minutes).

Yield: one 9-inch pie.

# Dried Fruit Custard Pie

Preheat oven to 450°F.
1 9-inch, unbaked pie shell (barley-oat or whole-wheat crust—see recipes in this section)
2 eggs
2 tablespoons honey
1/4 teaspoon salt
1/2 cup skim milk powder
1 cup water
1/4 teaspoon pure vanilla extract
1 1/2 cups dried fruit, soaked in water to cover for 30 minutes.

With wire whisk, beat eggs lightly and add honey, salt, skim milk powder, water and vanilla.

**2**

Lay drained, dried fruit in pie shell. Strain custard mixture over the fruit.

**3**

Bake 10 minutes in preheated oven, then reduce heat to 300°F., and bake until firm when tested with a silver knife (about 30 minutes).

Yield: one 9-inch pie.

# Lemon Chiffon Pie

1 9-inch baked pie shell (see recipes in this section)
4 egg yolks
1/2 cup honey
1 tablespoon unflavored gelatin
1/3 cup lemon juice
2/3 cup cold water
1 tablespoon grated lemon rind
4 egg whites
1/4 teaspoon salt
1/3 cup toasted unsweetened coconut (optional)

In saucepan, blend egg yolks, honey, gelatin, lemon juice and water.

**2**

Cook over medium heat, stirring constantly, just until mixture comes to a boil. Remove from heat and stir in lemon rind.

**3**

Place pan in bowl of ice and water or chill in refrigerator, stirring occasionally, until gelatin mixture is thick and mounds when dropped from a spoon.

please turn page

Beat egg whites and salt with electric beater, set at high speed, until stiff peaks form. Fold about one-half cup of beaten whites into gelatin mixture. Using an under-and-over motion, gently fold gelatin mixture into beaten whites, just until combined.

**5**

Turn mixture into pie shell; refrigerate several hours, or until firm. Sprinkle with toasted coconut before serving.

Yield: one 9-inch pie.

## Orange Chiffon Pie

1 9-inch, baked pie shell (see recipes in this section)
4 egg yolks
$\frac{1}{3}$ cup honey
$\frac{7}{8}$ cup orange juice
1 tablespoon unflavored gelatin
$1\frac{1}{2}$ tablespoons grated orange rind
4 egg whites, at room temperature
$\frac{1}{4}$ teaspoon salt
$\frac{1}{3}$ cup toasted, unsweetened coconut

In top of double boiler, combine egg yolks and honey. Mix together thoroughly. Stir in orange juice. Sprinkle unflavored gelatin over the top and allow to stand one or two minutes to soften. Stir mixture.

**2**

Place double boiler top over boiling water. Cook, stirring constantly with a wooden spoon, until mixture thickens—about 8 to 10 minutes. (Water in bottom section of double boiler should not touch base of top of double boiler.)

**3**

Remove from hot water. Stir in grated orange rind. Set double boiler top in a bowl of ice cubes to which a little cold water has been added. Stir occasionally until mixture is thick and mounds when dropped from a spoon. (If desired, the gelatin mixture may be placed in the refrigerator to thicken, stirring gelatin mixture occasionally.)

**4!**

Meanwhile, combine egg whites and salt in large bowl of electric mixer. Beat at high speed until stiff peaks form when beater is raised. Spoon about one-fourth of the beaten whites into the gelatin mixture blending thoroughly. Using an under-and-over motion, with a rubber spatula, gently fold gelatin mixture into remaining beaten whites, just until blended.

**5**

Turn mixture into pie shell. Place in refrigerator several hours or overnight before serving.

Just before serving, sprinkle toasted coconut over filling.

Yield: one 9-inch pie.

# Pies

## Lemon Meringue Pie

Preheat oven to 425°F.
1 9-inch baked pie shell (barley-oat or
    whole-wheat crust—see recipes in
    this section)
6 tablespoons cornstarch
$\frac{1}{2}$ teaspoon salt
$\frac{3}{4}$ cup honey
$1\frac{1}{2}$ cups boiling water
$1\frac{1}{2}$ teaspoons freshly-grated lemon rind
$\frac{1}{3}$ cup lemon juice
4 egg yolks, slightly-beaten
4 egg whites
2 tablespoons honey (softened by placing
    container in bowl of hot water)
$\frac{1}{2}$ teaspoon pure vanilla extract

Mix cornstarch, salt and honey in top of
double boiler. Add boiling water and cook
over direct heat until the mixture boils,
stirring constantly. Set over hot water,
cover, and cook 20 minutes.

Add lemon rind, lemon juice and beaten egg
yolks. Cook until thick, stirring constantly
(about 10 minutes). Cool.

Beat egg whites until soft peaks form when
beater is raised. Gradually beat in honey and
vanilla.

Pile lemon filling into pie shell and top with
meringue. Bake 5 minutes in preheated
oven.

Yield: one 9-inch pie.

see color photograph

# Pineapple Chiffon Pie

1 9-inch, baked pie shell (see recipes in
    this section)
4 egg yolks
½ cup honey
1 tablespoon unflavored gelatin
¼ cup lemon juice
¾ cup pineapple juice (from can of drained,
    unsweetened, crushed pineapple)
2 teaspoons grated lemon rind
1 cup unsweetened, crushed pineapple,
    drained
½ cup yogurt (beaten   th whisk to
    remove lumps)
4 egg whites
¼ teaspoon salt
⅓ cup coconut, toasted

In saucepan, blend yolks, honey, gelatin,
lemon juice and pineapple juice.

**2**

Cook over medium heat, stirring constantly
just until mixture comes to a boil. Remove
from heat. Stir in lemon rind and drained
pineapple.

**3**

Place pan in bowl of ice and water or chill
in refrigerator, stirring occasionally, until
gelatin mixture is thick and mounds when
dropped from a spoon.

**4**

Fold smooth yogurt into gelatin mixture
carefully and refrigerate again until the
mixture sets as before.

**5**

Beat egg whites and salt with electric beater,
set at high speed, until stiff peaks form.
Fold about one-half cup of beaten whites
into gelatin mixture. Using an under-and-over
motion, gently fold gelatin mixture into
beaten whites, just until combined.

**6**

Turn mixture into pie shell. Refrigerate
several hours until firm. Sprinkle with toasted
coconut before serving.
Yield: one 9-inch pie.

## Pumpkin Chiffon Pie

1 9-inch, baked pie shell (see recipes in
     this section)
1/4 cup skim milk powder
1/2 cup water
3 egg yolks
6 tablespoons honey
2 tablespoons molasses
1 1/2 cups pumpkin purée (see method of
     cooking pumpkin in vegetable
     section)
1/2 teaspoon salt
1 teaspoon cinnamon
1/2 teaspoon ginger
1/2 teaspoon mace
3 teaspoons unflavored gelatin
1/2 cup cold water
3 stiffly-beaten egg whites
chopped walnuts to garnish

Mix skim milk powder with water, using wire
whisk. Set aside.

Beat egg yolks until thick and lemon-colored;
add honey, molasses, pumpkin purée,
milk mixture, salt and spices. Cook in
double boiler until thick, stirring constantly.

**3**

Soften gelatin in cold water, then stir into hot
mixture. Chill until partially set.

**4**

Beat egg whites until stiff. Fold into gelatin
mixture. Pour into baked 9-inch pie shell.

**5**

Chill until set. Sprinkle with chopped walnut
meats.

Yield: one 9-inch pie.

# Pumpkin Pie

Preheat oven to 450°F.
1 9-inch, unbaked pie shell (barley-oat or
　　whole-wheat crust—see recipes in
　　this section)
½ teaspoon salt
½ teaspoon ginger
1 teaspoon cinnamon
1½ cups pumpkin purée (see method of
　　cooking pumpkin in vegetable
　　section)
½ cup skim milk powder
1¼ cups water
3 eggs, beaten
¼ cup honey
1 tablespoon molasses
1 teaspoon pure vanilla

Add seasonings to pumpkin.

Combine skim milk powder with water, using
a wire whisk.

Add milk mixture to beaten eggs. Stir in
pumpkin and seasonings, honey, molasses and
vanilla.

![4]

Place filling in unbaked 9-inch pie shell and
bake 10 minutes in preheated oven, then
turn back heat to 350°F. and bake 30
minutes longer.

Yield: one 9-inch pie.

# Pies

## Raisin Pie

Preheat oven to 375°F.
1 9-inch, unbaked pie shell (barley-oat or
      whole wheat crust—see recipes in
      this section)
1 cup raisins
1 cup water
1 egg, beaten
¼-½ cup honey
3 tablespoons lemon juice
1 teaspoon grated lemon rind
pinch of salt
2 tablespoons cornstarch
½ cup cold water

Soak raisins in water until soft and plump.

In a medium-sized saucepan, mix egg and
honey. Add soaked raisins, lemon juice,
rind and salt.

Cook over medium heat, adding cornstarch
dissolved in water. Continue cooking until
cornstarch is cooked and raisin filling
is thickened. Cool. Fill pie shell.

Bake in a preheated oven for ½ hour. Cool.
Yield: one 9-inch pie.

## Soybean Pie

Preheat oven to 400°F.
1 9-inch, unbaked pie shell (barley-oat or
      whole wheat crust—see recipes in
      this section)
3 whole eggs
¾ cup honey
2 teaspoons pure vanilla extract
½ teaspoon salt
1 tablespoon oil
2 tablespoons whole wheat flour
1 cup roasted soybeans, chopped (see
      recipe in soybean section)

Beat eggs in medium-sized bowl; add honey.
Combine thoroughly, then add vanilla,
oil, salt and flour. Mix thoroughly.

Pour mixture into unbaked pie shell and
sprinkle chopped soybeans over filling. Bake
10 minutes in preheated oven, then reduce
heat to 350°F., and bake until knife
comes clean when inserted in pie (about 45
minutes). Serve hot or cold.

Yield: one 9-inch pie.

# Strawberry Pie

1 9-inch, baked pie shell (see recipes in this section)
2 pints fresh strawberries, washed and drained
½ cup honey
1½ teaspoons lemon juice
1 tablespoon unflavored gelatin
3 tablespoons cold water

**1**

In electric blender, purée one pint strawberries. Stir in honey and lemon juice; set aside.

**2**

Combine gelatin with 3 tablespoons cold water in a small bowl. Place bowl over boiling water and stir until gelatin is dissolved.

**3**

Add dissolved gelatin to puréed strawberry mixture and combine thoroughly. Place in refrigerator and chill until mixture consistency is slightly thicker than unbeaten egg white.

**4!**

Spoon one-half of the strawberry mixture into baked pie shell. Arrange remaining pint of washed and well-drained strawberries over strawberry purée; spoon remaining strawberry purée mixture over strawberries. Chill until set before serving.

**5**

Serve plain or with whipped topping (see recipe in this section).

Yield: one 9-inch pie.

# *Confections*

## Buying and Preparing a Fresh Coconut

Preheat oven to 400°F.

Before purchasing a coconut, shake it to make sure it is full of liquid (coconuts without liquid or those with moldy or wet "eyes" are likely to be spoiled).

To open the coconut: With ice pick, puncture two of the three dark eyes of the coconut by hammering the tip of the ice pick through them. Drain all the coconut liquid into a measuring cup.

Bake the empty coconut in preheated oven for 15 minutes; transfer to a chopping board. While the coconut is still hot, split the shell with a sharp blow of a hammer. The shell should fall away from the piece of meat. If bits of meat still cling to the shell, cut them away with a paring knife.

To grate coconut: Pare off the brown outer-skin of the coconut meat with a potato or vegetable peeler—or small sharp knife. Grate the coconut meat, one piece at a time, with a hand grater.

## Apricot Chews

½ lb. dried apricots, soaked in water to cover for 30 minutes
½ lb. pitted dates
¼ cup honey
1½ cups unsweetened coconut shreds

Force dried fruits through a food chopper or grinder, using a coarse blade.

Gradually blend honey into ground fruit mixture. Add coconut shreds and mix thoroughly.

Press mixture into a lightly-oiled, 9-inch square pan. Place in refrigerator to chill, about one hour.

Remove from refrigerator and cut into bars or squares and serve.

Yield: approximately 1¼ lbs.

# Carob Confection

½ cup carob powder, sifted
½ cup honey
½ cup peanut butter
½ cup sunflower seeds
½ cup sesame seeds
¼ cup wheat germ
¼ cup soy flour, sifted
1-2 tablespoons water (until the mixture
        is the right consistency to roll nicely)
unsweetened, shredded coconut for coating,
        or finely-chopped roasted peanuts*

Heat carob powder and honey in the top of a
double boiler, stirring occasionally, for
about 10 minutes to take away the raw taste
of the carob.

Add rest of ingredients except coconut or
chopped peanuts. Mix well, form into balls
and roll balls in coconut or peanuts.

*Note: Roast raw peanuts on a paper-towel-
  lined cookie sheet for 30 minutes in a
  250°F. oven.

Yield: about 40 balls.

# Fudgies

⅓ cup skim milk powder
½ cup soy flour or soy powder, sifted
⅓ cup carob, sifted
¼ cup oil
⅓ cup honey
2 tablespoons hot water
½ cup chopped peanuts
1 teaspoon vanilla
⅔ cup chopped peanuts

In a medium-sized bowl, combine skim milk
powder, soy flour or powder and carob.

Add oil and honey. Stir in the hot water,
then the peanuts and vanilla.

Form into balls the size of an English walnut
and roll balls in chopped peanuts. Store
in airtight container in the refrigerator.

Yield: 2 dozen balls.

# *Confections*

## Peanut Butter Sesame Balls

¾ cup peanut butter
½ cup honey
1 teaspoon pure vanilla extract
¾ cup skim milk powder
1 cup oatmeal
¼ cup toasted sesame seeds*
2 tablespoons boiling water
chopped nuts or toasted sesame seeds for
       coating balls

In a medium-sized bowl, combine peanut butter, honey, and vanilla extract; blend thoroughly.

**2**

Mix skim milk powder and oatmeal together. Gradually add to the peanut butter-honey mixture, blending thoroughly, using hands if necessary to mix as dough begins to stiffen. Blend in the toasted sesame seeds.

Add two tablespoons boiling water to mixture, blending well.

**4!**

Shape in one-inch balls. Roll in finely-chopped nuts or toasted sesame seeds. For variety, roll half the mixture in chopped nuts and the other half in toasted sesame seeds.

*Toast sesame seeds in a preheated 200°F. oven for about 20 minutes or until lightly-browned.

Yield: approximately 3 dozen balls.

# Tutti-Frutti
# (A Dried Fruit Confection)

½ lb. prunes
½ lb. dried figs
1 lb. pitted dates
1 lb. seeded raisins
½ lb. dried apricots (soaked in water to
    cover for 30 minutes)
2 cups walnut meats
½ cup sunflower seeds
unsweetened coconut shreds

**1**

Pit prunes; set aside. Remove stems from figs.

**2**

Force the dried fruits through a food chopper
or grinder, using a coarse blade. If the
dried fruit is alternated with the nuts as
it goes into the grinder or chopper, it will
require less mixing. Add small amounts of
nutmeats and sunflower seeds along with
mixed fruits. (This method will prevent
fruit from becoming too sticky.) Mix
together.

**3**

Place mixture in a covered jar and store in
the refrigerator until ready to use. This
fruit mixture will keep for several months
if refrigerated.

**4**

When ready to serve, form mixture into
one-inch balls and roll in dry, shredded,
unsweetened coconut; or, press mixture into
an oiled, nine-inch square pan and sprinkle
shredded coconut over top. Chill—for
easier handling—before cutting into one-inch
squares.

Note: This fruit mixture may be used as a
filling for apples or pears before baking,
or thinned with fruit juice or water and
used as a sauce over puddings, custards, etc.
It may be heated, if desired.

Yield: one quart or more.

## Cookies

## Sunflower-Sesame Treats

¾ cup sunflower seed meal
¼ cup tahini (ground sesame seed)
½ cup unsweetened coconut shreds
¼ cup honey
⅓ cup toasted wheat germ
1 cup finely-chopped dates or raisins

In medium-sized bowl, combine ingredients in order given. Mix together thoroughly.

Separate mixture into two portions. Place each portion on a separate piece of wax paper. Form into rolls. Wrap securely in wax paper and store in refrigerator.

When sufficiently chilled, remove from refrigerator; unwrap roll and cut into one-half inch pieces. Serve as snack or accompany with fresh fruit after a hearty meal.

Yield: two 4-inch rolls.

## Almond Meringues

Preheat oven to 425°F.
2 cups unblanched almonds
¾ cup honey
2 egg whites
1 teaspoon pure vanilla extract
⅔ cup unsweetened, shredded coconut

Pulverize almonds in blender, ½ cup at a time. Sift to remove any large pieces.

Gradually blend honey into ground almonds.

In electric mixing bowl, beat egg whites, at high speed, until stiff peaks form. Slowly beat in the almond mixture until thoroughly combined. Add vanilla extract.

**4!**

Using a teaspoon, shape mixture into one-inch balls; (if too thin, add more ground almonds to the mixture) roll, in shredded coconut, and arrange two-inches apart on an oiled cookie sheet. Flatten with a damp spatula.

**5**

Bake in preheated oven for about 10 to 12 minutes or until golden. Remove cookies from pan and place on wire rack to cool.

Yield: about 2 dozen cookies.

# Brazil Nut Cookies

Preheat oven to 400°F.
1 cup potato starch
$\frac{1}{2}$ cup soy flour, sifted
$\frac{1}{2}$ cup brown rice flour
$\frac{1}{2}$ teaspoon salt
$\frac{1}{2}$ cup skim milk powder
1 cup oil
10 tablespoons honey
2 eggs, slightly-beaten
1 teaspoon pure vanilla extract
$1\frac{1}{2}$ cups ground or finely-chopped Brazil
        nuts

**1**

Sift potato starch, flours, salt and skim milk powder together.

**2**

In large mixing bowl, combine oil, honey, slightly beaten eggs, and vanilla extract. Using electric beater, set at medium speed, beat mixture until ingredients are thoroughly blended.

please turn page

# Cookies

Gradually beat in sifted flours and powdered skim milk. Stir in Brazil nuts. Refrigerate dough for one to two hours.

**4!**

Take rounded teaspoonfuls of cookie dough and roll into one-inch balls. Place two inches apart on oiled cookie sheet; flatten with a glass. Bake in a preheated oven for 8 to 10 minutes or until golden brown around the edges. Remove from oven and place cookies on a wire rack to cool.

Yield: about 5 dozen.

## Cream Puffs

Preheat oven to 400°F.
2 tablespoons cornstarch
$\frac{1}{2}$ cup rye flour
$\frac{1}{2}$ cup oil
1 cup cold water
$\frac{1}{2}$ teaspoon salt
4 eggs

Mix cornstarch into rye flour until they are well blended.

Combine oil, cold water and salt in medium-sized saucepan. Place over medium heat and bring mixture to boil.

Remove saucepan from heat; reduce temperature to low. Add cornstarch-rye flour mixture all at once, beating with wooden spoon constantly until all of it is incorporated into oil-water mixture. Return saucepan to low heat and continue to beat until mixture forms a ball and leaves the sides of pan (about one minute).

**4!**

Remove from heat. Pour mixture into a mixing bowl and cool slightly.

**5**

Add eggs, one at a time, beating well (with electric beater) after each addition. Continue to beat until mixture becomes smooth and glossy.

**6**

Drop by rounded tablespoons, two inches apart, onto ungreased cookie sheet.

**7**

Bake in a preheated oven for 30 to 35 minutes until puffed and golden brown. Turn oven off and allow cream puffs to remain in oven for ten minutes longer. Remove from oven and transfer onto wire rack, away from drafts, to cool completely before filling.

**8**

To serve: With sharp knife, cut off tops of cream puffs crosswise; remove any soft dough. Fill with custard filling (see recipe in dessert section) and replace tops.

Yield: approximately 14-16 puffs.

# Cookies

## Butterscotch Brownies

Preheat oven to 350°F.
2 eggs, beaten
2 tablespoons oil
1 tablespoon molasses
2/3 cup honey
2 teaspoons pure vanilla extract
2/3 cup peanut flour (raw peanuts
      finely-ground either in a blender or
      electric nut grinder)
1/2 cup skim milk powder
1/4 teaspoon salt
3 tablespoons oat flour
1/2 cup walnuts, chopped

Oil a 9 x 9 x 2-inch pan.

**2**

Beat eggs in medium-sized bowl until light.
Add oil, molasses, honey, and vanilla and
combine.

**3**

In another bowl, combine peanut flour,
skim milk powder, salt, oat flour and walnuts.
Stir wet ingredients into dry ones.

**4**

Spread batter evenly in prepared pan. Bake
in preheated oven 30 minutes or just until
surface is firm to the touch.

**5**

Remove from oven and cool before serving.

Yield: 16 squares.

# Carob Brownies

Preheat oven to 325°F.
1 cup carob powder, sifted
1 cup oil
⅔ cup honey
4 eggs
1 cup peanut flour (peanuts ground fine
either in blender or electric nut
grinder)
5 tablespoons rye flour
1 cup walnuts, chopped
2 teaspoons pure vanilla

**1**

Oil a 9 by 9 by 2-inch pan.

**2**

In a small bowl, combine carob powder, oil and honey.

**3**

In large mixing bowl, beat eggs until light. Beat into carob mixture.

**4**

Stir in peanut flour, rye flour and mix well. Add nuts and vanilla.

**5**

Spread batter evenly in the prepared pan. Bake in preheated oven 30 minutes or just until surface is firm to the touch.

**6**

Remove from oven and cool about ten minutes. Cut into squares.

Yield: 16 squares.

# *Cookies*

## Carob Date-Nut Squares

Preheat oven to 325°F.
½ cup oat flour
½ cup brown rice flour
¼ teaspoon salt
1 cup dates, chopped
¾ cup nuts, chopped
¼ cup wheat germ
½ cup carob powder, sifted
½ cup oil
⅓ cup honey
2 eggs, beaten
1 teaspoon pure vanilla extract

Oil the bottom of an 8 x 8-inch pan.

Sift together oat and brown rice flours, and salt; set aside.

Combine dates, nuts and wheat germ; toss slightly.

**4!**

In medium-sized bowl, combine carob powder and oil. Gradually blend in the honey. Add beaten eggs and mix thoroughly.

**5**

Add sifted flour and blend well. Stir in date mixture. Add vanilla extract.

**6**

Pour batter into prepared pan and bake in preheated oven for 25 minutes.

Yield: 16 squares.

# Carob Nut Cookies

Preheat oven to 350°F.
1⅓ cups carob
1½ cups oil
1½ cups honey
6 tablespoons hot water
2 eggs, beaten
½ teaspoon salt
1 cup brown rice flour
1¼ cups oat flour
⅔ cup soy flour, sifted
½ cup skim milk powder, sifted
1 cup potato starch
1 cup walnuts, chopped
1 teaspoon vanilla
walnut halves for garnish

Combine carob, oil and honey in medium-sized bowl. Add hot water, eggs, and salt.

In another bowl, combine brown rice flour, oat flour, sifted soy flour, sifted skim milk powder and potato starch. Stir into carob mixture. Add nuts and vanilla.

**3**

Form into balls the size of a walnut, flatten slightly on top, and lay on an ungreased cookie sheet. Place a walnut half on top of each cookie.

**4!**

Bake in preheated oven for 20 minutes. Cool on a rack.

Yield: approximately 8 dozen.

# Cookies

## Dried Fruit Cookies

Preheat oven to 350°F.
1/2 cup oil
1/2 cup honey
2 eggs, slightly-beaten
1 teaspoon pure vanilla extract
1/2 cup soy flour, sifted
1/2 cup oat flour
1/2 cup skim milk powder
1/2 teaspoon salt
1/2 cup chopped dried fruit—dates, figs,
        soaked apricots, raisins (use any one
        or a combination)
1/2 cup wheat germ

Mix oil and honey until well-blended, by beating with a whisk. Add eggs and vanilla and mix well.

Combine and sift soy flour, oat flour, skim milk powder, and salt. Add chopped fruit to flour and mix it, separating fruit. Add wheat germ.

Add flour-fruit mixture to wet mixture and stir until combined.

Drop by teaspoonfuls onto lightly-oiled cookie sheet. Bake in preheated oven for 15 minutes.

Yield: 3 dozen cookies.

# Filled Fruit Bars

Preheat oven to 375°F.
5 dried figs, stem removed and cut in half
¼ cup raisins
½ cup dates, pitted
½ cup dried apricots
water to cover
rind of one lemon
½ teaspoon lemon juice
½ cup oil
⅓ cup honey
2 eggs, beaten
10 tablespoons oatmeal
½ cup rye flour
½ cup soy flour, sifted
½ cup potato starch
½ teaspoon salt

Cook figs, raisins, dates and apricots in water to cover for 15 to 20 minutes, stirring occasionally.

Force fruit through food mill, or use blender to chop fruit.

After fruit is chopped, add rind of 1 lemon and ½ teaspoon lemon juice and mix well. Set aside to cool.

In medium-sized bowl, combine oil and honey, stirring well. Then add eggs and oatmeal. Mix well.

Sift flours, potato starch and salt together and add to egg and oatmeal mixture, mixing until well blended.

Oil 9 x 9-inch baking pan, press half of dough into pan. Bake 10 minutes in preheated oven.

**7**

Remove from oven; cool slightly.

**8**

Cover baked cookie dough with filling, spreading evenly over entire layer. Spread remainder of dough over top of filling. Bake in preheated oven for another 20 minutes. Cool and cut into squares.
Yield: 16 squares.

# *Cookies*

## Peanut Butter Cookies

Preheat oven to 325°F.
½ cup oil
1 cup honey
¾ cup peanut butter
2 eggs, beaten
6 tablespoons skim milk powder
½ teaspoon salt
1 teaspoon cinnamon
½ teaspoon mace
¼ teaspoon cloves
½ cup oatmeal
½ cup raisins
¾ cup whole wheat flour

In the large bowl of an electric mixer, blend oil and honey until creamy and light. Add peanut butter and continue to beat until mixture is blended.

Beat in eggs, milk powder, salt and spices.

**3**

With a wooden spoon, stir in oatmeal, raisins and whole wheat flour. Blend thoroughly.

**4!**

Drop by teaspoonfuls on an unoiled cookie sheet. Bake in preheated oven for 12 minutes.

Yield: about 50 cookies.

# Soy-Peanut Butter Cookies

Preheat oven to 350°F.
½ cup oil
½ cup honey
¼ cup molasses
2 eggs, slightly-beaten
½ cup peanut butter
1 teaspoon pure vanilla extract
½ cup soy flour, sifted
½ cup oat flour
¾ cup skim milk powder
½ teaspoon salt
¾ cup chopped, roasted peanuts* (optional)

Mix oil, honey and molasses. Add slightly-beaten eggs. Mix well.

Add peanut butter, blending well. Then add vanilla.

**3**

Sift soy flour, oat flour, skim milk powder and salt. Add dry ingredients to wet ones. Add chopped peanuts, if desired.

**4!**

Drop by teaspoonfuls onto lightly-oiled cookie sheet. Bake in preheated oven for 15 minutes.

*Note: Roast raw peanuts on a paper-towel-lined cookie sheet for 30 minutes in a 250°F. oven.

Yield: 3 dozen cookies.

# *Cookies*

## Wheat Germ and Oatmeal Cookies

Preheat oven to 350°F.
¾ cup oil
1 cup honey
2 tablespoons molasses
2 eggs
2 teaspoons pure vanilla
¾ cup soy flour, sifted
½ cup skim milk powder, sifted
½ cup raisins or dates, pitted and chopped
½ cup walnuts, chopped
1 teaspoon salt
1½ cups wheat germ
2 cups oatmeal

Combine oil, honey and molasses. Add one egg at a time, beating after each addition. Add vanilla.

Combine soy flour and milk powder. Add raisins (or dates), walnuts, salt, wheat germ and oatmeal.

Stir wet ingredients into dry ingredients and blend well.

**4!**

Drop by teaspoons onto lightly-oiled cookie sheet. Bake in preheated oven for 10 minutes.

Yield: approximately 6 dozen.

# *Cakes*

## Brazil Nut Torte

Preheat oven to 350°F.
6 egg yolks
¼ teaspoon salt
6 tablespoons honey
2 cups ground Brazil nuts (ground in
     electric blender, ½ cup at a time)
2 teaspoons pure vanilla extract
6 egg whites

Have eggs at room temperature.

**2**

Oil bottom of spring form pan. Line bottom of pan with parchment or brown paper, cut to fit. Do not oil paper.

**3**

Beat egg yolks until thick and lemon-colored. Add salt and honey, pouring in slowly and stirring to blend.

**4!**

Add ground Brazil nuts to egg mixture, adding about ¼ cup at a time, beating well after each addition. Add vanilla extract.

Beat egg whites until stiff peaks are formed.

**6**

Add about ¼ of beaten egg whites to yolk mixture, folding in lightly.

**7**

Now add above mixture to remaining beaten whites, folding in with an under and over motion, until well blended.

**8**

Pour into pan, place in preheated oven and bake 10 minutes. Reduce heat to 300°F. and continue baking for 40 minutes, or until surface springs back when gently touched with fingertips.

**9**

Remove from oven, cool in pan, on wire rack about one hour. Using spatula, carefully loosen torte and remove side of spring form pan. Then remove bottom of pan and paper. Cool completely before serving.
Yield: 10 servings.

# *Cakes*

## Carob-Almond Cake

Preheat oven to 325°F.
$\frac{2}{3}$ cup carob powder, sifted
$\frac{1}{2}$ cup boiling water
6 tablespoons honey
$\frac{1}{3}$ cup oil
1 teaspoon pure vanilla extract
6 egg yolks
$1\frac{1}{3}$ cups ground almonds (other ground
        nuts may be substituted or use half
        ground almonds and half soy grits*)
        almonds may be ground in electric
        blender $\frac{1}{2}$ cup at a time
$\frac{1}{4}$ cup potato starch
6 egg whites
$\frac{1}{4}$ teaspoon salt

Prepare one nine-inch square pan by lightly
oiling the bottom, then lining the pan with
parchment or brown paper and oiling
it lightly.

Let egg whites warm at room temperature
about an hour.

Combine carob powder and boiling water in
small bowl, stirring until smooth. Cool.

**4!**

Combine honey, oil and vanilla in mixing
bowl. Beat egg yolks until thick and
lemon-colored. Add to honey-oil mixture.
Blend in carob mixture and beat just until
smooth.

**5**

Combine ground nuts and potato starch. Add
to batter.

**6**

Beat egg whites and salt until soft peaks
form. With rubber scraper or wire whisk,
using an under-and-over motion, gently fold
batter into beaten whites until just blended.

Pour batter into prepared pan; bake on
middle rack of preheated oven for 45 to 50
minutes, or until toothpick inserted in
center comes out clean.

**8**

Remove cake from oven and allow to cool for
15 minutes. With spatula, carefully loosen
cake from pan, invert on wire rack,
remove paper and cool thoroughly before
serving. Serve plain or frost as desired.

*Note: This is an extra nutritious variation
and one which results in an even moister
cake and a less expensive one. Simply
simmer $\frac{1}{3}$ cup soy grits in $\frac{1}{3}$ cup water for
8 minutes. Then drain on a paper towel.
(The raw soy grits double their volume
after cooking, so you will have $\frac{2}{3}$ cup.)
Combine with $\frac{2}{3}$ cup ground almonds and
add to potato starch, then to batter, as
in step 5.

Yield: 10-12 servings.

# Cheese Cake, Fitness House Style

Preheat oven to 300°F.

*CRUST:*
1 cup wheat germ
1 tablespoon honey
4 tablespoons oil
$\frac{1}{2}$ teaspoon cinnamon

Combine ingredients and pat into spring-form
pan, covering bottom of pan and bringing
up sides about $1\frac{1}{2}$ inches.

*FILLING:*

$\frac{1}{4}$ cup cornstarch
1 cup yogurt
1 lb. cottage cheese
rind of one lemon, grated
1 tablespoon lemon juice
$\frac{1}{4}$ teaspoon salt
$\frac{1}{2}$ cup honey
2 teaspoons pure vanilla extract
4 egg yolks
4 egg whites

please turn page

# Cakes

**1**

Using a blender, blend cornstarch and yogurt until cornstarch is dissolved.

**2**

Then add cottage cheese and blend until smooth.

**3**

Add lemon rind, juice, salt, honey, vanilla. Blend to combine.

**4!**

Beat egg yolks in mixing bowl until thick and lemon-colored. Add to cheese mixture and mix well.

**5**

Beat egg whites until stiff but not dry. Fold into cheese mixture and pour into prepared pan. Bake in preheated oven for 50 minutes, or until center is firm. Turn off heat and, with oven door closed, let cake cool in oven for 1 hour or more.

**6**

When cake is cool, loosen sides of spring-form pan, and remove from cake. Refrigerate cake for a few hours or overnight. When cake is cold, lift it off pan bottom onto serving plate.

Note: Cheesecake may be topped with fruit or berry glaze (see recipe in this section).

Yield: 12 servings.

# Date Torte

Preheat oven to 325°F.
4 egg yolks
½ cup honey
1 cup walnuts, chopped fine
1 tablespoon lemon juice
¼ cup coconut shreds
1 teaspoon grated lemon rind
½ cup brown rice flour
¼ teaspoon salt
1 cup dates, chopped
4 egg whites

Prepare a nine-inch-square pan by oiling
bottom of pan with pastry brush. Cut a piece
of parchment paper or heavy brown
paper to fit bottom of pan; brush with oil
and set to one side.

Beat egg yolks until thick and lemon-colored.
Gradually add honey, beating at low speed.

Stir in chopped nuts and lemon juice. Add
coconut and lemon rind.

Measure and sift brown rice flour and salt.
Add chopped dates to flour mixture and
mix until each piece is separate and coated
with flour. Sitr into egg-yolk mixture.

Beat egg whites until stiff peaks form when
beater is raised.

Fold egg-yolk mixture into beaten egg whites,
using an over-and-under motion, until
well-combined.

Pour the batter into the prepared pan,
spreading evenly to edges. Bake in preheated
oven for 25 minutes.

8

Remove from oven and invert pan on wire
rack. Lift pan and remove paper from
cake immediately. Allow to cool before
serving. This cake may be served plain or
with a basic lemon sauce. (See recipe in
this section.)
Yield: 10-12 servings.

# *Cakes*

## No-Bake Fruit Cake

1 lb. dates, pitted
1 lb. dried apricots, soaked in water for 30
      minutes; then drained. (Reserve
      juice for future use.)
1 cup seedless raisins
2 cups pecans or walnuts
1 cup unblanched almonds
2 cups sunflower seeds
1 large orange, washed, cut into eighths and
      seeds removed
1 cup currants
2 cups unsweetened coconut shreds
1 teaspoon cinnamon
3 tablespoons lemon juice
⅓ cup honey
¼ cup sesame seeds, toasted for 20 minutes
      in a 200°F. oven

Force the dried fruits, nuts and orange
sections alternately through a food chopper
or grinder, using a coarse blade. (By
alternating the dried fruits, nuts and orange
sections as they go into the grinder or
food chopper, it will require less mixing
and will also prevent fruit from becoming
too sticky.) Include sunflower seeds with nuts.

**2**

Add currants, coconut shreds, cinnamon and
lemon juice to ground fruit mixture and
mix together thoroughly. Blend in the honey.

**3**

Pack mixture firmly into a nine-inch loaf
pan which has been lightly oiled. Cover with
sesame seeds and refrigerate overnight
to chill thoroughly before serving.

**4!**

Cut into slices and serve.

Note: This fruit cake will keep for three to
four weeks if stored in refrigerator.

Yield: 12 to 14 slices.

# Two-Layer Sponge Cake

Preheat oven to 325°F.
¾ cup potato starch
¼ teaspoon salt
7 egg yolks
¼ cup honey
2 tablespoons lemon juice
2 teaspoons grated lemon rind
½ teaspoon pure vanilla extract
7 egg whites

Ingredients should be at room temperature.

**2**

Prepare two 9-inch layer cake pans by
cutting two circles from heavy brown paper
(or baking parchment paper) to fit bottom
of each pan. Oil pans lightly with pastry
brush and place a circle of paper on the
bottom of each pan. (Do not oil paper.)

Sift potato starch with salt; set aside.

**4**

Beat yolks at medium speed, until light and
lemon-colored. Gradually add honey,
beating until thoroughly dissolved. Add
lemon juice, lemon rind, and vanilla.

**5**

Add sifted potato starch-salt mixture slowly,
blending thoroughly.

**6**

Using high speed on mixer, beat egg whites
until stiff peaks form when beater is
raised slowly.

Fold about one-fourth egg whites into yolk
mixture; then, with an under-and-over
motion, using a rubber spatula, fold the yolk
mixture into the remaining beaten whites.
(Do not overmix, as it will cut down the
lightness of batter.)

please turn page

# *Cakes*

**8**

Pour batter into prepared pans, spreading evenly to edges. Place pans on middle rack of preheated oven and bake for 30 to 35 minutes, or until toothpick inserted in center comes out clean.

**9**

Remove cakes from oven; cool 10 minutes. Loosen sides with a spatula to ease the cake out of the pan. Invert pans onto wire rack and remove paper immediately; cool.

**10**

Frost with egg-white frosting (see recipe this section) and top with fresh shredded coconut.

Yield: one 9-inch layer cake—12 servings.

## Sunflower Seed Meal Torte

Preheat oven to 375°F.
7 egg yolks
½ cup honey
1 teaspoon lemon rind
1¾ cups sunflower seed meal
¼ cup potato starch
1 teaspoon pure vanilla extract
¼ teaspoon salt
7 egg whites

Have eggs at room temperature.

Prepare a 9-inch spring-form pan by oiling bottom lightly. Cut circle from brown paper or parchment paper, to fit bottom of pan. Place over oiled surface bottom of spring-form pan. (Do not oil paper.)

Beat egg yolks until thick and lemon-colored. Gradually beat in the honey until mixture is smooth and very thick. Add lemon rind.

**4**

Combine sunflower seed meal with potato starch. Using a rubber spatula, thoroughly blend into the egg mixture. Add vanilla.

**5**

With mixer set at high speed, beat whites until frothy; add salt and continue to beat just until stiff peaks form when beater is slowly raised.

**6**

Gently, but thoroughly, fold one-fourth of the beaten whites into yolk mixture (this procedure helps to thin the batter for easier blending). Then fold yolk mixture into remaining beaten whites until thoroughly combined.

Pour batter into prepared spring-form pan. Place in preheated oven on middle rack and bake for 10 minutes; reduce oven temperature to 350°F. and continue to bake 30 to 35 minutes longer, or just until

surface springs back when gently touched with fingertip.

**8**

Remove torte from oven and cool completely in pan, on wire rack, before removing side —about one hour. Using a spatula, carefully loosen torte from pan; remove side of spring-form pan. Invert on wire rack and remove bottom part of spring-form pan and brown paper. Turn torte upright; or if desired, torte may be kept on bottom of spring-form pan.

**9**

Cut torte in wedges and serve plain or top with plain vanilla custard sauce or any fruit sauce. (See recipes in this section.)


Yield: 10 servings.

# *Cakes*

## Walnut Torte

Preheat oven to 325°F.
6 egg yolks
½ cup honey
½ cup skim milk powder
½ cup wheat germ
2 cups walnuts (ground fine in electric
       blender, ½ cup at a time)
1 teaspoon pure vanilla extract
6 egg whites

Prepare two 9-inch layer cake pans by oiling bottoms of pans with pastry brush. Cut two circles from heavy brown paper or parchment paper. Place the paper on the bottom of each pan and brush the paper thoroughly with oil.

Beat egg yolks until thick and lemon-colored. Gradually blend honey into the egg mixture. Stir in the skim milk powder, wheat germ and ground walnuts; blend together. Add vanilla extract.

**3**

Beat egg whites until stiff. Using an over and under motion, gently fold egg yolk mixture into beaten egg whites until well-combined.

**4!**

Pour batter into the prepared pans, spreading evenly to edges. Bake in preheated oven for 30 minutes.

**5**

Remove from oven and loosen sides with a spatula to ease the cake out of the pan. Invert on wire rack and remove paper immediately. (Allow to cool completely before adding filling or topping.)

Note: Layers may be put together with custard filling, or served singly, topped with fruit glaze (see recipes this section).

Yield: 10-12 servings.

# *Dessert Sauces*

## Fresh Berry or Fruit Sauce

2 cups fresh or frozen fruit or berries
1 cup water or fruit juice
⅓ cup honey (cut down on amount if fruit
    is not tart)
2 tablespoons cornstarch
1 tablespoon lemon juice

In a 1-quart saucepan, combine fruit or berries, water or juice, honey and cornstarch. Cook over medium heat, stirring constantly, until thickened and clear (about 20 minutes). Stir in lemon juice.

Cook 2 additional minutes. Chill.

Note: This recipe may be used for fruit topping or glaze: simply add 1 additional tablespoon cornstarch.

Yield: 2 cups.

## Lemon Sauce

¼ cup honey
1 tablespoon cornstarch
1 cup boiling water
dash of nutmeg
dash of salt
2 tablespoons lemon juice

In small pan, mix honey and cornstarch. Add boiling water and cook 5 minutes, stirring constantly.

Remove from heat. Stir in nutmeg, salt and lemon juice.

Yield: 1¼ cups.

# *Dessert Sauces*

## Custard Filling for Cakes

⅓ cup cornstarch
⅔ cup skim milk powder
¼ teaspoon salt
1¾ cups water
⅓ cup honey
2 egg yolks, slightly-beaten
1 teaspoon pure vanilla extract

**1**

In medium-sized saucepan, combine cornstarch, skim milk powder and salt.

**2**

Add ¼ cup of water, gradually, stirring with wooden spoon until mixture is smooth and free from lumps. Add remaining 1½ cups of water, mixing thoroughly.

**3**

Add honey to mixture and place over medium heat, stirring constantly until custard thickens, (about 10-12 minutes).

**4**

Remove custard from heat. Add three tablespoons of hot mixture to beaten egg yolks; mix well. Gradually pour yolk mixture into custard, blending well.

**5**

Return to medium heat and cook three minutes, stirring constantly. Remove from heat. Add vanilla. Cool custard completely before using to fill cake.

Yield: about 2 cups.

# Custard Sauce

1 tablespoon cornstarch
3 tablespoons honey
$\frac{1}{8}$ teaspoon salt
2 egg yolks
$\frac{1}{2}$ cup skim milk powder
$1\frac{1}{2}$ cups water
$\frac{1}{2}$ teaspoon pure vanilla extract

**1**

Combine cornstarch, honey and salt in top of double boiler. Add slightly-beaten egg yolks and blend together. Mix skim milk powder and water using wire whisk. Gradually stir in the milk mixture, blending until smooth.

**2**

Bring water to a boil in lower part of double boiler; reduce heat. Place double boiler top over hot water—water in lower part of double boiler should not touch upper part.

**3**

Cook, stirring constantly with a wooden spoon, until mixture is slightly thickened—about 8 to 10 minutes. (Do not overcook.)

**4**

Remove from heat; pour custard immediately into a bowl to cool. Stir in vanilla extract. Cover to prevent film from forming on surface of custard. Refrigerate when sufficiently cooled.

**5**

Serve over cake or torte wedges, fruit puddings or other gelatin desserts.

Yield: 2 cups sauce.

# *Dessert Sauces*

## Whipped Topping I

½ cup ice water
⅔ cup skim milk powder
2 tablespoons lemon juice
2 tablespoons honey
1 teaspoon unflavored gelatin
1 tablespoon boiling water
1 teaspoon pure vanilla extract
1 teaspoon grated lemon rind

In medium-sized mixing bowl, combine ice water, skim milk powder and lemon juice; mix together.

Beat with electric beaters, set at high speed, until mixture is firm (approximately 5 to 10 minutes). Blend in the honey.

In individual custard cup, dissolve gelatin in one tablespoon boiling water, stirring continuously. Beat into mixture, blending thoroughly until well-combined. Add vanilla and lemon rind.

**4!**

Refrigerate topping, covered, for 15 to 20 minutes before serving.

Note: Use as topping for desserts.

Yield: approximately 3 cups.

# Whipped Topping II

⅔ cup skim milk powder
½ cup ice water
1 egg white
3 teaspoons lemon juice
2 tablespoons honey
1 teaspoon grated lemon rind
1 teaspoon pure vanilla extract

In small mixing bowl, combine skim milk powder, ice water and egg white. With beater set at high speed, beat mixture three to four minutes.

Add lemon juice; beat one minute longer (at high speed). Gradually add honey, beating continuously; blend in lemon rind and vanilla.

Serve immediately or refrigerate for 15 minutes. Stir before using.
Note: *Do not allow topping* to stand too long, as mixture will become soft. Leftover topping may be frozen for later use in a salad or frozen dessert.
Yield: approximately 4 cups

# Frosting

2 egg whites
½ cup honey
½ teaspoon pure vanilla extract

In top of double boiler, combine egg whites and honey. Beat one minute with rotary beater (hand or electric type), to combine ingredients.

Cook over rapidly boiling water (water in bottom should not touch top of double boiler), beating constantly until soft peaks form when beater is slowly raised. Allow about 10 minutes for beating to get proper consistency.

Remove from boiling water. Add vanilla; continue beating until frosting is thick enough to spread—about 4 minutes.

Yield: frosting for a 9-inch two-layer cake.

# Natural Food Stores

The growers, distributors and shops
listed here advertise that
they market natural foods.
No further authentication is implied
by their inclusion.

## ALABAMA

Foods for Life, Inc.
P.O. Box 5126
Huntsville 35804
Phone: 837-2234

Fresh vegetables & fruits. Nuts, dried
fruits, seeds, baked goods & frozen
foods. Will ship.


The Health Food Store
Lois Cobb Milson
1225 University Boulevard
Tuscaloosa 35401


## ALASKA

Super Natural Food Store
3906 Greenland Drive
Anchorage 99503
Phone: (907) 277-7978


## ARIZONA

Rancho Verde
Peter T. & Phyllis S. Robinson
Star Rt. 2, Box 675
Camp Verde 86322

Fresh vegetables, grains, meats,
poultry, eggs, breads, and other baked
products. Beef and wheat all year
'round. Vegetables in season. Will ship.

Sones Health Foods
3900 Roosevelt
Kingman 86401
Phone: 757-2308

Fresh vegetables & fruits in season.
Nuts, dried fruits, seeds, juices.
Will ship.


Desert Health Food Store
525 E. Dunlap Ave.
Phoenix 85020
Phone: 944-3642

Fresh vegetables & fruits. Nuts, dried
fruits, seeds, eggs, breads, juices.
Will ship.


Ehrlich's Date Garden
868 Ave. B
Yuma 85364
Phone: 783-7327      783-4778

Oranges, grapefruit and lemons.
Nuts, dried fruits, seeds. Will ship.


## ARKANSAS

Olde Fashioned Foods
123 N. 18th St.
Fort Smith 72901
Phone: (501) SU2-6183

Vegetables & fruits in season (potatoes,
cabbage, carrots, turnips, rutabaga,
tomatoes, cucumbers, corn, greens).
Beef, poultry, honey, grains, nuts.
Will ship.


Shiloh Farms
Route 59
Sulphur Springs 72768
Phone: (501) 298-3297

Fruits & vegetables in season.
Beef, eggs, poultry, honey, grains,
nuts. Will ship.

## CALIFORNIA

Health Town
"A Super Market of Health Foods."
1008 No. Santa Anita Avenue
Arcadia 91007
Phone: (213) 445-0215

Vegetables & fruits in season. All
types dairy. Beef, eggs, poultry, honey,
grains, nuts. Will ship.


Berkeley Health Foods
2311 Shattuck Ave.
Berkeley 94704

Vitamins, minerals, herb teas, stone
ground bread, vegetable juice
extractors. Free delivery & mail orders.


The Mustard Seed
Town & Country Shopping Center
Mill Valley & Haste & Telegraph Ave.
Berkeley 94704


Beverly Hills Nutrition Center
430 N. Canon Dr.
Beverly Hills 90210
Phone: CR4-2962

Vegetables & fruits in season. Eggs,
honey, grains, nuts. Will ship.


Fraley Lane Organic Orchard
Robert E. Fraley
928 Mission Dr.
Camarillo 93010
Phone: 482-5640

Avocados, cherimoyas. No shipping.

C. H. Lage
12583 E. Heather Dr.
Clovis 93612
Phone: 299-7041

Variety of vegetables, fruits and berries in season. Armenian cucumber seeds. No shipping.

Lee Anderson's Covalda Date Co.
P.O. Box 908, Hwy. 86
Coachella 92236
Phone: (714) 398-3551

Citrus fruits, dates and date products, own pecans. Will ship.

Sun'n Soil Natural Foods
Cupertino Crossroads
20700 Stevens Creek Blvd.
Cupertino 95014

Nutriville
7822 E. Florence Ave.
Downey 90240
Phone: 927-9666

Complete stock of organic foods. No shipping.

Pavone Ranch
Rt. 4, Box 472-P
Escondido 92025
Phone: (714) 745-5710

Navel & Valencia oranges, tangerines and tangelos in season. Order ahead. Nuts, dried fruits, seeds. Order ahead. Will ship.

Fallbrook Farms Store
936 S. Main St.
Fallbrook 92028
Phone: 728-9309

Fresh vegetables & fruits. Nuts, dried fruits, seeds, grains, meats, poultry, eggs, breads and juices. No shipping.

Natural Foods
821 E. Broadway
Glendale 91205
Phone: 244-8601

Organic produce, vitamin supplements, special diet foods.

Rancher Waltenspiel—Fruit
Pac Brand Dried Fruits
Timer Crest Farms
4791 Dry Creek Rd.
Healdsburg 95448
Phone: (707) 433-2800

Dried fruits all times of year. Will ship. Visitors welcome to visit ranches or packing plant anytime.

Sun & Earth Natural Foods
6576 Trigo Road
Isla Vista 93017
Phone: 968-7369

Organic foods.

Tahoe Health Food Center
1020 Wildwood Ave.
S Lake Tahoe 95705

Lodi Health Food Store
521 S. Central
Lodi 92540
Phone: 369-3168

All varieties grains. Eggs, breads, juices.

Healthway Foods
Village Corner
4546 El Camino Real
Los Altos 94022

Natural food supplements—special diet foods- fresh juice—raw milk.

Erewhon Trading Company
8003 Beverly Boulevard
Los Angeles 90048
Phone: (213) 651-3787

Vegetables, nuts, seeds, grains, breads, juices. Will ship.

Organic-Ville
4177 W. Third St.
Los Angeles 90005
Phone: (213) 386-1441

Variety of vegetables, fruits and nuts in season. Beef, eggs, poultry, honey, grains, nuts. Restaurant.

Sun Circle
Max Kozck Produce Co.
651 S. Kohler Ave.
Los Angeles 90021
Phone: 622-6093

Vegetables & fruits in season.

Cactus Ranch
3445 Pacific Coast Highway
Malibu 90265

Vegetables in season. Eggs, brown
rice, honey. No shipping.


Malibu House of Health
22716 Pacific Coast Highway
Malibu 90365
Phone: 436-6909

Nuts, dried fruits, seeds, grains,
meats, poultry, eggs, breads, frozen
foods, dairy products and juices. No
shipping.


Ahlers Organic Date Grapefruit Garden
P.O. Box 726
Highway 111
Mecca 92254
Phone: (717) 396-2337

Fruits in season. Dates & grapefruit.
Will ship.


Golden Valley Market
64 E. Blithdale
Mill Valley 94941

Organic fruits & vegetables.


Good Morning Natural Foods
242 Commercial Street
Nevada City 95959


The Good Life
5147 Lankersham
No. Hollywood 91601
Phone: 766-4389 or 877-4134

Vegetables and fruits in season. Beef,
eggs, poultry, honey, grains, nuts,
sausage, cheeses, juices and dietary
foods. Perishable foods not shipped.


Vitamin Village
732 N. Tustin Ave.
Orange 92667
Phone: (714) 639-2582

Vegetables & fruits in season. Beef,
eggs, poultry, honey, grains, nuts.
Will ship.


The Grainery
1124 Forest Avenue
Pacific Grove 93950

Natural grain breads and pastry
(cookies, rolls, etc.), natural cheeses.
Natural produce and grains. Organic
eggs.


Paradise Natural Foods
5729 Almond St., P.O. Drawer JJ
Paradise 95969


Organic Pasadena
1380 N. Lake
Pasadena 91104
Phone: 794-8849

Complete stock organic foods. No
shipping.


J. B. Broderson
723 Cleveland Lane
Petaluma 94952
Phone: 763-0529

A variety of vegetables in season.
Honey, grains, nuts. Will ship.


Petaluma Health Foods
137 Kentucky St.
Petaluma 94952


Healthway Food Center
2630 S. Market
Redding 96001


Horn of Health
416 East State St.
Redlands 92373
Phone: 792-2579

Fresh vegetables & fruits. Nuts, dried
fruits, seeds, grains, eggs, breads,
pastries & cookies. No shipping.


Lindberg Nutrition No. 7
18515 Sherman Way
Reseda 91335
Phone: (213) 345-6403

Complete selection of all organic
foods. No shipping.


Laurelwood Acres
P.O. Box 577
Ripon 95366
Phone: (209) 599-4423

Certified raw goat's milk. A few eggs
& vegetables in summer. No shipping.


Dave's Diet and Nutrition Foods
1743 Arden Way
Sacramento 95815

Complete stock organic foods. No
shipping.


Evelyn Porter's Nutrition Shops
San Anselmo Ave.
San Anselmo 94960

Fresh vegetables & fruits, nuts, dried
fruits, seeds, grains, meats, poultry,
breads, dairy products, juices.
Will ship.

Mac's Nutrition Center
1245 E. Street
San Bernardino 92405
Phone: 885-7165

Vegetables & fruits in season. Beef, eggs, poultry, honey, grains, nuts. No shipping.


Vital Food Shop
534 North El Camino Real
San Clemente 92672


Nutrition Shoppe
4935 Newport Ave.
San Diego 92107
Phone: 222-4121

Complete stock organic foods. Will ship.


Tirrell's Health Foods
1016 Lucas St.
San Fernando 91340
Phone: 361-4680

Fresh vegetables & fruits. Nuts, dried fruits, seeds, poultry, eggs, breads, dairy products, juices. No shipping.


Arko Health Foods
5515 Geary Blvd.
San Francisco 94121
Phone: 751-0767

Complete stock organic foods. No shipping.


Wells Nutrition Center
2309 Irving St.
San Francisco 94100
Phone: 661-0224

Vegetables & fruits in season. Eggs, poultry, honey, grains, nuts, raw milk & dairy products. No shipping.


San Rafael Health Foods
1132 Fourth Street
San Rafael 94901
Phone: 457-0132

Vegetables & fruits in season. Beef, eggs, poultry, honey, grains, nuts. No shipping. Juice bar.


Pacific Grain & Grocery
817 Pacific Avenue
Santa Cruz
Phone: 423-9858

Organic foods.


Rock Island Line Organic Food Trip
1915A Bridgeway
Sausalito 94965
Phone: 332-2195

Organic foods.


Foods for Health
14543 Ventura Blvd.
Sherman Oaks 91403
Phone: (213) 784-4033

Fruits & vegetables in season. Beef, eggs, poultry, honey, grains, nuts. No shipping.


Ray's Nutrition Center
580 Thousand Oaks Blvd.
Thousand Oaks 91360
Phone: (805) 495-1508

Vegetables & fruits in season. Beef, eggs, poultry, honey, grains, nuts. Will ship.


Jaffe Bros. Natural Foods
28560 Lilac Rd.
Valley Center 92082
Phone: (714) 746-1393

Fruits in season. Dried: apricots, peaches, pears, bananas, figs, prunes, raisins. Honey, grains, nuts, butters & oils. Will ship.


Back to Eden
David H. Stern
Barron G. Bingen
2025 Pacific Avenue
Venice 90201
   (corner of North Venice Blvd.)
Phone: (213) 399-9622

Fruits and vegetables in season.


Vita Green Farms
P.O. Box 878
Vista 92083
Phone: 724-2163

Information center for organically raised foods. Large variety of fruits and vegetables. Spanish and Jumbo peanuts. All vegetable seeds and sprouting seeds. Dried beans and peas. Also opening a ranch & frozen food deal in Australia 1970-1971.

# CANADA

Filsinger's Natural Foods
R.R. 3
Ayton, Ontario
Phone: (519) 665-7763

10 varieties of apples 8 mos. of year.
Will ship. Complete stock organic
foods.

Health Food Supplies
10114 Richmond Avenue
Grande Prairie, Al.
Canada

Grassroots Natural Foods
124 Yale Road, East
124 Yale Road, East
Chilliwack, BC
Canada

Edenvale Health Foods
691 West Broad
Vancouver 9, BC
Canada

Shum Organic Foods
4366 Main Street
Vancouver, BC
Canada

Nutra-Mart
285 Edmonton Street
Winnipeg, Manitoba
Canada

The Bean Sprout
1709 Barrington Street
Halifax, NS
Canada

Ceres Health Foods
463 Manor Road, East
Toronto 7, Ontario
Canada

Gibson's Natural Foods
2571 Victoria Park
Toronto, Ontario
Canada

Rollys Health Food Store
634 Yonge Street
Toronto, Ontario
Canada

Sesame Natural Foods Reg'd.
5518 Sherbrooke Street, West
Montreal 260, Quebec
Canada

Soliel & Sante Health Foods
6038 St. Andre
Montreal, Quebec
Canada

Old Fashion Foods
511 Victoria Avenue
Regina, Saskatchewan
Canada

Naturex, Inc.
1125 Mount Royal East
Montreal 34, Quebec
Phone: (541) 526-5513

Vegetables and fruits in season. Out of
season fruits & vegetables imported
from Florida, California & Jamaica.
Beef, eggs, poultry, honey, grains,
nuts. Will ship.

# COLORADO

Natural Food Shop
G. W. Leffler
1655 24th St.
Boulder 80302

Organic foods & meats.

Specialty Food Shop
19 E. Bijoa
Colorado Springs 80902
Phone: 632-5769

Complete health food store.

Living Foods Store
2624 W. 23rd Ave.
Denver 80211
Phone: 455-8110

Irish potatoes, carrots, beets, turnips,
dry onions and apples. Wheat berry
and whole millet. Beef, lamb and
mutton. Snack and fresh juice bar.

Natural Food Shop
G. W. Leffler
North Valley Shopping Center
516 15th St.
Denver 80200

Organic foods & meat.


The Vitamin Cottage
8800 14th Ave. West
Lakewood 80215
Phone: 237-6266

Vegetables in season. Beef, eggs,
honey, grains, nuts. Will ship.


Sunshine Health Foods
430 Yucca St.
Pueblo 81005
Phone: 545-8812

Vegetables in season. Nuts, dried
fruits, seeds, grains, eggs, breads, dry
milk, cheese. No shipping.


# CONNECTICUT

Natural Organic Foods
648 Beachwood Ave.
Bridgeport 06600
Phone: (203) 335-5687
Turnpike Exit 25

Vegetables and fruits in season, meats,
dairy products and baked goods. Beef,
eggs, poultry, honey, grains, nuts.
No shipping.


Four Seasons Health Foods
91 South St.
Danbury 06810
Phone: (203) 743-7803

Fruits & vegetables in season. Beef,
eggs, poultry, honey, grains, nuts.
No shipping.


Mother Nature's Nutrition Center
1275 Post Road
Fairfield 06430

Vegetables & fruits in season.
No shipping.


Country Health Foods & "The
   Organic Farm"
Portland Avenue Box 32
Georgetown 06829
Phone: (203) 544-8976

Large variety vegetables & fruits
available all year. Dried fruits & nuts,
and many health foods. Frozen meat
and our own poultry. Some shipping.
Local deliveries.


Natural Organic Foods
Mr. Joseph Costa
1311 State St.
New Haven 06511

Complete food store.


Our Food Shop
338 Whalley Ave.
New Haven 06511

Natural and organic foods. Grains,
beans, dried fruits, fresh fruit and
vegetables, dairy products.


Country Health Store
Store Road Rte. 156
Old Lyme 06371
Phone: (203) 434-5436

Vegetables & fruit year 'round. Beef,
eggs, poultry, honey, grains, nuts. No
shipping.


Valley Health Food Shop
1402 Hopmeadow St.
Simsbury 06070
Phone: 658-9390


Azusa Diet & Vitamin Center
19 Cedar Heights Rd.
Stamford 06905
Phone: (203) 322-9177

Complete Organic store. Will ship.


Stamford Nutrition Center
35 Bedford
Stamford 06901

Nuts, dried fruits, seeds, grains. Eggs,
breads, juices. Will ship.


Colonial Healthway, Inc.
254 E. State St.
Westport 06880
Phone: (203) 227-7100

Fruits in season. Beef, eggs, poultry,
honey, grains, nuts. Will ship.

Leonard's Eco-Farms
Leonard Urbanovitz
81 W. State Street
Westport 06880
Phone: 226-5233

Complete stock organic foods. No shipping.


## DELAWARE

Sunshine Natural Foods and
    Equipment
Frank A. Linn
2 Tri State Mall
Interstate 95 and Naamans Road
Claymont 19703
Phone: (302) 789-9390


## DISTRICT OF COLUMBIA

Vita Food Co. Inc.
1010 F St. NW
Washington 20004
Phone: RE7-1212

Fresh vegetables occasionally. Apples in season. Grains, eggs, juices. Will ship.


## FLORIDA

Nutrition Cottage
231 W. Camion Real
Boca Raton 33432
Phone: (305) 391-2819

Thomas Barry
Maplehurst Gardens
Hampshire 60140
Phone: 741-0740

Very large variety of green vegetables & root crops. Grapefruit, oranges, lemons and apples. Peanuts, cashews, walnuts, pecans, and almonds. Beef, pork, lamb, goat, rabbits, chickens, turkeys, geese & ducks. No shipping. Closed on Mondays & mornings during summer months.


Swanson's Organic Farm Stand
Arthur Swanson
115th & Archer Avenue
1 mile south of Rt. 83 on 171
Lemont 60439
Phone: (312) 257-2007

3 acres of vegetables, peppers, corn, tomatoes, potatoes, onions, beans, zuchini, squash, cucumbers, strawberries. No wholesale, retail only. No shipping.


Alboe Acres Organic Foods
5515 No. Wilmot Road
McHenry 60050
Phone: (312) 497-3103

Fresh vegetables. Sunflower seeds, honey, oats, hogs, rabbits, poultry, eggs. No shipping.


Halbleib Organic Farm
McNabb 61335
Phone: (815) 882-2487

Cheese, Stone ground whole grain flours, cereals, other grains and seed corn. More—send for listing. Will ship.

Scarborough's Health Food Store
1441 N. Dixie Hwy.
Fort Lauderdale 33304
Phone: (305) 523-2173

Complete organic store. No shipping.


Berry's Health Food Center
417 Avenue C
Ft. Pierce 33450
Phone: 461-4355

Fresh fruits, nuts, dried fruits, seeds, grains. No shipping.


Nutrition Center, Inc.
23 West Duval St.
Jacksonville 32202
Phone: 355-4020

Nuts, dried fruits, seeds, grains. Will ship.


Robert Strang
1321 N.W. 29th Terrace
Miami 33142
Phone: 635-7890

Vegetables & fruits in season. Citrus, papaya, avocado, mango, lychee nuts, bananas, eggs, honey. Some shipping.


Reeser Health Foods
1319 E. Silver Spgs. Blvd.
Ocala 32670
Phone: 629-1040

Fresh vegetables & fruits. Nuts, dried fruits, seeds, grains, eggs, breads. Will ship.

Chamberlain Natural Foods
25 W. Church St.
Orlando 32802
Phone: (305) 425-6661

Large stock: vit., minl., supplements, books, herbs, cereals, grains, dried fruits, food for special diets.


Dandelions Unlimited
450 N.E. 28th Street
Pompano Beach 33064
Phone: (305) 781-9820


Lewis Natural Health Foods
Robert O. Lewis
211 Third Street South
St. Petersburg 33701
Phone: 894-2454


Nature's Health Foods
Herman Fernandez
6304 N. Armenia
Tampa 33604


## GEORGIA


Health Unlimited, Inc.
Toco Hills Shopping Center
2993 N. Druid Hills Rd. NE
Atlanta 30329
Phone: (404) 633-6677

Vegetables & fruits in season. Eggs, honey, grains, nuts. Will ship.

Staff of Life
3619 Calvin Drive
Columbus 31904
Phone: (404) 323-9194


Health Foods Dept.
Conner-Walker Studio
Folkston 31537


## HAWAII


Fourth World General Store
Jeff Danm
72 Kapiolani Street
Hilo 96720


The Good Earth
3520 Waialae Ave.
Honolulu 96816


Garden Isle Natural Foods
1384 Kuhio Highway
Kapaa, Kauai 96746


## IDAHO


Chase's Health Food Store
723 Main
Boise 83702

Natural nutritional foods. Vitamins, herbs & books. Prompt mail order service.

Wilma's Natural Foods
159 S. Corner Ave.
Idaho Falls 83401
Phone: 522-6964

Cold pressed oils, Health breads. Herb teas, etc. One block south of swimming pool.


Wood River Natural Foods
Neil Wolf
Dan Gruener
Box 471
Ketchum 83340
Phone: (208) 726-3032


Cottage Health Foods
583 Roosevelt Ave.
Pocatello 83201


## ILLINOIS


Walnut Grove Farm
Edward F. Johnson
Benson 61516
Phone: 394-2523

Beef, lamb, pork, poultry, eggs. Local delivery. No shipping.


Natural Food Store
102 E. Jackson
Carbondale 62901

Honey, grains, nuts and vegetables in season. No shipping.

Hyde Park Health Foods
LaVonne Braaten
1360 East 53rd Street
Chicago 60615
Phone: 955-0021

No shipping.


Irving Park Dietary Foods
3931 W. Irving Park Road
Chicago 60618
Phone: 539-1490

Vegetables & fruits in season. Beef, eggs, poultry, honey, grains, nuts. Will ship except for perishables.


Downers Grove Health Foods
1326 Ogden Ave.
Downers Grove 60515
Phone: (312) 969-7614

Beef, eggs, poultry, honey, grains, nuts. Will ship.


Diet House
1029 Davis St.
Evanston 60201
Phone: GR 5-1121

Complete stock organic foods. Will ship.


Moss Hill Organic Food & Provisions Co.
6115 S. Cass Ave.
Westmont 60559
Phone: (312) 852-5850


Wagoner's Organic Acres
Box 116
Williamsfield 61489
Phone: (309) 639-4337
West edge of town on State Rte. 180.

Vegetables in season from own farm. Eggs, poultry, sorghum, fowl, black walnuts. No shipping.


# INDIANA


Schwartz Natural Food Center
Sarah E. Schwartz
260 E. Water St.
Berne 46711
Phone: (219) 589-2868

Complete stock of organic foods. No shipping.


John McMahan
McMahan's Farm Market
Box 111
Clifford 47226
Phone: 372-4368

Own vegetables & strawberries in season. Beef, eggs, honey. No shipping.


A&B Natural Foods
2445 Broadway
Fort Wayne 46807
Phone: (219) 744-1413

Vegetables & fruits in season. Nuts, seeds, grains, eggs. Will ship.


Hammond Natural Foods
631 Gostlin St.
Hammond 46327
Phone: 931-8383

Fresh vegetables in season.


Grepke Health Mart
2223 Lafayette Rd. (in rear)
Indianapolis 46222
Phone: (317) 638-2081

Vegetables, honey, grains, nuts, own eggs. Will ship (limited).


Rosary Acres Natural Foods
5224 E. Carter Road
Kokomo 46901
Phone: 452-5821


Moses J. Troyer
Lone Organic Farm
R. 1, Box 58
Countryroad 37—46 west.
Millersburg 46543

Whole grain products, whole wheat flour, cornmeal, cereals, steel cut oats, sorghum, molasses, honey, and herbs. Herbs shipped.


# IOWA


McCready Health Foods
37 SE 2nd Avenue
Cedar Rapids 52401


Sparling Health Foods
Stanley Sparling
1601 Harrison Street
Davenport 52803
Phone: 323-8933

Complete stock organic foods. Will ship vitamins.

Wonder Life Foods
4931 Douglas Avenue
Des Moines 50310


Van's Health Foods
Clarence or Tillie Van Sant
Route No. 2
Grinnell 50112
Phone: 526-8522

Sweet corn, dried fruits by lb. or
25 lb. case. Beef & Pork, eggs, poultry,
honey, breads, nuts. No shipping.


Harmony Natural Foods
R. R. No. 2
Hull 51239
Phone: (712) 439-2703

Own grown Jerusalem artichokes &
carrots. Wheat, corn, beef, lamb.
Prefer orders for meats. No shipping.


## KANSAS


Central Health Foods
1219 Central Ave.
Kansas City 66102
Phone: 342-2800

Grains, Breads for Life, vegetarian
frozen foods. Goat's milk. No shipping.


Downtown Health Foods
Anna W. Berger
20 East Ninth
Lawrence 66044
Phone: 842-2771

Nutritional Food Center
8740 Santa Fe Dr.
Overland Park 66212
Phone: DU 1-0021

Vegetables & fruits, nuts, dried fruits,
seeds, grains, meats, poultry. Breads
for Life and other baked products.
Will ship.


Health Foods Store
2211 West 10th St.
Topeka 66604


## KENTUCKY


Grimm's Health Foods
1482 South 7th Street
Louisville 40208


Natural Food Store
515 Davies St.
Owensboro 42301


## LOUISIANA


Evelyn's Vitality Food Shoppe
Evelyn Rabialais
4213 Government Street
Baton Rouge 70806

Fine Foods
3236 S. Carrollton Ave.
New Orleans 70118
Phone: 486-5436

Apples in season. Nuts, dried fruits,
seeds, grains. Eggs, baked products.
Will ship.


Nutritional Health Products, Inc.
Helen Keller
1534 Melpomene Street
New Orleans 70130


Nutritional Foods East, Inc.
June Dakin
3926 Gentilly Road
New Orleans 70126


Harris Health Foods
3421 Greenwood Rd.
Shreveport 71109
Mail orders filled.


Natural Organic Health Foods
2314 Front Street
Slidell 70458


## MAINE


Wolf's Neck Farms
Freeport 04082
Phone: (207) 865-6653

Meats. Will ship.

Donn's Health Foods
Don & Leta Crafts
14 Oak Street
Lisbon Falls 04252
Phone: (207) 353-2806

Vegetables and fruits in season. Beef, poultry, honey, nuts. Will ship.

## MARYLAND

Miss Fannie L. Harn
(Edmondson Village)
4402 Rokeby Rd.
Baltimore 21229
Phone: 947-4391

Vegetables & fruits in season from garden. Nuts, seeds, honey, grains, dried herbs. Will ship.

Special Diet Shop
1 N. Howard St.
Baltimore 21201
Phone: (301) 727-0383

Natural vitamins, natural & organic foods, natural cosmetics, stone ground flour.

Laurelbrook Foods
Rod and Margy Coats
Box 47
Bel Air 21014
Phone: 879-7818
Will ship.

Beautiful Day Trading Co.
4915 Berwyn Rd.
College Park 20740
Phone: 345-6655

Fresh vegetables. Fruit in season. Nuts, dried fruits, seeds, grains, eggs, breads, goat products, apple cider. No shipping.

Springbottom Natural Foods
Box 53, Bottom Rd.
Hydes 21082
Phone: 592-7580

Kennedy's Natural Food, Inc.
Baltimore Road & Route 28
Rockville 20851

Maple Lane Farms
Carlton Barnes
Rt. 2, Box 312
Sykesville 21784
Phone: (301) 635-2364

Vegetables and fruits in season. Beef, eggs, poultry, honey, fish. Will ship.

## MASSACHUSETTS

Joseph Marques
644 Middle Rd.
Acushnet 02743
Phone: 995-8937

Vegetables in season. Goat's milk, cheese, certified raw cow's milk. Eggs. No shipping.

Whole Wheat Inc.
181 North Pleasant Street
Amherst 01002

Stern's Natural Food Center
Sumner Stern
261 Cabot Street
Beverly 01915
Phone: 927-4991

Wide line of vitamins and food supplements, canned foods, breads, snacks, meats, dried fruits, teas, honeys, macrobiotic foods, drinks, preserves, dietetic foods, toiletries and cosmetics.

Erewhon Trading Co.
342 Newberry St.
Boston 02115
Phone: (617) 262-3420

Complete stock of organic foods. No shipping.

Grazing Fields
Bay End, Box 244
Buzzards Bay 02532

The Corners of the Mouth
1419 Cambridge St.
Cambridge 02139

Fresh vegetables. Nuts, dried fruits, seeds, grains, baked goods. No shipping.

The Source
50 Central Street
Leominster 01453


Cape Cod Health Food Center
1620 Bay Road
Osterville 02655
Phone: (617) 428-9888


Healthway Food Shop
235 Elm Street, Davis Square
W. Somerville 02144
Phone: 625-1181

Honey, grain, nuts. Will ship.


Red Owl
Southampton Road
Westfield 01085
Phone: 562-9712


Organic Food Center
Winston F. Burrell
557 Bedford St.
Whitman 02382
Phone: (617) 447-2152 or 447-3344

Vegetables & fruits all year. Beef,
eggs, poultry, honey, grains, nuts. No
shipping. Open daily 9 to 9.


Living Earth
Albert E. Maykel, Jr.
321-327 Pleasant St.
Worcester 01609
Phone: (617) 753-1896

Will ship.

# MICHIGAN

Allen Park Health Foods
6537 Allen Rd.
Allen Park 49010
Phone: 673-3475 evenings

7 mi. west of Otrego on 27th between
104 & 106 Aves. Blueberries in season
at farm, by order or pick your own.
Vegetables in season.


Your Health and Nutrition
523 North Ashley Street
Ann Arbor 48103


Vital Food Stores
4911 Schaefer
Dearborn 48126
Phone: KE 3-1989

Fresh vegetables in season. Apples,
carrots. Will ship.


Vital Food Stores
1454 Broadway
Detroit 48226
Phone: KE 3-1989

Fresh vegetables in season. Apples,
carrots. Will ship.


Dale's Foods for Health
Dale D. Wolfe
421 Harrison Street
Flint 48502

Harvest Health Inc.
1944 Eastern Ave. SE
Grand Rapids 49507
Phone: 245-6268

Fresh vegetables in season. Oranges,
grapefruit, grains, seeds, nuts and
dried fruits. No shipping.


Randall Health Foods
223 So. Washington
Lansing 48933


Zerbo's
34164 Plymouth Rd.
Livonia 48150
Phone: (313) GA 7-3144


Sunflower Shop
116 E. Main
Northville 48167


Nutri Foods Inc.
120 So. Main St.
Royal Oaks 48067
Phone: 541-6820

Organic fresh fruits & vegetables.

## MINNESOTA

Norman Seppanen
Rt. 3
Alexandria 56308
Phone: 763-7736

5 mi. west of Alexandria on Hwy. 27
1½ mi. north of gravel road due
north of Lake Mary or take
Garfield-Lovery Exit off 94 go south
on 144 to Hwy. 27 then 1 mi. east
then north on gravel road.

Vegetables & fruits in season. Beef,
honey, grains. Will ship.

"Sno-Pac" Farms
Calendonia Cold Storage Co.
379 S. Pine St.
Calendonia 55921
Phone: 724-3984

Fresh & frozen asparagus, peas, and
sweet corn. Wheat, berries. Will ship.

Cayol Natural Foods
811 La Salle Ave.
Minneapolis 55402
Phone: 335-7452

Sunflower seeds, pumpkin, Brazils,
grains. Breads of Life. Juices. Will ship.

Tao Traditional Organic Foods
2223 East 35th Street
Minneapolis 55407

Beans, nuts, honey, some dairy
products.

Health Food Center
39 South Cleveland Ave. at Grand
St. Paul 55105

Natural & organic foods, inc. some
dairy products.

Mastel's Health Foods
1828 St. Clair Avenue
St. Paul 55105

Natural & organic foods & supplements.

## MISSISSIPPI

Rodruge's Health Foods
USM Shopping Center
2509 West 4th Street
Rt. 10, Box 87
Hattiesburg, Miss. 39401

## MISSOURI

Columbia Specialty Food Center
802 Business Loop
70 East
Columbia 65201

Main Health Foods & Vita. Ctr.
Vern L. Hight
110½ E. Lexington
Independence 64050

Burgins Nutritional Center
1650 E. 63rd Street
Kansas City 64110

Holswon Health Food Store
319 N. 17th St.
St. Joseph 64501
Phone: AD 2-1272

Honey, grains, nuts. Will ship.

A-A Natural Foods
8135 Big Bend
St. Louis 63119
Phone: 961-3541

New-Dawn Natural Foods
Sterling J. Ryan
3175 S. Grand Blvd.
St. Louis 63118
Phone: PR 2-9110

Complete stock organic foods. Will
ship.

Evans Health Studio
500 Mt. Vernon St.
Springfield 65806

Complete line of health foods,
sprouted beans.

Winslow Health & Diet Foods
1501 So. Glenstone
Springfield 65804
Phone: 881-5643

## MONTANA

Schroeders Health Food Center
202 North 18th
Billings 59101

Withey's Health Foods
Mr. & Mrs. Withey
1231 S. Main
Kalispell 59901

Vegetables in season. Nuts, grains,
eggs, breads, juices. Will ship.

Natural Health Foods
117 West Main Street
Lewistown 59457

The Hut
1222 West Kent
Missoula 59801

## NEBRASKA

Murdock's Natural Foods
128 East Sixth St.
Fremont 68025

## NEVADA .

Washoe Health Food Center
1298 South Virginia
Reno 89501

Natural vitamins, cosmetics, herb teas.

## NEW HAMPSHIRE

The Source
Chuck & Margie Dempsey
Rt. 12A Alstead Center
Alstead 03602
Phone: 835-6681

Complete stock of organic foods. Local
eggs, meat, fruit & vegetables. No
shipping.

Richardson Food Service
11 Woodbury Lane
Bedford 03102
Phone: (601) 623-1495

Nuts, dried fruits, grains, eggs, juices.

The Source
40 Main Street
Lancaster 03584
Phone: 788-4400

## NEW JERSEY

The Health Shoppe
16 Portland Ave.
Bergenfield 07621
Phone: (201) 385-3040

Fruits & vegetables in season. Beef,
eggs, poultry, honey, grains, nuts.
No shipping.

Country Health Foods
626 U. S. Highway 206
Bordentown 08505
Phone: 298-4201

Natural Food Shop or Olive May Co.
13 Washington Place
East Orange 07017
Phone: (201) OR 3-0326

Eggs, cheese, meats, chicken.

Natro Health Foods
268 Morris Avenue
Elizabeth 07200
Phone: 352-4771

Honey, grains, nuts, weekly supplies
of vegetables, cheese & eggs. No
shipping.

California Health Center
35 West St.
Englewood 07631
Phone: 567-1489

Vegetables & fruits all year 'round.
Beef, eggs, poultry, honey, grains &
nuts. No shipping.

Aylward's Natural Food, Inc.
335-A Main St.
Hackensack 07601
Phone: 342-1932

Advanced Health Foods
193 Jackson Avenue
Jersey City 07305

Vegetables & fruits in season. Eggs,
poultry, honey, grains & nuts. No
shipping.

Lakewood Health Foods
222 Clifton Ave.
Lakewood 08701
Phone: 364-5877

Vegetables & fruits in season. Beef,
eggs, poultry, honey, grains, nuts.
Will ship.

Nutrition Center of West End
155 Brighton Avenue
Long Branch 07740
Phone: (201) 870-1587

Montclair Health Food Center
E. A. Zarro
549 Bloomfield Ave.
Montclair 07042
Phone: 744-7122

Complete stock of organic foods.
Will ship.

The Health Shoppe, Inc.
151 Morris Street
Morristown 07960
Phone: (201) 538-9131

Vegetables and fruits in season. Beef,
eggs, poultry, honey, grains, nuts.

Basic Health Center
53A E. Ridgewood Ave.
Paramus 07652
Phone: 265-1330

Felicia's Vital Health Foods
32 Market Street
Paterson 07505
Phone: 525-1976

The Third Day
10 Franklin Place
Rutherford 07070

Westfield Health Foods
Dr. Irving Lapidus
271 South Ave. E.
Westfield 08830
Phone: 232-8008

Complete stock organic foods. Some
shipping.

## NEW MEXICO

Alamogordo Health Food Center
1210 Ninth Street
Alamogordo 88310
Phone: 437-6699

Carrots, cereal, food supplements,
tea, honey, and oils.

Downtown Health Foods
110 12th NW
Albuquerque 87102
Phone: 242-7735

Radiant Health Products
Jim and Flo Johnson
33 Winrock Center
Albuquerque 87110
Phone: 296-2073

Vegetables & fruits in season. Will
ship.

Health Center
Edwin & Margaret Head
105 East Willow
Deming 88030
Phone: 546-7035

Grains, nuts, seeds, juices.

Las Cruces Health Food Center
211 North Main
Las Cruces 88001
Phone: 522-1222

Cereal, food supplements, tea, honey,
carrots.

Natural Foods
Ella Hanford
1203 Cerrillos Rd.
Santa Fe 87501
Phone: 982-2931

Complete stock except for meat &
poultry. Own yogurt and carrot juice.
Will ship.

## NEW YORK

The Store
30 Central Ave.
Albany 12210
Phone: (518) 463-7822

Large assortment of grains, seeds,
nuts. Honey, natural cheese, fertile
eggs, vitamins, dried fruits, ice cream
and yogurt. No shipping.

A-Bree Health Foods, Inc.
R. A. Bressler
33 E. Main St.
Bay Shore 11706
Phone: 666-4721

Complete stock organic foods. Will ship.


Brighton Special Foods
508A Brighton Beach Ave.
Brooklyn 11235
Phone: (212) SH 3-6749

Vegetables & fruits in season. Beef, eggs, poultry, honey, grains, nuts. No shipping.


Stamena Health Foods
8314 5th Ave.
Brooklyn 11209
Phone: (212) BE 8-1522

Vegetables & fruits in season. Eggs, poultry, honey, grains, nuts. No shipping.


Hildegard's Health Foods
56 University Plaza
Buffalo 14226
Phone: (716) 837-8649

Vegetables & fruits in season. Beef, eggs, poultry, honey, grains, nuts. No shipping.


Thousand Island Apiaries
Clayton 13624

Honey. Will ship.


Lang Apiaries
8448-NY Rt. 77
Gasport 14067
Phone: (716) 772-7518 evenings

Honey. Buckwheat honey a specialty. Will ship.


Great Neck Health Food Center
Mr. H. Burger
46 Great Neck Road
Great Neck 11021
Phone: (516) 829-9299

Will ship.


Deer Valley Farm & Country Store
Carsten Families
Guilford 13780
Phone: 764-2720

Complete stock organic foods. Will ship.


Westchester Health Shop
367 Elwood Ave.
Hawthorne 10532
Phone: (914) RO 9-6292

Vegetables & fruits in season. Beef, eggs, poultry, honey, grains, nuts. Will ship except produce.


Village Health Food Shop
Evelyn Ripnitz
368 New York Ave.
Huntington 11743
Phone: (516) 423-6667

Cheese, butter, organic meats. Walk-in refrigerator, pure goat products.


Stur-Dee Health Products, Inc.
Island Park 11558
Phone: (516) 889-6400

Mail order.


Jackson Heights Health Foods
8306 37th Avenue
Jackson Heights 11372
Phone: (212) 429-9511

Eggs, honey, grains, nuts. No shipping.


Sante Health Products
Sy Schlaifer
170-18 Hillside Avenue
Jamaica 11432
Phone: (212) 657-7507

Complete stock. Will ship.


Belly of the Whale
Sea Life Enterprises, Ltd.
271 Floral Ave.
Johnson City 13790

Nuts, dried fruits, grains, herbs, spices, teas, books and imports. Dry goods. Vegetables, fruits, cider in season. No shipping.


Dorothy's Natural Food Shop
Dorothy J. Hull
214 Main St.
Johnson City 13760
Phone: (607) 785-9597

Complete stock organic foods. No shipping. Open 6 days a week.

Vita-Life Health & Diet Shop
Dennis & Mona Jones
377 Central Ave.
Lawrence 11559
Phone: 569-3073

Fruits, carrots, meats, eggs, goat
yogurt, milk and cheese. Will ship.


Levittown Diet & Health Foods Center
90 Gardiners Avenue
Levittown 11756

Organic foods, vitamin supplements,
fresh breads, imported honey and
goat's milk.


Lo'Cal Dietetic Shop
209 Gramatan Ave.
Mt. Vernon 10550
Phone: MO 7-9683

Eggs, honey, grains, nuts, natural flour,
natural vitamins. No shipping.


The Real Food Store
53 Main Street
New Paltz 12561

Bulk grains, beets, herb teas, organic
vegetables, dried fruits, nuts, vitamins.


Mother Nature's Nutrition Center
1291 North Avenue
New Rochelle 10804

Vegetables & fruit in season.
No shipping.


The Brickyard Natural Foods, Ltd.
171 8th Ave.
New York 10011


Brownie's Natural Foods
Restaurant & Food Store
21 E. 16th St.
New York 10001
Phone: (212) AL 5-2838

Complete stock of organic foods. Will
ship.


Good Earth Natural Foods, Inc.
1336 First Ave.
New York 10021
Phone: (212) BU 8-7408

A complete organic store. No shipping.
Serve snacks. Free 40-page catalog.


Gramercy Natural Food Center
Marvin E. Wilkenfeld
387 Second Avenue
New York 10010
Phone: 725-1651

Health foods, organic produce, natural
vitamins, beef, poultry, sea food.


Greenberg's Health Food Store
125 First Avenue
New York 10003
Phone: AL 4-2959

Grains, flours, world wide organic
specialties.


Kubie Health Shop, Inc.
1234 Lexington Ave.
New York 10028
Phone: RH 4-3268

Vegetables & fruits in season. Nuts,
grains, eggs, juices. Will ship.


Living Foods
165 9th Ave.
New York 10011
Phone: (212) 675-2223

Vegetables & fruits in season. Beef,
eggs, poultry, honey, grains, nuts.
Will ship.


Mother Nature & Sons, Ltd.
351 Bleecker
New York 10014
Phone: (212) 924-7572

Natural foods, organic fruits and
vegetables, meats, vitamins, grains,
goat products, cosmetics, books. No
shipping.


Nature's Way Foods, Inc.
236 W. 10th St.
New York 10014
Phone: (212) 242-1111

Vegetables & fruits in season. Beef,
eggs, poultry, honey, grains, nuts.
Will ship.


Nature's Cupboard
80 East 7th St.
New York 10003
Phone: 473-9278

Vegetables & fruits in season. Nuts,
grains, dairy products. No shipping.


Nutrition Center
Dan Squillanty
247 East 50th Street
New York 10022
Phone: PL 3-5363

Panacea-Health Foods & Herbs
Mary Anne & Cornelis Knynenburg
323 Third Avenue
New York 10010
Phone: 725-2320

Will ship.


Niagara Health Food Center
2775 Main St.
Niagara Falls 14305
Phone: (716) 282-7824

Beef, eggs, poultry, honey, grains, nuts.


House of Nutrition
5 Collegeview Ave.
Poughkeepsie 12603

Vegetables in season. Beef, eggs,
poultry, honey, grains. Regular supply
of fruits and vegetables to subscribers.


Dietary Specialties
E. Niblack
20 Magnolia St.
Rochester 14608
Phone: (716) 328-5745

Vegetables & fruit in season. Nuts,
dried fruits, meat, poultry, eggs. Will
ship.


Mother Nature's Nutrition Centers
70 Garth Rd.
Scarsdale 10583
Phone: 723-5556

Vegetables & fruits in season. Will ship.


Patton's Products
221 Broadway
Schenectady 12305
Phone: (518) FR 4-4883

Vegetables & fruits in season. Beef,
eggs, poultry, honey, grains, nuts.
No shipping.


Threefold Corner
Alex Flaum
841 S. Main St.
Spring Valley 10977
Phone: 352-9708

Vegetables & fruit in season. Nuts,
poultry, breads, cheese. No shipping.


Gericke's Organic Farm
2876 Arthur Kill Rd.
Staten Island 10309
Phone: (212) YU 4-2672

Complete stock organic foods. Own
vegetables and fruit. No shipping.


Hilda Van Health Food
Hilda Van Gelderen
102 Lafayette Ave.
Suffern 10901
Phone: (914) 357-4646

Vegetables & fruits in season. Meat,
eggs, fish, poultry, honey, grains, nuts.
No shipping.


Troy Nutritious Foods, Inc.
451 Fulton St.
Troy 12180
Phone: (518) 272-9839

Vegetables & fruits in season. Beef,
eggs, poultry, honey, grains, nuts.
Will ship.


Amity Store
R. D. No. 2, Box 226
Newport Bridge Road
Warwick 10990

Breads, herb teas, honey, flours, eggs,
grains, produce in season.


Preferency Foods
742 Morrison St.
Watertown 13061
Phone: (315) 788-2617

Some fruits in season. Eggs, poultry,
honey, grains, nuts. Will ship.


Seneca Lodge
South Entrance Watkins Glen State
   Park
Watkins Glen 14891
Phone: 535-2014

Surplus vegetables and eggs. Pick your
own grapes in early fall. Whole beef
and hogs; reserve. No shipping.


White Plains Health Food
108 Mamaroneck Ave.
White Plains 10601


# NORTH CAROLINA


Good Health Food Store
26 Wall St.
Asheville 28801
Phone: 254-2543

Breads, juice bar. Will ship.

Natural Nutrition
Howard F. Basile
Lakewood Shopping Cntr., Box 722
Durham 27707
Phone: 489-7805

Vegetables & fruit in season. Nuts, grains. Local breads, squash cakes, acidophillus milk & yogurt. Some shipping.

## NORTH DAKOTA

Yorktown Mills
Mr. & Mrs. Harold Weis
Fullerton 58441
Phone: 375-7660

Fresh vegetables, grains, breads. Will ship.

## OHIO

Alexander Health Foods
282 S. Main Street
Akron 44308
Phone: (216) 762-7451

Beef, honey, grains, nuts. Will ship.

Lawrence B. Greve
R. 1
Botkins 45306
Phone: 693-4785

Small supply of vegetables & fruits in season. Eggs, poultry, grains. No shipping.

Quality Natural Food Center
Glenn Infield
221 13th St. NW
Canton 44703

Complete stock organic food.

Vitality Health Food Shop, Inc.
No. 51 Arcade-Euclid Ave.
Cleveland 44114
Phone: (216) MA 1-0348

Some vegetables & fruits in season. Eggs, honey, grains, nuts, dairy products. Will ship.

Beechwold Natural Foods
4185 N. High St.
Columbus 43214
Phone: (614) 262-0192

Vegetables & fruits in season. Beef, eggs, poultry, honey, grains, nuts. Limited shipping.

Olympia Nature Foods
600 Watervliet Ave.
Dayton 45420
Phone: 254-2421

Vegetables & fruits in season. Beef, eggs, poultry, honey, grains, nuts. Limited shipping.

Vassar Health Food Store
13902 Euclid Ave.
East Cleveland 44112
Phone: (216) 761-2206

Schlarman's Natural Foods
R. R. 1, Box 77
Ft. Recovery 45846
Phone: (419) 375-2659

Dietrich's Organic Farm
R. R. 1
Genoa 43430
Phone: (419) 855-4369

Vegetables & fruits in season, comfrey, grains, green soy beans. No shipping.

Slade's Natural Foods
912 Gray Ave.
Greenville 45331
Phone: (513) 548-1763

Marshall Health & Oceanic Foods
Al Smith
15721 Madison Ave.
Lakewood 44107

Phone: (216) 226-8146
Complete stock organic foods. Will ship.

Nature Nutrition Shoppe
404 W. Main St.
Louisville 44641
Phone: 875-9234

Some vegetables & fruits in season. Eggs, honey, grains, nuts. Will ship.

Variety Health Foods
1407 Springmill Rd.
Mansfield 44903
Phone: (419) 747-7363

Nichols Health Foods
268 N. State St.
Marion 43302
Phone: (614) 382-2715

Vegetables & fruits in season. Beef,
eggs, poultry, honey, grains, nuts.
Will ship.


Harris Health Foods
110 N. Center St.
Mt. Vernon 43050
Phone: (614) 392-5151

Vegetables & fruits in season. Beef,
poultry, honey, grains, nuts, dairy
products. No shipping.


Mother Natures Cupboard
408 S. Main
Orrville 44667
Phone: 682-6896

Vitamins, wheat germ oil, protein, dried
fruit, all kinds of seeds, juices, coffee
substitutes, etc. Honey, grains, nuts.
Some shipping.


Draper's Foods
14868 Pearl Rd.
Strongsville 44136


Dietrich's
519 Monroe Street
Toledo 43604
Phone: (419) 243-7183

Vegetables & fruits in season. Beef,
eggs, poultry, honey, grains, nuts, fresh
juices. Will ship.


Helen's Health Foods
Helen Kessens
614 North Street
Wapakoneta 45895
Phone: (419) 738-6001

Complete stock organic foods. Will
ship.


Ideal Health Center
Ann Mandrick
219 N. Park Ave.
Warren 44481
Phone: 392-3786

Complete stock organic foods. Will
ship.


Health Food Center
Cyril Nickoloff
12 Parade
Youngstown 44503
Phone: (216) 746-1515

Complete stock organic foods.


Natural Health Foods
Max & Ruth Huberman
6981 Market St.
Youngstown 44512
Phone: (216) 758-9897

Complete stock organic foods. Fresh
juices.


# OKLAHOMA


Natural Food and Vitamin Shop
Patricia Bond
P.O. Box 114
330 South 81 By-Pass
Duncan 73533


L & L Health Foods Company
Lawrence Burrell
Route 1, Box 197
Fairview 73737
Phone: (405) 227-3200

Honey, nuts, own produced wheat and
rye. Will ship.


Lewis' House of Better Living
307 S. Air Depot
Midwest City 73110
Phone: 732-5694

Natural vitamins & minerals, cosmetics,
raw nuts, whole wheat bread, cold
pressed oils.


Wilder F. Curtess
Tauscher's Natural Foods
512 Classen
Oklahoma City 73106


Earl's Health Store
Earl H. Haworth
3701 E. Admiral Place
Tulsa 74115
Phone: 935-0794

Apples, nuts, grains, meats, eggs,
juices. Will ship.

# OREGON

Beaverton Health Foods
3055 S.W. Cedar Hills Blvd.
Beaverton 97005


Van's Natural Foods
824 Wall
Bend 97001
Phone: 383-0564

Foods for health. Mail orders filled.


Casa Yerba
Star Route
Box 21
Day's Creek 97429

Herbs and blended herb teas. Fertile eggs, Valencia oranges, limited amounts of fresh produce.


Life-Sake
809 River Avenue
off River Road
Eugene 97402

Goat milk and cheese. Juice bar, organic produce in season.


Nature Food Centres
Valley River Shopping Center
Eugene 97401

Certified organic beef and produce. Fertile eggs. Raw goat milk, goat milk cheese. Fresh breads.

Staff-O-Life Foods
285 Super Hiway
Gladstone 97027


Merrick's Natural Foods
220 N.W. "D" Street
Grants Pass 97526
Phone: (503) 476-2585

Complete stock organic foods, grains, seeds, beans. Raw cow's milk & goat's milk, goat's milk ice cream, own yogurt. Will ship.


Hillsboro Nutrition Center
125 S. 3rd
Hillsboro 97123
Phone: 648-1966


La Grande Health Foods
303 North Fir
La Grande 97850


Parkway Health Foods
111-3rd St.
McMinnville 97128

Refrigerated natural foods, grains, flours, raw honey, food supplements, vitamins, minerals, homeopathic tablets, organic cosmetics.


Moan's Health Foods
32 South Central
Medford 97501
Phone: 773-3061

Organic fruits & vegetables. All major lines & brands. Fresh carrot juice on order. Mail orders.

Roy Wilkins Organic Farm
Rt. 1, Box 60
Newberg 97132

Vegetables & fruits in season. Dried fruit, eggs & nuts. Will ship.


Healthway Food Center
Eastport Plaza Shopping Center
4048 S.E. 82nd
Portland 97266
Phone: 794-0117

Local vegetables in season. Complete store. Will ship.


Lawson's
A. J. & Ida Lawson
471 Canin St.
Salem 97301
Phone: 363-8229

Nuts, seeds, eggs, juices. No shipping.


Salem Health Food Store
409 Center St. N.E.
Salem 97301


# PENNSYLVANIA

Queen's Nutritional Products
Jack Queen
1424 Pennsylvania Ave.
Allentown 18103
Phone: 691-6644

Complete store.

Main Line Diet Shop
11 W. Lancaster Ave.
Ardmore 19003
Phone: MI 9-2554

Vegetables & fruits all year around.
Beef, eggs, poultry, honey, grains &
nuts. No shipping.


Thompson's Health Foods
619 11th St.
Beaver Falls 15010
Phone: (412) 843-4781


Millers Natural Foods
Christ B. Miller
Box 77A, RD No. 1
Bird-In-Hand 17505

Complete stock of organic foods. Some
homemade foods and own eggs and
chickens. Will ship small orders.


Snowhill Farm
Norman and Marjorie Aamodt
RD 4
Coatesville 19320
Phone: 384-7910

Beef, veal, potatoes, corn. Will ship.


Natural Health Foods
422 Main St.
Edwardsville 18704
Phone: (717) 288-0228

Beef, eggs, poultry, honey, grains &
nuts. No shipping.


Better Food Foundation Inc.
300 N. Washington St.
Greencastle 17225

Soy flour, raw wheat germ, oils, spray
dried milk, etc. Mail order, too.


The Health Kitchen
Barbara Heller
313 S. Pennsylvania Avenue
Greensburg 15601
Phone: 837-0525

Nuts, seeds, grains. Sends customers
to sources of produce. No shipping.


Health Food Store
143 Baltimore St.
Hanover 17331
Phone: 637-7230

Fresh vegetables & fruits in season.
Nuts, dried fruits, seeds, eggs, dairy
products & juices. No shipping.


The Earth Shop, Inc.
318 York Road
Jenkintown 19046
Phone: 885-5355


Arnold Voehringer
R.D. No. 2
Kempton 19529
Phone: (215) 756-6342

Organic beef—Angus/Holstein.


Natural Foods
108 W. Orange St.
Lancaster 17603

Nuts, seeds, grains, eggs, breads,
juices. Will ship.


The Organic Market
K. T. Carroll
601 West Lemon Street
Lancaster 17603
Phone: (717) 397-4641

Brown rice, wheat, rye, barley, millet,
buckwheat, oatmeal. Freshly ground
whole grain flours, variety of beans,
vegetables, nuts, cheeses, fruits.


North Penn Health Food Center
711 W. Main St.
Lansdale 19446
Phone: (215) 855-1044

Vegetables & fruits in season. Beef,
eggs, poultry, honey, grains, nuts. Will
ship.


Waldron's Organic Farm
Charlotte B. Waldron
609 Lancaster Pike
Malvern 19355
Phone: NI 4-9111

Enclose stamp with inquiries. Many
vegetables picked to order. Poultry,
brown eggs, honey. No shipping.


New Hope Health Food Shop
Rt. No. 202
New Hope 18938
Phone: (215) 862-5750


Walnut Acres
Paul Keene
Penns Creek 17862

Complete stock of organic foods,
except fresh fruit. Will ship except for
beef, poultry.

P. F. Braungardt
Reading Terminal Market Stall 361
12th & Filbert St.
Philadelphia 19103
Phone: 257-6189

Vegetables in season.


Concept Chestnut Hill Natural Foods
 & Nutrition Center
3 E. Gravers Lane
Chestnut Hill, Philadelphia 19118
Phone: CH 7-3215


Lahr's Nutritional Foods
5537 No. 5th St.
Philadelphia 19120
Phone: WA 4-0322

Foods for special diets. Natural &
organic foods. Juicing machines.


Martindale's Health Foods
25 South 11th Street
Philadelphia 19107

Complete array of products.


Maplewood Nutrition
Sydney Ciment
51 Maplewood Ave.
Philadelphia 19144
Phone: VI 8-0857

Nuts, dried fruits, seeds, grains, juices.
No shipping. Goat milk products.


Good Earth Natural Foods
Dennis Portnoy
2635 Murray Ave.
Pittsburgh 15217
Phone: (412) 521-9762

Fertile eggs, nuts, produce, cheese,
honey, grains. Shipping.


Kay's Natural Health Foods
315 High St., Rt. 422
Pottstown 19464
Phone: 323-1180

Honey, grains, nuts, vitamins. Will ship.


Nonesuch Natural Foods
Clyner Health Clinic
Clyner Rd.
Quakertown 18951
Phone: 536-8003

Meats, poultry, bread, nuts, flours
ground to order, vegetarian specialties.


Bucks County Natural Food Center
Charles & Audrey Boxer
9 Cherry St.
Richlandtown 18955
Phone: 536-3819

Produce, beef, poultry, eggs, raw milk
cheeses, honey ice-cream, special
herbal blends, fresh frozen fish. Snack
bar. No shipping.


Cornucopia Natural Food Corner
Dr. & Mrs. Richard Letizi
9 Huntington Pike
Rockledge 19111
Phone: 379-8175

Nuts, grains, dairy products, juices,
natural vitamins, dietetic specialties.


Mease's Natural Foods, Inc.
Richard & Isabel Mease
Schoeneck 17574
Phone: (215) 267-5125

7 varieties of whole grain, flourless
breads. Will ship.


Feldi's Health Food Center
Souderton Shopping Center
Souderton 18964
Phone: 723-9444

Grapefruit and carrots. Beef, eggs,
poultry, honey, grains, nuts. Will ship.


Bunn's Natural Food Shoppe
1007 Street Rd.
Southampton 18966
Phone: 355-1165

Vegetables & fruits in season & out.
Beef, eggs, poultry, honey, grains, nuts.


Sonnewald Service Natural Food
Harold & Grace Lefever
Rt. 1 (at Stoverstown)
Spring Grove 17362
Phone: (717) 225-3456

Own vegetables and fruits in season.
Meats, eggs, honey, grains, nuts, etc.
No shipping.


McKees Natural Food Center
115 McKinley Avenue
Vandergrift 15690


Sustenance
RD 4 West Chester 19380
Phone: 692-1944

Mail orders. Vegetables, fruits, nuts
and complete line of organic foods.

Myers Health Food Store
271 W. Market St.
York 17401


Tom's Organic Foods
Thomas Smidl
RD 1, Box 264
Zelienople 16063
Phone: 775-6218

Vegetables & fruit picked daily, sold at home.


## RHODE ISLAND


One Clear Grain
34 Governor Street
Providence 02906


Mother Nature's Nutrition Center
1119 Main St.
Wakefield 02879


## SOUTH CAROLINA


Natural Food Center
Mrs. W. C. Davis, Jr.
1158 Rutherford Rd., Stone Plaza
Greenville 29609
Phone: 233-9820

Nuts, dried fruit, grains, eggs, breads. Will ship.


Lee's Health Foods
Mr. & Mrs. Lee Lowry
Box 981
Ballentine 29002

Vegetables & fruits in season. Nuts, dried fruits, seeds, grains, beef, eggs, homemade bread. Some shipping.


## TENNESSEE


Nutri-Shop
3619 Ringgold Road
Chattanooga 37412

Vitamins, minerals, protein, natural foods, enzymes. Free catalog.


Tri-Cities Health Food Stores
Mary E. Kensinger
1812 West Market Street
Johnson City 37601
Phone: (615) 926-5521


Natural Foods
708 Locust St. S.W.
Knoxville 37902


Health Food Store
Dorothy N. Rogers
679 S. Mendenhall
Memphis 38117


New Morning Organic Food Store
Penn Waugh, Mary Ann Clark
1004 16 Avenue S.
Nashville 37212
Phone: (615) 255-9027

No shipping. Carrots, lettuce, onions, broccoli, celery, cauliflower, tomatoes, beets, radishes, potatoes, apples, pears, oranges, grapefruit.


## TEXAS


Natural Food Center
3120 B North First St.
Abilene 79603
Phone: (915) OR 2-9281


Plimmers Enterprises
P. M. Plimmer
P.O. Box 701
Alpine 79830
(2 miles W)

Pecans, sunflower seeds, some herbs all year round. Apples, radishes, corn, tomatoes, etc., seasonally. Will ship.


Natural Organic Foods
212 E. Hiram, P.O. Box 210
Atlanta 75551
Phone: (204) 796-2879


Austin Natural Foods
Max Watson
2602 Guadalupe
Austin 78705
Phone: (512) 477-0045

Vegetables & fruits in season. Beef, poultry, honey, grains, nuts. Will ship.

Big Spring Health Food Center
Eva Nail
1305 Scurry
Big Spring 79720
Phone: 267-6524

Nuts, dried fruits, seeds, grains, eggs, breads, cheese, juices. Will ship.

Back to Nature
102 Old Town, 5500 Greenville Avenue
Dallas 75206
Phone: (214) 691-2800

Health Food Cottage
235 Preston Royal Center
Dallas 75230

Beef, eggs, poultry, honey, grains, nuts. Will ship. Serve snacks.

Pure-As-Can-Be Gourmet Foods
12011 Coit Road No. 109
Dallas 75230
Phone: (214) 233-6461 or 233-6491

Complete stock of organic foods. Mail orders also.

Cupboard Health Foods
913 Sunset Drive
Denton 76201
Phone: (817) 387-5386

Vegetables & fruits in season. Beef, eggs, poultry, honey, grains, nuts. No shipping.

Health Food Center
V. Rovertson
2700 Montana Avenue
El Paso 79903
Phone: 566-3511

Cereals, food supplements, tea, honey. Juice bar.

Ken's Natural-Organic Juices
Kenneth Sallman
3101 E. 1st
Fort Worth 76111

Juices, vegetables & fruits. Rice, meats, poultry, eggs. Custom juicing and nut butters. No shipping.

Taylor's Natural Foods
6801 Oak Crest Dr. E.
Fort Worth 76119
Phone: JE 1-3455

Stock vitamins & honey, fresh eggs & vegetables. No shipping.

Arrowhead Mills
Box 866
Hereford 79045
Phone: 364-0730

Grains. Will ship.

Pam's Health Foods
Pam Bookhart
7958 Westheimer
Houston 77042
Phone: 781-0061

Vegetables & fruits in season. Meats, eggs, poultry, honey, grains, nuts. Some shipping.

Health Food Store, J. Roberts
4901 W. Marshall Avenue W. Hwy. 80
Longview 75601
Phone: PL 6-1171

Eggs, honey, grains, nuts. Vegetables in season. Dried fruits.

Polly's Health Foods
Lewis L. Gilbert
3409-33rd Street
Lubbock 79410

Natural Food Center
900 Morrison St.
Marshall 75670
Phone: WE 5-3339

Vegetables & fruits in season. Beef, eggs, poultry, honey, grains, nuts. Will-ship.

Wright's Organic Food & Bake Shop
Mr. & Mrs. J. N. Wright
Rt. 1, Box 260 (near Dallas)
Mesquite 75149
Phone: 286-5805

Vegetables picked as sold. Poultry, eggs, homemade breads & cookies. No shipping.

Garden-Ville
Farm and Market
7561 E. Evans Road
P.O. Box 1056
New Braunfels 78130
Phone: (512) 651-6307

Organically grown foods, vegetables, fruits, grains, organic garden supplies. Organically grown grains—bulk, fresh flours-stoneground, corn, wheat, rye, rice, vegetables and fruit juices.

Mr. T's Health Store
3339 Gulfway Dr.
Port Arthur 77640
Phone: 982-3933

Vegetables & fruits in season. Some
year 'round. Beef, eggs, poultry, honey,
grains, nuts. Will ship.

The Cottage Health Foods
29 Arapaho Village
Richardson 75080

Beef, eggs, poultry, honey, grains, nuts.
Will ship.

More Natural Foods
516 N. Alamo
San Antonio 78215
Phone: 227-3189

Vegetables & fruits in season. Eggs,
honey, grains, nuts.

A-1 Health Foods
The Wester's
Box 363-J, Route 8
Tyler 75701
Phone: LY 2-8495

Vegetables and fruits year 'round. Beef,
eggs, honey, grains, butter, juices.
No shipping.

# UTAH

Ray's Organic Vegetables
East State Road
American Fork 84003

Vegetables in season. No shipping.

Starkweather Organic Gardens
Robert Starkweather
2185 S. 7400 W.
Magna 84044

Vegetables in season. Duck and goat
meat on order. Goat's milk & cheese.
No shipping.

Goddard's Health Food Mart
Lillian Goddard
3427 Riverside Rd.
Ogden 84403

Nuts, dried fruits, seeds, grains, eggs,
juices. Will ship.

Whole Earth Natural Foods
David L. Ronninger
1026 Second Avenue
Salt Lake City 84103
Phone: (801) 355-7401

# VERMONT

Solanaceae Natural Foods, Inc.
115 So. Winooski Ave.
Burlington 05401
Phone: 863-5130

OM Natural Health Foods
David Vilner
15 Court St.
Middlebury 05753
Phone: 388-9060

Complete selection of nuts, dried
fruits, seeds, and grains. Flour ground
to order. Bread, juices. No shipping.

Earth Artisan Co.
Gary Miller
RD 2, Plainfield 05667
Plainfield 05667
Phone: 454-7776

Vegetables & fruits in season. Grains,
eggs, breads, juices, goat's milk &
yogurt. No shipping.

Wholemeal
Amanda Hamilton
30 College Street
Poultney 05764
Phone: 287-5758

Vegetables & fruits in season. Nuts,
grains, flours, breads, juices.

Bungaree Natural Foods
RFD 1, Rt. 5
Putney 05346
Phone: 722-4058

Own: vegetables, herbs, chickens, eggs,
breads, cheese, goat milk, apple &
vegetable juices. Other foods. No
shipping.

Tweedmeadow
Stockbridge 05772
Phone: (802) 746-5541

Stoneground flours, 5 grain pancake
mix, whole grain cereals, unprocessed
oils, brown rice, Vermont cheese, maple
syrup, honey and other natural foods.

Mother Nature's Food Store
Miss Robin E. Hayes
P.O. Drawer L, Mountain Rd.
Stowe 05672
Phone: (802) 253-4370

Nuts, dried fruits, grains, bread, juices.
Will ship.

## VIRGINIA

Natures Harvest
4551 Duke Street
Alexandria 22304
Phone: (703) 370-5752


Woodlawn Natural Foods
1219 North Glebe Road
Arlington 22201


Sylvania Organic Foods
Richard C. Allen, Peg Tillotson
1110 W. Main St.
Charlottesville 22903
Phone: 295-3808

Local vegetables & fruits in season.
Complete stock of organic foods. 7
kinds bread baked there daily.


Kennedy's Natural Foods
Jim & Elinor Kennedy
1051 West Broad St.
Falls Church 22046
Phone: (703) 533-7790

Beef, pork, lamb, poultry, rabbit, fish
& wild game. Breads. Vegetables &
fruits all year. No shipping.


Golden Acres Orchard
A. P. Thomson
Front Royal Rt. 2, Box 70
Front Royal 22630
On Rt. 639 intersects with Rt. 522
east. About 16 mi. south from
Winchester or 6 mi. north of Front
Royal.

Apples, apple juice and apple cider
vinegar, mineral water. Will ship.


Sylvania Organic Angus Ranch
Richard C. Allen
Gordonsville 22942
Phone: TE 2-2443

Beef. Frozen 2 lb. labeled packages,
minimum, 100 lbs. No shipping.


The Honey Shop
61 W. Mercury Blvd.
Hampton 23369
Phone: 723-9104

Honey, grains, nuts. Will ship.


Shenandoah Valley Natural Foods
Dutch Inn
Washington St.
Lexington 24450


The Honey Shop
Rosemarie B. West
3150 West Cary Street
Richmond 23221
Phone: 358-3943

Honey, grains, nuts, eggs, breads. Will
ship.


Heritage Store, Inc.
Tom Johnson
Box 444
Virginia Beach 23458
Phone: (703) 428-0100

Will ship.


## WASHINGTON

Cook's Nutrition Center
Darwin B. Cook
118 105th NE
Bellevue 98004
Phone: GI 4-8141

Complete stock of organic foods. Fresh
vegetable juices. Some shipping.


Fred A. Rauch Farm
RT 1
Chattarny 99003
Phone: CE 8-6759

Beef, alive or slaughtered. 1 per month.


Gourmet's Galley
Patty DeStaffany
Spring St.
Friday Harbor 98250
Phone: 378-2251

Organic foods & juice bar. Home-baked
dark bread. Will ship.


Scandia Natural Health Foods
310 Montgomery St.
Mt. Vernon 98273


Health-Way Food Center
220 E. 4th.
Olympia 98501


Ames Nutrition Center
Renton Shopping Center
Renton 98055

Natural and dietary foods, vitamins.

Pilgrim's Natural Foods
4532 University Village Ct.
Seattle 98105
Phone: 523-5770


Snohomish Health Food Shoppe
Lloyd & Marjorie Anderson
731 2nd
Snohomish 98290
Phone: LO 8-6303

Dried fruits, seeds, grains, breads.
No shipping.


Groff's Nutrition
612 Tacoma Mall
Tacoma 98409
Phone: GR 5-3282

Natural vitamins, health & diet foods.


Vancouver Health Food
2010 Main Street
Vancouver 98660

Food store.


Everybody's Store
Jeffrey & Amy Margolis
Van Zandt 98244
Phone: 592-2482

Vegetables & fruits in season. Nuts,
grains, poultry, eggs, bread. Will ship.


# WEST VIRGINIA


Foods for Life, Inc.
407 East Lee Street
Charleston 25301

Health foods, vitamins, proteins, dried
fruits, nuts, seeds, oils, whole grain
breads & flours.


Hillbilly Mountain Products
Mr. & Mrs. R. W. Feliy
Box 1
Mill Creek 26280

Apples & berries in season. Black
walnuts, hickory & butternuts. Corn,
herb teas. Will ship.


# WISCONSIN


Schwartz's Natural Foods
Mr. & Mrs. Chester A. Schwartz
2126 Liberty Ave.
Beloit 53511
Phone: 365-7550

Vegetables & fruits in season. Nuts,
dried fruits, grains, eggs, bread. No
shipping.


Mother Natures Food Inc.
2434 London Road
Eau Claire 54701

Food supplements, fresh raw nuts,
Wisconsin organic cheese made from
raw milk, fresh fruit (grapefruit &
oranges from Texas), apples raised in
Wisconsin, soil builder, distributors for
Guild Soap Products.


Hickory Hill Farm
Mr. & Mrs. Harold G. Kruse
Rt. 2
Loganville 53943
Phone: (608) 727-2289

Vegetables & fruits in season, flours,
sorghum, poultry, lamb, honey, grains.
These from self, neighbors & relatives.
Will ship grains & pkg. goods.


Langlois' Health Food Mart
5506 W. Center St.
Milwaukee 53210
Phone: 871-2510

Nuts, dried fruits, grains, breads,
juices. Will ship.


Leon R. Horsted Whole Grain Foods
Rt. 2
Waunakee 53597
Phone: 846-3287

Own vegetables in season; honey,
corn meal, wheat germ, whole grain
flours, brown rice, sunflower kernels,
dried fruits, cheddar & colby cheese.
Will ship. Send stamp for seasonal list.


Bauer's Natural Foods Farm
Floyd & Ione Bauer
Rt. 1
Wonewoe 53968
Phone: 464-7628

Vegetables & berries in season. Dried
fruits, seeds, flours, pork, rock cornish
roasters, eggs. No shipping.


# WYOMING


Wyoming Natural Foods
242 So. Wolcott
Casper 92601

# Index